GAMES OF INTELLIGENCE

Which country has the best intelligence service in the world? How can they be judged? Is Mossad's reputation for ruthless efficiency really justified? Does the KGB have any role in Mikhail Gorbachov's Soviet Union? Is the CIA too reliant on sophisticated technical methods of gathering intelligence? How do the French get away with murder? Are the British still paralysed by fear of penetration by moles?

These are some of the compelling questions posed in this revealing study of six major intelligence agencies. The answers are detailed and often surprising. *Games of Intelligence* is a thought-provoking account of how key secret services conduct their operations. It provides a formula for judging their relative performance. Does the tax-payer get value for money? Do ministers even know the right questions to ask?

Nigel West has given us a unique insight into the world's intelligence communities, based on interviews with professional case officers, their agents, KGB defectors and a few convicted spies, backed up with fascinating documented evidence, some of it still classified secret.

**Also by the same author,
and available from Coronet:**

The Friends
GCHQ: The Secret Wireless War
A Matter of Trust: MI5 1945–72
Molehunt

About the Author

Nigel West is a military historian specialising in security matters and is the European editor of *Intelligence
Quarterly*. He was voted 'The Experts' Expert' by the
Observer's panel of spy writers. He has written several
controversial espionage histories including *MI6:
British Secret Intelligence Service Operations
1909–45*; *GARBO*; *Unreliable Witness: Espionage
Myths of World War II*. His first novel, *The Blue List*,
was published in 1989.

The Sunday Times has commented on his books: 'His
information is often so precise that many people
believe he is the unofficial historian of the secret
services. West's sources are undoubtedly excellent.
His books are peppered with deliberate clues to
potential front-page stories.'

Games of Intelligence

The Classified Conflict of International Espionage

Nigel West

CORONET BOOKS
Hodder and Stoughton

Copyright © 1989 by Westintel
Research Limited

First published in Great Britain in
1989 by George Weidenfeld &
Nicolson Limited

Coronet edition 1990

British Library C.I.P.

West, Nigel
    Games of intelligence: the
classified conflict of
international espionage.
1. Intelligence services
Rn: Rupert Allason I. Title
327.12

ISBN 0-340-53026-X

Printed and bound in Great Britain
for Hodder and Stoughton
paperbacks, a division of Hodder and
Stoughton Ltd., Mill Road, Dunton
Green, Sevenoaks, Kent TN13 2YA
(Editorial Office: 47 Bedford Square,
London WC18 3DP) by Richard
Clay Ltd., Bungay, Suffolk.

'The importance of intelligence services in the fortune of nations can't be over-stated.... The existence or absence of a well-working spy network on the territory of a potential enemy may spell the difference between victory and defeat.'

Alexander Orlov in *Handbook of Intelligence and Guerrilla Warfare* (1963)

Contents

Acknowledgments

I am grateful for the generous help and advice of the following: Elizabeth Bancroft of the National Intelligence Book Center, Washington; Miles Copeland; Peter Deriabin; Roger Faligot; William Geimer of the Jamestown Foundation, Washington; Dr Katherine Herbig; Etienne M. Huygens; Alexandra Kosta; Professor Vladislav Kraznov; Stanislas Levchenko; Professor Ariel Levite of Tel Aviv University; Dr Lawrence Martin; Carolyn McMartin; John Moe; Hayden Peake of the National Intelligence Study Center, Washington; Dr Walter Pforzheimer; Vladimir Rezun; and the U S Department of Defense Security Institute.

Introduction

Largely unseen by the general public and the taxpayer, a clandestine conflict has been fought by the world's security and intelligence agencies. Very occasionally the espionage war has reached the surface and glimpses have been caught of covert activity: spies have been arrested, diplomats expelled, traitors executed and defectors revealed.

What makes all this so remarkable is that intelligence-gathering – or spying, call it what you will – is a pastime indulged in by virtually every nation. Indeed, it has been called 'the game of nations', and in some respects it does resemble a sport. It is played to certain rules: some written, like the international conventions covering diplomacy; others unwritten, such as those governing the exchange of captured personnel. There are winners and losers, and the stakes can be high. Most participants have similar objectives, involving the penetration of an opponent's intelligence apparatus, and adhere to the same tradecraft, using dead-letter drops, coded signals, double-agent operations, honeytraps, false-flag recruitments, deception ploys, covert surveillance, deep-cover moles and sophisticated communications equipment.

But there is also a deadly side to the business, which makes it more than a game. The consequences for losers are often fatal. Some assassinations, like that of Georgi Markov, in a crowded London street with a poison-tipped umbrella, become widely known. Others are never reported because the true cause of death has gone undetected. When the Labour opposition leader Hugh Gaitskell died suddenly in 1963, it was widely accepted that he had succumbed to a fatal blood infection. Only a few insiders knew the real story: that the British Security Service suspected he had been deliberately poisoned with a deadly toxin.

The implications of the duel for those opting out, by refusing to participate, are equally serious. In December 1941 the United States had no Central Intelligence Agency and lacked the means to produce, collate, assess and distribute secret intelligence. Thus it was caught unawares by the attack on Pearl Harbor, even though there was considerable evidence available to indicate Japanese intentions. Similarly, back in 1973, Mossad was unprepared for the Yom Kippur War. In a secret review of the Israelis' security and intelligence capabilities, which has never been declassified, the CIA observed that their

> failure is an example of inadequacies in their communications intelligence capability at that time. In recent years as well there also have been indications that Israeli intelligence on the Arabs, other than communications intelligence, has been somewhat inadequate in quality and their agent operations lacking in success.

Kipling's 'great game' has much in common with a duel. Intelligence agencies invariably have one principal target. For the Israelis it is the Arab world; for the British and the Americans it is the Soviets; for the South Africans it is the African National Congress. There are defensive and offensive stratagems, employing molehunts and the infiltration of agents. In some duels there are clear winners and losers, just as there are compromised sources and successful case officers. There are also the stand-offs, when neither opponent scores, and both sides agree to fight another day.

The duel of espionage knows no geographic boundaries and is undertaken largely behind the scenes, away from those who inevitably have to foot the bill, in either financial or other terms.

One difficulty about meeting the cost of international intrigue is the reluctance of those personally involved, be they individual agents, their handlers or the intelligence agencies themselves, to disclose the facts by which their performances can be judged.

How can a particular organization be assessed? How can the government or taxpayer be sure of value for money? By what standard can relative efficiency be gauged? Are there any relevant criteria which allow verdicts to be passed on the merits (or otherwise) of a nation's security apparatus?

The purpose of *Games of Intelligence* is to examine the structure, role and background of certain key participants so as to determine which countries excel in the arcane arts and which are handicapped by intrinsic flaws. Does Mossad really live up to its reputation of ruthless efficiency? Has the KGB legions of subversive moles planted in the West? Is Britain still dogged by ideological traitors? Will sheer economic pressure continue to produce mercenary spies in the US? Are the intelligence agencies of Soviet satellites like Poland and Czechoslovakia mere surrogates of the Kremlin, and perhaps more prone to the defector syndrome? Can the French DGSE rely on public and political support whatever the scale of its misconduct?

Games of Intelligence may well be conducted far from the light of public scrutiny and accountability, but the clues are there to be traced. They can be found in the historical backgrounds of the intelligence systems constructed in each country. They can be spotted in the execution of certain operations, and detected in the rare public utterances of skilled practitioners. Patterns can be discerned and, when placed in contrast, relative positions established. Which is the best, most efficient, most reliable, cost-effective intelligence organization in the world? This study of the duel is intended to assist the reader, be he an inquisitive politician, professional intelligence officer or long-suffering taxpayer, to find answers to some of these questions.

In February 1978, *Time* magazine attempted to assess the relative performance of the intelligence agencies of fourteen countries: the United States's CIA; the Soviet Union's KGB; Israel's Mossad; Britain's SIS; Czechoslovakia's STB; Poland's UB; West Germany's BND; France's SDECE; Japan's CRO; China's GRI; Norway's OS; Sweden's FOE[1]; Canada's CSIS and Australia's ASIS.

The top four organizations awarded *Michelin*-like rosettes were the CIA, KGB, SIS and Mossad. The KGB was credited with a budget of $10 billion and described by an anonymous State Department official as 'a worthy and persistent foe'. The CIA, then recovering from Director Stansfield Turner's Halloween massacre, in which 212 members of the clandestine service had been summarily dismissed, was characterized as a rudderless agency lacking morale and self-confidence after its involvement in a series of debilitating escapades.

In contrast, Mossad was described as 'well-organized, ruthless, dedicated, all but impossible to penetrate', while SIS was judged 'tops at analytical work and political judgments'. While these views probably coincided with popular perceptions held at the time, no attempt was made to explain the basis on which the highly subjective opinions were formed or the criteria used to make a comparative assessment. Indeed, what standards could be used for an evaluation that had any validity or practical purpose?

One possible model is based on a formula which takes into account three separate aspects of any intelligence organization: its integrity, its ability to conduct operations and its skill at making the best use of its product. All of these yardsticks can be usefully applied to different agencies facing differing challenges in different countries, and can be defined even further. For example, how is one to assess a service's integrity? Certainly, the views of insiders and other professionals will prove a useful guide. The receipt of defectors is also a valuable indication of whether there has been any hostile penetration. One of the items of circumstantial evidence for a Soviet source inside the British Security Service throughout the 1950s was the complete absence of any defectors willing to seek asylum in Britain. Those that did make tentative approaches were swiftly identified by the KGB and eliminated, and those that took refuge in Allied countries told much the same tale: that the British intelligence community was thoroughly contaminated.

If a lack of defectors is a likely sign of active penetration, the ability to mount a really successful operation and sustain it through to a satisfactory conclusion must be regarded as a signal that the relevant service has not been compromised. Such estimations are, of course, meat and drink to the counter-intelligence specialists, who continually seek to protect their own establishments and undertake penetrations into hostile agencies. Their standing depends upon a bewildering variety of arcane skills: to spot the false defectors dispatched deliberately to mislead; to catch the authentic spies; to deter potential traitors.

All of these components make up the jigsaw of a particular agency's integrity, and it is an appraisal that allied services routinely have to make so as to place a value on information emanating from that source and decide whether it can be trusted with confidence. In the pages that follow we shall turn to parallel and rival organizations to provide a hint as to their feeling on the issue. In some cases this is relatively straightforward. For example, when the US embassy in

Tehran was occupied by revolutionary students in 1979, an official CIA report on the current status of Mossad was discovered among classified documents awaiting destruction. Several KGB defectors, such as Oleg A. Gordievsky and Vitali S. Yurchenko, have also been sufficiently well placed to describe their agency's attitude to, say, the British.

The second category, which might be termed operational prowess, is an amalgam of different disciplines, some of which depend upon the host political environment. Certainly, the attitudes of governments to enterprises such as sabotage and assassination differ radically. For a while the Elysée Palace seemed blithely unconcerned when the DGSE was revealed to have sunk the Greenpeace ship, *Rainbow Warrior*, in 1985. French public opinion appeared to endorse the operation, and accepted without criticism the disclosure from a retired director-general of the organization that dozens of similar schemes had been executed successfully. Yet in America the admission that at one time the CIA had plotted the assassination of Fidel Castro and contemplated the murder of Patrice Lumumba provoked an unprecedented political storm. Suggestions that Britain had planned to topple President Nasser caused lasting disquiet, yet the murder of Georgi Markov and the attempt on the life of Pope John Paul II were only temporary sensations and were deliberately ignored by the Eastern Bloc's subservient media.

There is a similar attitude displayed to other clandestine activities, such as covert action and the dissemination of misleading information known as black propaganda. Strict rules have been enforced by Congress to limit American paramilitary interventions abroad, while the Cubans seem perfectly willing to embark upon lengthy engagements, especially in Africa, as Soviet stand-ins. Britain's principal instrument of propaganda, the euphemistically named Information Research Department of the Foreign Office, was closed in 1977, whereas Mossad was prepared to abduct Mordechai Vanunu, a renegade Israeli nuclear technician, from Rome a decade later. Clearly the degree of political support for potentially embarrassing schemes differs from nation to nation, and is a critical factor in assessing the capacity of organizations to mount them.

It would be a mistake for anyone to believe that intelligence organs only indulge in hazardous conspiracies, although open sources such as the Western media inevitably focus on the disasters because successes can rarely be publicized without diminishing their value.

Thus the triumphs go unnoticed and the catastrophes are emblazoned in headlines across the world. However, apart from the moments of high drama, there are the more mundane preoccupations that are applicable universally. Virtually all agencies receive defectors known as 'walk-ins', who turn up unannounced and volunteer their services. The unimaginative intelligence officer rejects the offer as an obvious provocation. The quick-witted may try and establish his *bona fides* and send him back into the field as a valued source, occasionally referred to as a 'defector-in-place'. Once an agent has outlived his operational usefulness, he may become a candidate for long-term resettlement; again this is an area where useful comparisons can be made. How well do certain agencies fare in treating their defectors? Why do some decide to redefect? What treatment can a Western defector expect in Moscow? What proportion of Soviet escapees opt to return home?

Part and parcel of these topics for study is the business of planting the deep-penetration agents often called moles, and the sometimes painful experience of managing double agents. Are some services better than others at practising these mysterious arts? Does the KGB have to overcome the same kind of obstacles when an American defector needs rescuing from North America as the CIA faces when attempting the exfiltration of an asset from the Eastern Bloc?

Examination of relative ability to stage complex operations takes one into the area of resources. In the technical field there is the question of training facilities and access to key *matériel*, such as sophisticated communications equipment. Any agency, however enthusiastic, will be handicapped if its personnel is insufficiently prepared for the purpose in hand, or if it lacks the logistical support needed to complete the allotted task.

Even with the best available paraphernalia much will depend upon the personalities involved. A committed, resourceful agent may well achieve the extra distance that turns failure into success. But what is the key element, the moral fibre that commands endurance beyond the call of duty? Patriotism, bloody-mindedness or sheer determination? Access to potential agents of the right calibre is vital, and both the Soviet and Israeli military establishments willingly provide a deep pool in which the intelligencers can fish. Traditionally a high proportion of French businessmen journeying overseas act as 'honourable correspondents', supplying the DGSE with reports of their observations abroad. Similar exercises conducted in Britain and the United States to debrief travellers have not met the same level of success, perhaps a reflection of the standing of the particular organization in the relevant community, and itself a factor that requires consideration.

Finally, there is the more routine capacity to deploy short-term spies to undertake specific, limited missions. How do the big six fare in this essential part of intelligence-gathering?

1

The Company

'The CIA is the only intelligence service in
the world which has never been penetrated
by the KGB. That's what I worried about....[1]

Richard Helms, Director of Central
Intelligence 1966–73

As recently as 1985, Olivier Schmidt, director of the Paris-based
Right to Information Association, wrote to all the world's major
intelligence agencies requesting whatever information about themselves they were prepared to disclose publicly. Only one reply was
received: the CIA's public affairs department sent three brochures–
Intelligence: The Acme of Skill; *Factbook on Intelligence*, and a
twenty-nine-page recruitment pamphlet entitled *Careers That Can
Make a Difference*.

In marked contrast to parallel organizations around the globe, the
CIA is really quite open about its activities. Its headquarters in a
compound of 219 wooded acres at Langley, Virginia, which was
opened in September 1961, is actually signposted from the George
Washington Parkway, outside Washington DC, and the overwhelming majority of its 25,000 or so employees make no effort to
conceal the nature of their work. The Agency is also legal, having
been created by statute in the 1947 National Security Act. A further
piece of legislation, the CIA Act, exempted the Agency from most
of the usual federal budgetary requirements and authorized it to
receive unvouchered funds from other government departments.
Since 1975, the CIA has conducted its operations under the scrutiny

of various congressional committees.

There is also an impressive literature about the CIA, a proportion of which has been written by insiders. They are contractually obliged to submit their manuscripts to a Publications Review Board before being released, but the only restriction on outside observers is the Intelligence Identities Protection Act passed in June 1982, which makes it a criminal offence to reveal the names of the Agency's covert personnel. To date, no one has been prosecuted for breaking this

---

Directors of Central Intelligence

Rear Admiral Roscoe H. Hillenkoetter, USN
1 May 1947–7 October 1950

General Walter Bedell Smith, USA
7 October 1950–9 February 1953

Allen W. Dulles
26 February 1953–29 November 1961

John A. McCone
29 November 1961–28 April 1965

Vice-Admiral William F. Raborn, Jr (USN, Ret.)
28 April 1965–30 June 1966

Richard Helms
30 June 1966–2 February 1973

James R. Schlesinger
2 February 1973–2 July 1973

William E. Colby
4 September 1973–30 January 1976

George Bush
30 January 1976–20 January 1977

Admiral Stansfield Turner (USN, Ret.)
9 March 1977–20 January 1981

William J. Casey
28 January 1981–29 January 1987

William H. Webster
26 May 1987–

Chief of Clandestine Service
(Deputy Director for Plans,
Deputy Director for Operations after March 1973)

Allen W. Dulles	1951
Kilbourne Johnstone	1951–2
Frank G. Wisner	1952–8
Richard M. Bissell	1958–62
Richard M. Helms	1962–5
Desmond FitzGerald	1965–7
Thomas H. Karamessines	1967–73
William E. Colby	1973
William Nelson	1973–6
William Wells	1976–7
John N. McMahon	1977–81
Max C. Hugel	1981
John H. Stein	1981–4
Clair George	1984–7
Richard F. Stolz	1987–

law. In addition to the books written about the organization, the Agency itself periodically publishes an internal magazine, *Studies in Intelligence*, censored copies of which are publicly available by application through the Freedom of Information Act procedure.

Perhaps the most sensitive part of the CIA is the Operations Directorate, the details of which are omitted from the officially disseminated versions of the Agency's structure chart.[2] However, its nine regional divisions and six 'Staff Elements' have been described in several publications. There is, in short, very little about the CIA that is completely secret. The identities of senior staff are well known, and congressmen and the media are regularly briefed on developments. The appointment of every Director of Central Intelligence (DCI) has to be confirmed by Congress, and the hearings are held in public, often on television. There is a recognized system of commenting publicly on particular events, such as the shooting-down of the Korean jumbo jet by a Soviet fighter in 1983. On that occasion the CIA's spokesman, Dale Peterson, was constantly being quoted on the subject.[3] The CIA's telephone number is in the public directory and most personnel are recruited overtly, usually on university campuses.

Recruitment to the CIA as an intelligence officer is a routine affair, accompanied by a series of interviews and backed up by loyalty screening and polygraph tests. Thereafter, a recruit may undergo training in one of several unmarked buildings in Alexandria and McLean, Virginia, or attend the special facility at Camp Peary, near Williamsburg, in anticipation of an overseas posting, usually under light State Department cover. This will take the form of an attachment to a military or diplomatic mission which provides convenient, discreet accommodation for the local CIA station.

Protection of overseas staff is of considerable importance, and the fifty-three stars etched in the Georgia marble of the north wall in the entrance lobby of the main headquarters building are testimony to the lives of CIA personnel lost while on active duty. For example Richard Welch, the Chief of Station in Athens, was ambushed and shot by terrorists in 1975 after his identity had been disclosed in the local newspapers. Others perished when the US embassy in the Lebanon was bombed by Muslim fanatics in April 1983. Among those who died were Robert C. Ames, a senior Middle East analyst who happened to be visiting while on a mission in the region, the local Station Chief, Kenneth Haas, his deputy and six other officers. The experience of William Buckley, kidnapped from outside his home in Beirut in March 1984 and subsequently held hostage and tortured for eighteen months before being brutally murdered, high-lighted the dangers of exposing CIA officials to unnecessary risk in potentially hostile territory. It was DCI Bill Casey's desperate attempts to rescue Buckley, who was listed as a political officer in the Beirut embassy, that eventually led to a plan to supply embargoed arms to Iran in exchange for his release. Casey considered the objective of freeing his Station Chief so important that he delib-erately circumvented the congressional oversight system by using the National Security Council, which was not subject to oversight, as a conduit for negotiations with the Iranians and thereby pre-cipitated a major political crisis.

The CIA has endured continuous congressional oversight in one form or another since Senator Frank Church's committee began investigating allegations of CIA misconduct in January 1975. Church finally submitted his report in April 1976, by which time the Senate had created a permanent Select committee on Intel-

The CIA's Organization

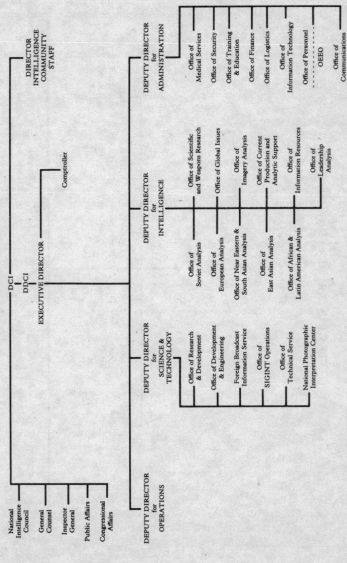

The CIA's Operations Directorate

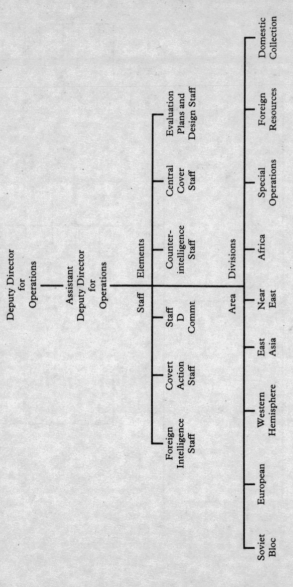

ligence, and the House of Representatives took a similar initiative the following year.

The catalyst for these developments was Watergate and the revelation, subsequently investigated by Vice-President Nelson Rockefeller, that for years the CIA had been indulging in illegal domestic operations. Once the CIA's Pandora's Box of barely deniable activities had been opened, the appalling details of discreditable undertakings were revealed. They ranged from schemes to employ the Mafia to assassinate Fidel Castro with a poisoned cigar to the preparation of a deadly virus intended for President Patrice Lumumba of the Congo. As we shall see, these disclosures set the agenda for a system of accountability that remains intact to this day, in spite of Casey's imaginative strategy to thwart it.

Judging the performance of the CIA with the assistance of insider opinion is easily the most difficult task of the six agencies to be reviewed in these pages because of the sheer scale of the literature. Every view is to be found, from the aggressively hostile, like the renegade Philip Agee, to the unashamedly partisan like David Atlee Phillips. Broadly, it falls into about four rough categories: autobiographies of distinguished (and occasionally notorious) intelligence officers; hostile critiques or exposés; academically orientated historical studies; and books by authors who do not acknowledge their insider status.

Placed prominently in the first group are no less than five former DCIs, and their books, together with other contributions from their colleagues, are listed in Appendix 1.

If it is difficult to discern a common strand of conviction from insiders on broad issues of performance concerning the CIA, it is possible to set out the facts relevant to the formula discussed earlier. Indeed, the subject of the CIA's integrity has been a matter of sustained debate for many years. The reason for this, quite simply, is the complete absence of any known Soviet penetration of the Agency during the greater part of its history. Whereas Soviet spies have been detected in all branches of the armed forces, and an estimated forty sources were believed to have operated in the Office of Strategic Services (OSS),[4] no major espionage case was uncovered in the CIA until December 1976, when Edwin G. Moore was discovered to have offered classified information to the Soviets. Moore had taken early retirement from the Agency three years before, following a lacklustre career as a map and logistics analyst. The FBI prevented any documents from changing hands, but Moore was sentenced to fifteen years' imprisonment.

Soon after Moore's arrest, two others who did succeed in getting Agency secrets to the KGB were caught, although one of the two culprits was strictly an employee of a contractor, TRW Defense Group.

Christopher Boyce and Andrew Lee had compromised CIA cryptographic arrangements while the former had been working on a classified satellite contract in California. Both were arrested in January 1977, and later the following year it was revealed that a serving CIA officer, William Kampiles, had volunteered more information concerning satellites to the KGB. He, too, was convicted of espionage, in an unconnected case, and sentenced to forty years' imprisonment, the second member of the CIA to be charged with such an offence. Since then several CIA personnel have been indicted: a retired Agency officer, David H. Barnett, offered to sell secrets to the KGB in Indonesia, but was arrested in 1980 and sentenced to eighteen years' imprisonment; Waldo H. Dubberstein shot himself in 1983 having been charged with selling secrets to Libya; Larry Wu Tai Chin was found suffocated in his prison cell in February 1986, having been identified as a source for the Chinese; Sharon M. Scranage was sentenced to a term of imprisonment in November 1985 for having given classified material to her Ghanaian lover; Edward L. Howard defected to the Soviet Union in September 1985; and Karl Koecher, a Czech agent who succeeded in penetrating the CIA as a translator and analyst, was traded in an East–West swap in February 1986. Five months later John H. Bothwell, a former CIA staffer who had left Langley in 1972 to work under business cover in Athens, was arrested in London and accused of selling secrets to Viktor P. Gudarev, a KGB colonel who had recently defected. The charges against Bothwell were later dropped and he was released. Thus in a space of six years, six spies had been discovered to have breached the CIA's security. What had happened in the previous thirty years? Was it, as David Atlee Phillips claimed, that 'the CIA has the best record of any intelligence service in history in defending itself against penetration by hostile services'? Or was the truth really that the spies had existed, but simply not been caught?

On the face of it there is something a little unusual about the CIA's counter-espionage record. Soviet agents were spotted in its predecessor, the OSS. Spies were caught in the US cryptographic organization, the National Security Agency (NSA), and virtually every branch of the armed forces. As we shall see, moles were planted successfully in most of the West's intelligence agencies. So how did the CIA escape unscathed?

In fact, it was the view of the CIA's Counterintelligence Staff that the Agency had not avoided contamination and that penetration had taken place. There was no firm proof of this, but the circumstantial evidence was considered sufficient to justify a debilitating series of molehunts, which wrecked the careers of several senior officers and eventually led to the downfall of Jim Angleton, the CIA's legendary counter-intelligence chief. Angleton was convinced of the existence of a Soviet spy codenamed SASHA and argued that as one of the KGB's prime targets it would be utterly complacent to believe that the Agency had been overlooked. He also pointed out that, according the KGB defector Anatoli Golitsyn, SASHA not only existed, but had been visited in 1957 by Viktor M. Kovshuk, then the head of the KGB section responsible for monitoring the US embassy in Moscow. Golitsyn had claimed that the KGB had been running an agent of unique importance, and this is what had brought Kovshuk to Washington under the false identity of Komarov.

What puzzled Angleton was the alternative explanation of the same incident described by Yuri Nosenko, whom he had good grounds for suspecting to be a deliberately dispatched disinformation agent, or 'plant'. Nosenko confirmed that Kovshuk had made the clandestine visit in 1957, but identified his agent as ANDREI, a low-grade source who had been recruited while on a tour of duty at the car pool at the US embassy in Moscow several years earlier, in 1953. ANDREI turned out to be Sergeant Roy Rhodes, who was then serving a prison sentence, having been arrested in the aftermath of the Rudolf Abel case back in June 1957.* When challenged, Rhodes admitted to having met Kovshuk, but only many weeks after 'Komarov' was known to have entered the US. What had the KGB man been doing in the meantime? Nosenko thought that ANDREI had been hard to track down, but his name had been listed in the telephone directory. Other doubts about Nosenko's *bona fides* led Angleton to believe that the ANDREI story

*For fuller details of the Abel case, see pages 90–91

had been little more than a cover to conceal the true nature of Kovshuk's mission: to service a high-level spy who had burrowed deep into the CIA. There was also the unusual irregularity of Kovshuk, from the KGB's Second Chief Directorate, travelling overseas to handle a spy who was known to have been run by Abel's particular branch, the First Chief Directorate.

It was this anomaly that led Angleton to pursue the enigma of SASHA further; but, although he harboured doubts about several of his colleagues – Richard Kovich, David Murphy, Peter Bagley and Igor Orlov were all investigated – no conclusive results were achieved. Angleston was forced into early retirement by DCI William Colby late in 1974 for having embroiled the CIA in illegal domestic operations, including mail intercept and telephone tapping, and left without ever having caught a single penetration agent inside the CIA.

There remains a high probability that the CIA did, indeed, experience hostile penetration at some stage, but there is little direct indication that this is the case. The opinion of insiders and outsiders alike is divided on the issue, a subject that is often clouded by the emotions expressed by those quoting the views of Angleton or his controversial associate, Golitsyn.

One almost universally accepted method of judging the integrity of an intelligence agency is to assess the number of defectors received from an opponent. Being the richest agency in the West, boasting the greatest resources to resettle asylum-seekers, the CIA has an unequalled record of attracting Eastern Bloc line-crossers. In fact, between the defections of Vladimir and Evdokia Petrov in Australia in April 1954 and Oleg Lyalin's safe reception in London in August 1971, the CIA enjoyed an absolute monopoly in this particular area. The Agency's continued success in the field can be judged by a glance at the comprehensive chart of GRU and KGB defectors received in the West since the end of the Second World War (see pages 122–3). In contrast, the French got none during the same period and the British actually lost three that had risked a tentative approach. Although Yuri A. Rastvorov managed to switch to the Americans at the last moment, neither Vladimir A. Skripkin nor Konstantin Volkov was so lucky and they are believed to have been executed, their intentions having been betrayed by well-placed moles like Kim Philby.

★　　★　　★

The entire area of handling Soviet intelligence defectors is fraught with difficulty, as is demonstrated by the extraordinary case of Vitali S. Yurchenko, who turned up at the Vatican Museum in Rome seeking asylum in August 1985 and then surrendered to the Soviet embassy in Washington three months later, on Saturday 2 November. He had been dining with his young CIA escort, Tom Hanna, at Au Pied de Cochon, a fashionable bistro in Georgetown, when he slipped away. In the intervening weeks he had given enough information to the Americans for them to identify Edward L. Howard and Ronald W. Pelton as important Soviet spies. Howard, who had been employed by the CIA for two years before being fired in 1983, managed to flee the country and evade arrest, but Pelton, who had retired from the NSA some six years earlier, was convicted and sentenced to life imprisonment.

Quite apart from the questions raised about the wisdom of allowing Yurchenko to be eating in downtown Washington, within a mile or so of his old office in the Soviet embassy, accompanied by a single minder, the episode highlighted the importance of handling useful defectors with tact and sensitivity. It also provided ammunition for those critics of the CIA who had advocated turning responsibility for the handling of defectors over to the Federal Bureau of Investigation (FBI). It was pointed out that the Bureau could hardly have performed worse than the CIA in this instance. Yurchenko had simply left Hanna sitting at their table, walked up Wisconsin Avenue unhindered and sought refuge at the Soviet Mount Alto compound in Tunlaw Road. It was later revealed that while Yurchenko had been posted to Washington, he had conducted an illicit affair with Valentina Yereskovsky, the wife of a colleague. Her husband, Aleksandr S. Yereskovsky, had been moved to the Soviet consulate in Montreal, and while Yurchenko was still undergoing his debriefing the CIA arranged for the two lovers to meet close to the Canadian border with Vermont. The rendezvous had not been a success, and Valentina reportedly refused Yurchenko's offer of a new life in the US. Disillusioned, he then returned to his suburban safe-house just outside Fredericksburg, Virginia. Evidently, his debriefers had not appreciated the impact of the confrontation on him.

Certainly, Yurchenko was a prize catch by any standards. He had spent five years in Washington as the embassy security chief until 1980, when he was transferred to Moscow to take charge of the Fifth Department of the KGB's elite First Chief Directorate, concerned with counter-intelligence investigations. In April 1985, he had been switched to head operations in North America. He was, therefore, unlikely to have been rebuffed in Rome when he made his initial approach. Nor would he have been persuaded to return home as a defector-in-place. He was of sufficient stature to ensure a warm welcome from the CIA, and some sceptical observers noted that being such an attractive plum he would have been hard to resist. Had the KGB made exactly this calculation when planning some Machiavellian scheme?

The conspiracy theorists presented a labyrinthine scenario in which Yurchenko willingly played the role of a dispatched agent, ready to furnish the CIA with details of two burnt-out cases, Howard and Pelton, neither of whom had any prospect of further value. Two persuasive factors mitigated in favour of this interpretation of events. Firstly, the supreme confidence of the two Soviet diplomats who flanked Yurchenko at the press conference he called on the Monday following his appearance at Mount Alto. If Yurchenko really was as unstable as some commentators suggested, why did the Soviets risk putting him on show, instead of hustling him back to Moscow as quickly as possible, which is the usual practice? Secondly, from his long experience in the KGB Yurchenko would know that the Soviet allows only one fate for a traitor, even one who has changed his mind. The fact that the Soviet authorities subsequently scotched rumours of his execution by presenting him to the media for a second time some months later, in March 1986, tended to support the 'deliberate plant' explanation, which had as its purported objective the creation of a climate antagonistic to defectors.[5] This conjecture rested upon the assumption that Moscow had sustained inordinate damage because of the activities of recent defectors such as Vladimir Kuzichkin, Anatoli Bogaty, Igor Gezha and Sergei Bokhan, and had decided to 'poison the well' so as to deter others of their ilk, or at least ensure that they got a frosty reception. Whoever had master-minded the scheme may well have reckoned, probably correctly, that a less than sympathetic response during the crucial first few hours might tip the balance in their favour and make a vulnerable potential defector reconsider. George Carver, the CIA's ex-Deputy Director for National Intelligence, claimed that 'the CIA conveyed an image of amateurish bungling that will be a great deterrent to future defectors'.[6] Considering the losses borne by the KGB and the GRU, such a scenario is not entirely far-fetched. In any event, Yurchenko was last heard of on 20 September 1987, when *Izvestia* quoted him dismissing speculation in the press about his fate. But not everyone accepted the 'plant' theory. Dick Helms, for example, is convinced that Yurchenko was a genuine defector who simply changed his mind. 'If you were chief of the KGB, would you pick an agent who knew all your agents and send him on a mission like this?'[7]

The conundrum of Yurchenko's motives is unlikely to be resolved, and the debate about the appropriate jurisdiction for defector resettlement between the Bureau and the Agency has been perpetuated. In October 1987, a Senate sub-committee investigated the débâcle and took evidence from both the DCI, William H. Webster, and several defectors, including Major Stanislav Levchenko, formerly of the KGB, and 'Dr Lawrence Martin' of Boston University, actually Ladislav Bittman, once the Czech STB's disinformation expert. Tom Polgar, who retired from the CIA in 1981 as Chief of Personnel Management in the Operations Division, testified that in the Yurchenko case 'a potent weapon is provided to the Soviet security services with which to discourage further defections'. He questioned 'the adequacy of integration of the various elements required for the secure and efficient exploitation of defectors'.[8] Mark Wyatt, another experienced CIA officer with direct experience of defector-handling, emphasized the significance of defectors in his evidence when he described them as 'the Soviet "Achilles' heel"'. Our adversaries know that some of the very best intention-level intelligence has been given to the US by defectors, including identification of Soviet "illegals" working in the US and key leads to "mole" operations in Western Intelligence and Security organizations.'[9]

What had motivated Yurchenko? Had he been depressed by the unexpected rejection of his former mistress? Had he been affected by the number of newspaper articles which had appeared during his interrogations accurately describing his co-operation in clearing up old counter-intelligence problems? Or was he part of an elaborate strategy to undermine the CIA's ability to deal with defectors? The answer is unlikely to be found.

Redefection is not uncommon, and in recent times two valued defectors have expressed an intention to return home. Anatoli Bogaty, the KGB officer who disappeared with his wife Larissa and two sons from the Soviet embassy in Morocco in September 1982, complained about debts they had accumulated since their resettlement in Falls Church, Virginia. Ludek Zemenek, a KGB illegal 'turned' by the FBI in May 1977, wants to return to his native Prague, citing his continued commitment to Marxism and his desire to bring up his two sons in a non-materialistic society. Zemenek, who called himself Rudolf Herrmann while under cover, first as a delicatessen operator in Toronto and then as a photographer, was regarded as an important coup by the FBI. His principal meal-ticket was the identity of another KGB illegal, Professor Hugh Hambleton, who was eventually prosecuted in England in 1982. The FBI resettled Zemenek as a house builder in Hartsdale, New York, and put him on their payroll at $35,000 a year. His business thrived, and now Zemenek and his wife Inga are quite wealthy, at least by Czech standards, but they still want to return home.

In spite of the shock waves caused by Yurchenko and felt throughout the West's counter-intelligence community, the CIA has continued to attract high-grade intelligence defectors. Oleg Agranyants of the KGB defected from Tunis in June 1986 and was followed in December the following year by Andrei A. Remenchuk, a GRU officer under translator cover at the Soviet consulate in Montreal. There have been others, perhaps as many as four senior intelligence defectors during 1988, whose details have yet to be disclosed.[10] This has to some degree compensated for an era of ceaseless failure, and the CIA's demonstrable inability to run successful operations in the so-called denied areas behind the Iron Curtain.

Edward Howard, the CIA traitor denounced by Yurchenko, is in part responsible for the latest defeats suffered by the CIA's Moscow Station. Before his dismissal for petty theft and drug abuse, Howard had been selected for an assignment to Moscow. Although it is surprising that someone so inexperienced could be chosen for hazardous duty in his first posting overseas, the CIA prefers to use unknown personnel in Moscow so as to reduce the chances of their being compromised instantly by the local security apparatus. The old hands, who have been on missions across the world, may have the advantage in terms of tradecraft and knowledge but, inevitably, they are also more likely to be spotted for what they really are by the KGB. Accordingly, Howard was selected for Moscow and underwent a special training course at Rosslyn, Virginia, in preparation for his transfer. During this period he was briefed on a number of current operations, including that of Adolf G. Tolkachev, an aeronautical engineer then supplying the CIA with secrets. In June 1985, Tolkachev was arrested while attempting a rendezvous with his case officer, Paul M. Stombaugh, who had operated under second secretary cover at the US embassy. Soon afterwards, two other cases went badly wrong. In March 1986, another CIA officer, Michael Sellers, was declared persona non grata for espionage and, on 7 May, his colleague Eric Sites was expelled for the same reason. Within a year three important operations, which had taken years of painstaking preparation by the Moscow Station, had been destroyed and, it has been alleged, no less than five of the CIA's local assets were shot because of Howard's treachery.

Of course, intensive surveillance is an accepted occupational hazard in Moscow and, like most Allied organizations, the CIA has found the task of running an agent in the Soviet Union exceptionally difficult. Most of the agents recruited have come to a sticky end. Aleksandr D. Ogorodnik, a regular diplomat recruited in Bogota, only survived twenty months before being arrested in 1977. He succeeded in committing suicide with a lethal pill supplied by the CIA.[11] Anatoly Filatov, another Foreign Ministry official run for a long period by the CIA, was eventually caught and executed in July 1978. Similarly, Major Piotr Popov was arrested in October 1959 and thrown live into a furnace before an audience of his GRU colleagues. The event was filmed and subsequently screened to new recruits *pour encourager les autres*. In short, a combination of ruthless deterrents, strict supervision and an oppressive scrutiny of suspect foreigners makes Moscow a daunting environment in which to mount agent operations. Naturally, the solution is to concentrate such activities in more congenial surroundings, which is why the overwhelming majority of successful cases are developed or serviced in neutral or Allied countries. Thus, the famous Oleg Penkovsky underwent his debriefings during visits to London and Paris while he was supposedly attending trade negotiations. In the case of Vladimir N. Sakharov, who eventually defected from Kuwait in July 1971, clandestine contact was largely restricted to the countries in the Middle East where he had been posted as a regular Soviet diplomat.

The difficulties inherent in Moscow operations have already been described; but, to emphasize the conditions in which the CIA has to operate, it is worth pausing a moment to look at the historical position. The US embassy in Tchaikovsky Street is an old, nine-storey, converted apartment block, which, until 1986, actually accommodated more Russians than Americans. No less than 206 Soviets worked there, just outnumbering the US personnel. All, of course, had been employed through the auspices of UPDK, the state-controlled agency responsible for the selection of all Soviet citizens working for foreigners.

The UPDK is regarded as a sub-section of the KGB's Second Chief Directorate by most Western counter-intelligence officers who know the catalogue of espionage, entrapments and provocations engineered by UPDK-sponsored staff. Before a potential walk-in could volunteer his services to an American, he had either to talk his way past the Soviet operator who manned the embassy's switchboard, or bluff his way past the KGB men, dressed in militia uniforms, who guarded the front entrance.

Of the full complement, less than a third of the US personnel are strictly State Department employees. A proportion are trade and agriculture experts seconded to Moscow, but a very large number are intelligence officers, working principally for the NSA, the Defence Intelligence Agency and other related organizations. Although Soviet workers once enjoyed the run of most of the premises, they were excluded, in theory at least, from three floors, access to which could only be gained via the top floor. The actual CIA station is relatively small, consisting of just a dozen staff, located on the seventh floor. Thus, when the Station Chief arrives at his desk each day, he has taken the lift to the ninth floor, passed through a security checkpoint manned by armed marine guards, and then made his way downstairs to the two sealed floors where the classified work is dealt with. It has always been an unproductive post, ever since the first CIA Station Chief was posted in 1953 and then swiftly transferred, when it was discovered that he had started an affair with his attractive Russian maid.

Up until the reciprocity agreement in 1986, which led to the withdrawal of the locally hired UPDK workers and their replacement by ninety Americans, there was overwhelming evidence of KGB-inspired espionage both inside and outside the building. Literally dozens of listening devices had been found in every conceivable hiding-place, and, after the arrest of several US marine guards in 1986, it was learned that even the most sensitive communications rooms had been entered by the KGB. Sophisticated miniaturized transmitters were discovered in the electric typewriters used by the CIA, and there were bugs embedded in the very fabric of the building. At one stage the level of concentrated microwave energy focused at the embassy, and used to provide remote power to the eavesdropping devices, was thought to be posing a health hazard to the staff. CIA personnel also protested about the invisible dust they were occasionally sprayed with so as to monitor their movements and contacts, but analysis showed it not to be toxic.

Apart from this kind of routine harassment, being literally physically surrounded by KGB premises from which intensive surveillance is conducted, the CIA station has to contend with all the difficulties of gathering information in a totalitarian environment. The fact that it manages to purchase 800 different Soviet publications on a regular basis, ranging from magazines to technical journals, is a partial justification for continuing to maintain the station. However, the fact remains that the embassy and consulate will always be a prime target for the KGB, and, whatever measures are taken to minimize the inconvenience, there is little prospect of the surveillance becoming less intrusive.

Even now that the Soviet capital has become an important tourist destination, and a growing number of inquisitive Americans make the journey each year, the local environment remains, in intelligence terms, unacceptably hostile. Accordingly, the CIA responds by deploying counter-intelligence experts elsewhere in the world where they are bound to find their counterparts.

The CIA's ability to deploy skilled counter-intelligence officers around the globe is probably unequalled. It can call upon plenty of resources and its data bank of identified Soviet intelligence personnel is extraordinarily thorough. On one occasion Melvin Beck reported on a conversation held in Havana bar by two Soviet trade officials, whom he suspected of not being quite as innocent as they appeared. Langley acknowledged the signal, but rejected his identification because the two arms experts CIA headquarters had been expecting to arrive in Cuba did not fit Beck's description. Apparently, one was known to be completely bald, yet both men staying in the Hotel Comora boasted full heads of hair. A week or so later, however, Beck was vindicated. A local agent informed him that one of the Russians was wearing a wig, which he invariably took off before going for a swim in the hotel pool. This news was duly transmitted to CIA headquarters by a jubilant Beck.

The research and technical support available to CIA personnel in the field is widely recognized to be first-rate, but it is no substitute for the intuitive case officer who can recruit and inspire assets. This is the key to the successful management of individual agents: assessing their psychological make-up, judging their temperament accurately and instilling in them a sense of personal loyalty. These are the fundamental skills of a worthwhile case officer, and it is upon his estimate of a perhaps dubious personality that crucial counter-intelligence decisions will be taken, maybe putting lives in jeopardy. Every US embassy in the world accommodates a secret defector committee, which prepares contingency plans for the day when 'a hot one' turns up unexpectedly and a CIA counter-intelligence expert from the local station will be required to give some instant answers. Can he spot the false defector? Is he able to discriminate between the agent provocateur or the genuine walk-in? Will he fail to recognize an authentic spy?

Character evaluation is a vital element, and the performance of a particular counter-intelligence branch will not only sway the performance of an entire agency, but directly affect the standing of the organization in the Allied community. Thus, the CIA's Counter-intelligence Staff, headed for so long by Jim Angleton, had a disproportionate influence over the rest of the Company, and by the nature of its unique liaison with Mossad, carried extra prestige and weight elsewhere.

Angleton's Counterintelligence Staff has often been characterized, unfairly, as having succumbed to the 'wilderness of mirrors' syndrome, which manifests itself through the warped testimony of disaffected defectors and causes a distortion in perspective. This phenomenon is not unique to the CIA. Sir Martin Furnival Jones, the British Security Service officer who headed MI5 between 1965 and 1972, has been quoted as suggesting that 'four or five years in counter-espionage is too long and causes insanity',[12] and one is bound to wonder about the outlook of a Soviet official raised on the jaundiced attitudes of the few Western defectors resident in Moscow. Apparently, Yurchenko told of having had dealings with both George Blake and Kim Philby when he was running the KGB's counter-intelligence directorate, and maybe this had an adverse impact on his state of mind.[13]

2

Company Business

> 'The respect for scholarship is one of the main distinguishing features that has given the CIA a marked superiority in intellectual quality over the Soviet KGB and other totalitarian intelligence agencies.'[1]
>
> Dr Ray Cline

Assessing counter-intelligence skills is bound to be a very subjective exercise, with the basic data needed to come to a proper evaluation hard to find. Even the most fundamental statistics, such as the number of suspected hostile intelligence personnel expelled from a particular country, can be difficult to calculate. The game of intelligence is played by professionals who conform to certain rules. One of them requires, in certain circumstances, informal notification that a particular person is about to be declared persona non grata, thus giving the individual concerned an opportunity to be withdrawn quietly without undue fuss. In the game of intelligence this is known as a 'silent PNG', and some countries, such as Canada, prefer this option to the more public alternative. Similarly, details of court proceedings can provide only the roughest guide to the relative performance of a counter-espionage agency. The FBI, for example, prosecuted no less than forty-nine people during the period 1975–88 and experienced only one acquittal. But that does not reflect figures from the military, which often opts for courts-martial and did so twice during this period, nor does it take account of the alternative conclusions to cases that ought to be regarded as counter-intelligence successes: the number of hostile agents turned into double agents; the spies neutralized by a preliminary interrogation where there is insufficient evidence to mount a full-scale prosecution; the convictions for related offences, such as perjury or contempt of court; and the deals made, perhaps in return for immunity or a swap.

Spy-swaps, incidentally, are not limited to those of the East–West variety negotiated by Wolfgang Vogel, the East German lawyer. For example, in June 1985 a Ghanaian, Michael Soussoudis, was arrested in a Virginian motel, where he was supposed to meet his lover, Sharon Scranage, a black CIA operations support assistant recently returned from the Accra Station, where she had supplied CIA secrets to Kojo Tsikata, head of Jerry Rawlings's intelligence apparatus. Scranage and Soussoudis were convicted of espionage; but when Soussoudis was flown home, four Ghanaians were simultaneously released from custody and sent into exile. Four US embassy staff, including two CIA officers, also left the country. It soon became known that the four detainees had admitted spying for the CIA, whilst Soussoudis was revealed as the Ghanaian leader's first cousin. Scranage's five-year sentence was later reduced on appeal to two years, with a recommendation for parole after eighteen months. Nor do spy-swaps involving the exchange of a prisoner of the US always have an obvious American angle. In 1978, Robert Thompson, a former USAF airman who had received a thirty-year sentence for espionage in 1965, was traded to East Germany in return for the release of Miran Marcus, a young Israeli pilot held in Mozambique. And in July 1969, Yuri N. Loginov, a KGB illegal arrested in Johannesburg two years earlier, was swapped for eleven people held in the East.

On the surface, the FBI's performance during the 1975–88 period looks impressive. A heavy workload and a high rate of convictions quite contrast with the period between 1966 and 1975, when there was not a single successful Justice Department prosecution for espionage. Does this mean there was no espionage undertaken during this time, or simply that the FBI was unable to detect it? The reality is that, quite apart from the operational considerations, politics often come into play in the intelligence arena. In one classic case in February 1972, the FBI trapped Valery I. Markelov, a KGB officer working at the United Nations under translator cover, in the act of receiving classified documents about the F-14A Tomcat fighter from a Grumman engineer. Coincidentally, President Nixon was planning a summit with Brezhnev, so the charges against Markelov were quietly dropped and he was allowed to return home as a gesture of goodwill. The case is far from unique. Igor A. Ivanov, the KGB officer implicated when John Butenko was caught in 1963 passing him secrets of Strategic Air Command's communications system, stayed out of gaol through clever legal manoeuvres even when Butenko had been convicted and sentenced to thirty years' imprisonment. Ivanov was subsequently allowed to travel to Moscow. More recently, in August 1986, Gennadi F. Zakharov was arrested for receiving classified jet-engine blueprints from an FBI double agent, Leakh N. Bhoge. A week later an American journalist, Nicholas Daniloff, was taken into custody in Moscow and then swapped for Zakharov. Also caught in the fall-out was the CIA Station Chief in Moscow, Murat Natirboff, who was withdrawn discreetly.

Not all cases come to court, or even come to the attention of the public. An USAF sergeant was intercepted in 1973 while on his way to the Soviet embassy on Washington's Sixteenth Street with a package of top-secret, counter-intelligence documents. Nothing more was heard of the affair and the sergeant's name was never disclosed. It may well be that the Justice Department was inhibited from taking public proceedings against a suspect for fear of compromising further information. In 1954, an agreement was reached between the CIA and the Justice Department allowing the Agency discretion to drop the charges where more damage might be done if the evidence was made public. This policy was terminated when William Kampiles was prosecuted in 1977, revealing a number of appalling security lapses committed by the Agency. An unknown number of cases have been allowed to lapse under the threat from defendants to reveal sensitive information in court. Three years later, Congress approved the 1980 Classified Information Procedures Act, which enabled lawyers, at the discretion of the judge, to study very secret evidence in private without the requirement to put it all on the public record. However, even the CIPA's provisions failed to give adequate protection to the ultra-secret NSA in the trial of Ronald Pelton in 1986. The NSA, whose initials are sometimes believed to stand for 'No Such Agency', was exceptionally cautious about public disclosures of its activities, and it went to great lengths to avoid statements in open court regarding its operations. The only previous incident of this kind led to the conviction in 1948 of an employee of the Armed Forces Security Agency (the NSA's predecessor), William Weisband, for contempt, not espionage.[2] In

1978, the prosecution against a black American USAF non-commissioned officer, formerly based with the 6950th Electronic Security Squadron at RAF Chicksands in Bedfordshire, who had volunteered his services to the GRU, was dropped because of its sensitivity. The British Security Service was reluctant to disclose their tapes, which had recorded the man's telephone conversations with the Soviet military attaché, and the trial might also have revealed details of the highly secret work undertaken at Chicksands. In another case involving the CIA, in which the CIPA was invoked, R. Craig Smith insisted that his contacts with Soviet intelligence officers had been part of an authorized operation and Smith was acquitted.

The rate of court hearings or the number of PNGs in any given period cannot be used as anything but the vaguest guide for the level of activity in a particular country. And, by definition, they are only likely to be of limited value in determining past reputation rather than giving a valuation of the current position. With these caveats in mind, we can now turn to look at the US experience in dealing with the intelligence threat to its security.

The exact scale of the threat is difficult to quantify, but the number of Eastern Bloc diplomats is closely monitored. At present it stands at 4,250, of whom 2,100 come from Warsaw Pact countries. The CIA regularly releases its own analysis of Soviet commercial representation and, in 1980, this showed a total of 148 trade officials resident in the US.[3] Soviet diplomatic establishments in the capital include the new embassy and residential complex on Mount Alto, the old embassy on Sixteenth Street, the consulate at 1825 Phelps Place and the Soviet military office at 2552 Belmont Road NW. There is also an information centre on Eighteenth Street NW, a trade office at 2001 Connecticut Avenue, a fisheries section on Decatur Street NW, a marine attaché at 1555 L Street NW and a forty-acre estate at Pioneer Point, in Centreville, Maryland.

Elsewhere there are the consulates on East 67th Street, New York, and 2790 Green Street, San Francisco; the UN mission in Manhattan and the Glen Cove compound on Long Island. About two hundred or so of the Soviet diplomats based in Washington are regarded by the FBI as KGB or GRU professionals. In addition, there are about 140 diplomats accredited to the UN, plus a similar number of international civil servants employed by the UN based in New York.

A further twenty work for Aeroflot and Intourist, with a similar corps of journalists reporting for the TASS and Novosti news agencies, *Izvestia, Pravda* and the various Soviet radio and television organizations, most of which maintain duplicate premises in New York and Washington. In October 1986, a parity agreement was made in respect of the Soviet diplomats which limited their total to 225 in Washington and twenty-six in San Francisco, identical to the US presence in Moscow and Leningrad.

Ranged against them is the FBI's Intelligence Division and, in particular, the twenty counter-intelligence CI squads based at the Washington field office at 1900 Half Street SW. The exact number of the FBI's 9,220 special agents, spread over fifty-nine field offices and 400 resident agencies, employed on intelligence duties is classified. However, it is estimated that rather more than 3,000 special agents are devoted to counter-intelligence work, and half the 500 special agents posted to the Washington field office are assigned to CI operations, where they are divided into squads, each with up to thirty members, deployed against specific targets. Thus, CI-2 concentrates on the KGB's elite Line KR personnel;[4] CI-3 keeps surveillance on GRU staff at the Soviet military office; CI-4 watches the KGB contingent at the embassy; and CI-6 monitors all other GRU suspects. As well as tapping all the Soviet telephones, the FBI maintains a permanent observation post in the AFL–CIO headquarters in the Philip Murray building, which directly overlooks the embassy and routinely photographs all visitors.

The FBI is assisted in its operations by two restrictions imposed on their Soviet opponents. All cars used by diplomats carry distinctive licence plates, coloured red, white and blue, and bearing the prefix 'FC'. Like their counterparts at the CIA's Moscow Station, they are also limited to travel within the capital itself. Any journey further afield requires special permission and rented cars cannot be used.

During the years 1945 to 1986, a total of 104 Soviet intelligence personnel were expelled from the US. Of this group, a high proportion operated under UN or other international cover (see chart on pages 54–6).[5] The location of so many UN establishments on US territory is an added burden for the counter-espionage authorities. Responsibility for the supervision of these threats is chiefly in the hands of the FBI, although the CIA overlaps when the counter-intelligence interest centres on Soviet Bloc defectors. It is this sometimes uneasy liaison that has been known to go wrong on occasion, despite the efforts made in the early 1960s among like-minded 'keepers of the seal' to work collectively against the common adversary. At that time, between 1961 and 1971, William C. Sullivan, J. Edgar Hoover's Assistant Director in charge of the FBI's Intelligence Division, and Jim Angleton created a highly secret international co-operative known as CAZAB, which included selected members of the security and intelligence agencies of Britain, Canada, Australia, New Zealand and the United States. There were, and continue to be, three levels of access: Level One was indoctrination into CAZAB's existence; Level Two was limited access to certain kinds of CAZAB codeword material; and Level Three was unrestricted involvement. The only condition of entry to CAZAB, which undertook joint operations and conducted regular conferences, was to have every CAZAB candidate cleared by all five participating countries. One 'blackball' would exclude, and there was no appeal.

CAZAB's very existence has been a tightly guarded secret because Hoover's attitude to inter-Agency co-operation was, according to Sullivan, 'laughable'. 'Hoover didn't like the British, didn't care for the French, hated the Dutch and couldn't stand the Australians. He wouldn't meet with the director of British intelligence, not even as a courtesy.'[6] CAZAB was thus the only method of circumventing Hoover's malign influence over counter-intelligence liaison which, after all, is the key to successful counter-espionage operations. Nevertheless, there have been several avoidable lapses. One CAZAB principle is that an expellee should not be granted a visa in an associated country. Yet, although Richardas K. Vaygauskas had been PNG'd in 1962 while operating in New York under UN cover, he was granted permission to come to London in 1969 with the rank of consul. He was subsequently filmed emptying dead-letter drops by M15 and added to their list of expellees in 1971.[7] Since Hoover's death, CAZAB has enhanced its status and is regarded as an essential weapon in the game of intelligence.

That, of course, is not to say that the US does not remain susceptible to penetration. As has been seen, the CIA itself has experienced hostile penetration, and the apparent absence of any detected spy within the Agency until 1976 is a continuing cause for anxiety among those keen to tie up loose ends. Certainly, Yurchenko assisted in clearing up a lot of old mysteries, but it has yet to be determined whether his débâcle has had a long-term beneficial effect on Allied counter-intelligence or, more specifically, on the CIA's ability to spot false defectors, catch spies and deter treachery, three of the principal objectives of its Counterintelligence Staff.

A curious feature of the CIA's experience of contamination is the way in which all the spies involved were walk-in volunteers. And an ominous aspect is the haphazard way in which they were eventually detected. Edwin Moore tossed a package containing instructions on how to make contact with him over a fence into a Soviet compound in Washington. A suspicious guard, believing it might be a bomb, reported it to his security chief, Yurchenko, who promptly called the American authorities and handed it over unopened. The FBI then followed the directions and caught Moore when he came to collect what he anticipated was the KGB's response to his offer. In a similar episode, Daulton Lee was apprehended by a vigilant policeman, who spotted him throwing a cigarette pack through the railings of the Soviet embassy in Mexico City. He was arrested on suspicion of being a terrorist, but examination of Lee's litter revealed a microfilm containing classified data about satellite surveillance systems. Once again, it was sheer chance that led to his discovery. Under questioning Lee admitted his role as a courier for Christopher Boyce, who was then promptly arrested in California. In the case of William Kampiles, he actually volunteered a confession. He had only been working at Langley for eight months when he resigned, taking a highly secret satellite technical manual with him. This he sold to a GRU officer in Athens for $3,000. Upon his return to the US he approached the CIA to suggest that he be used as a double agent, but was charged with espionage instead.

David Barnett had also retired from the CIA when he originally made contact with the KGB in Jakarta in 1976, but three years later he rejoined the Agency as a contract employee to teach a course on interrogation resistance. The exact details of how he was spotted are unknown, but it is believed that he was identified contacting Vladimir V. Popov while the latter was under routine CI-3 surveillance. When challenged by the FBI, Barnett admitted his guilt and Popov was withdrawn discreetly. The scale of the damage inflicted by Barnett is supposed to have been immense. He was a career officer with twelve years' experience, and he certainly compromised much of the work he had undertaken in Jakarta while posted there as an operations officer between 1967 and 1970. He is known to have betrayed thirty of his colleagues, together with details of a still classified operation known as HU/BRINK. He also confessed to telling the Soviets why their SAM-2 anti-aircraft missiles had been so ineffective in Vietnam: the CIA had examined the guidance system of one 'borrowed' from the Indonesian navy and developed an ingenious counter-measure. He had also disclosed the extent of the CIA's knowledge about the Soviet Whisky-class diesel submarine and the resourceful method used to obtain it.

Lee, Boyce, Kampiles and Barnett were all walk-ins in the classic mould. So was Edward Howard, who had simply hand-delivered a letter to the Soviet consulate in downtown Washington in 1983 to establish contact and his *bona fides* as an authentic CIA source. Waldo Dubberstein was rather less a spy, and rather more a willing tool exploited by Edwin P. Wilson and Frank Terpil, two renegades who sold out to the Libyans. Dubberstein's activities probably would have escaped attention if he had not been so heavily involved with the two arms suppliers. His full story can only be guessed at, because he committed suicide with a shotgun in the basement of his Arlington home on 29 April 1983, the very day he was due to answer a grand jury indictment. [8] Only Karl Koecher has the distinction of being a deep-penetration agent deliberately planted inside the CIA. He arrived in the US in 1965 from Austria, in transit from Czechoslovakia, and applied for a post in the CIA in April 1972. By February the following year, he had passed the mandatory screening process and had been accepted as a translator. However, he also attempted to improve his standing with the Agency by declaring a suspicious approach from a Czech diplomat, Vesek Kralik, and offering to become a double agent. [9]

John Bothwell's difficulties were caused by allegations from a defector, as were those experienced by Larry Wu Tai Chin, a retired CIA translator still employed part-time as a consultant at the time of his arrest. A Chinese defector named Ou Quiming had denounced Chin as a long-term, ideologically motivated agent, who had been spying on the Americans since he was first taken on by the US consulate in Shanghai back in 1948.

The CIA and the FBI's performance in the detection of spies can hardly be described as very impressive, the overwhelming majority of cases mentioned here having been discovered fortuitously. Nevertheless, some comfort can be taken from the amateurish approach of most spies, even those from a professional background, and the continuing success of very basic precautions like photographic surveillance of Soviet premises and the interception of all telephone lines. Oddly enough, these rather fundamental measures, which might be thought to have been anticipated by those contemplating a walk-in overture, has accounted for a high proportion of successful detections, particularly in London.

Of course, surveillance cannot guarantee identification of every caller, and the KGB does what it can to reduce its exposure. Ronald Pelton's experience in January 1980 is a case in point. He made two short telephone calls to the Soviet embassy and then made his pitch straight through the front entrance. Once inside he had been able to establish his NSA credentials quite quickly, but outside the FBI was at an acute disadvantage. 'We saw him go in, saw his backside, and we could not identify his exit,' the FBI Director, William H. Webster, explained afterwards.[10] During three hours of preliminary interrogation Pelton was accepted as a potentially crucial source, and the KGB made elaborate arrangements for him to elude the FBI's waiting cameras. His beard was shaved off and, dressed in the scruffy clothes of a Soviet embassy workman, he was smuggled into a van filled with other Soviet employees. He was driven to the Mount Alto complex for a meal and further questions before being returned to where he had parked his car. According to Yurchenko, who had participated in the operation, the KGB had monitored the FBI's radios throughout and noticed a perceptible increase in the traffic when Pelton had first approached the embassy building. It was only after Yurchenko had labelled the mysterious visitor as a former NSA analyst with access to IVY BELLS, the NSA's top-secret underwater eavesdropping project in the Sea of Orkhotsk, that the tapes recording the visitor's brief conversation were matched to Pelton's voice. Even then, it took the FBI eight days to trace him. In short, blanket surveillance is far from foolproof. Nor is there anything secret about it, despite rather lame attempts to limit admissions on the subject. The tapes released by the FBI during Pelton's trial were described as having come from 'a targeted premise', and Melvin Beck's account of the surveillance conducted by the CIA on the Soviet embassy in Mexico was censored:

Photographic coverage of [FOUR WORDS DELETED] of the Soviet Embassy provided daily reports of the sighting of individual Soviets and others, with accompanying photographs. From certain [TWO WORDS DELETED] lines to the Soviet Embassy, the station had a complete daily account of conversations between

Soviets inside the embassy and callers from without.

Since the Pelton case, which inflicted grave, irreparable damage on the NSA's operations, the FBI has improved its comprehensive cover of its targets, and several lower-level approaches have been averted. Nevertheless, short of the introduction of a hostile, Moscow-style regime in the locality of every Soviet diplomatic mission, no system based on covert observation posts can be regarded as complete protection against the determined walk-in.

Turning to the CIA's operational status and its ability to fulfil its intelligence-gathering role effectively, a brief review of the political environment in which it has to operate would be in order. There are, for our purposes, three significant criteria by which to compare the oversight demanded by the government and the legislature in the highly controversial area of assassination, covert action and black propaganda.

Disclosure of the CIA's involvement in discreditable operations in the early 1970s provided the catalyst for a series of debilitating official investigations, which resulted in the introduction of a strict framework requiring top-level consultation before the CIA could embark upon future high-risk schemes. The Church Committee's enquiries, which took evidence from over a hundred witnesses and examined thousands of classified CIA cables and memoranda, established beyond all doubt that the Agency had planned to kill Patrice Lumumba and Fidel Castro. The Congolese Premier was murdered in mid-January 1961 after the plane carrying him from the custody of UN forces in Leopoldville to Bakwanga had been diverted to Elisabethville in the secessionist Katanga province, where he had been delivered into the hands of Joseph Mobutu's hostile troops. In fact, when Lumumba died, the CIA had been plotting to get rid of him for more than six months and had even hired two experienced European killers, codenamed QJ/WIN and WI/ROGUE, to complete the job. Various methods were discussed, including the use of a lethal virus which was stored in the safe belonging to Larry Devlin, then the CIA Station Chief in Leopoldville.[11] When asked about the poison, Michael Mulroney, the CIA officer assigned the task of 'neutralizing' Lumumba, recalled that he 'knew it wasn't for somebody to get his polio shot up to date'.[12] In the event, the plot proved unnecessary because the Congolese dealt with Lumumba without any assistance from the Company, although help would have been given gladly, as indicated by the signal transmitted to Langley by the CIA Station Chief in Elisabethville two days after the murder: 'THANKS FOR PATRICE. IF WE HAD KNOWN HE WAS COMING WE WOULD HAVE BAKED A SNAKE.'[13] The Senate Select Committee concluded that

> the chain of events revealed by the documents and testimony is strong enough to permit a reasonable inference that the plot to assassinate Lumumba was authorized by President Eisenhower.... It is clear that the Director of Central Intelligence, Allen Dulles, authorized an assassination plot.[14]

No less than three successive presidents, Eisenhower, Kennedy and Johnson, sanctioned the CIA's plan euphemistically known as 'executive action' between 1960 and 1965 to get rid of Fidel Castro. Or, to be more precise, the eight separate projects, all covered with 'plausible deniability', to eliminate the Cuban leader. Of the eight, only two actually progressed beyond a preparatory stage. However, even before the decision had been taken to kill Castro, the CIA had proposed some extraordinary strategies to undermine his standing: the first was for a cigar spiked with LSD to be handed to him shortly before he was to make a speech; the second was for a radio studio he was due to use to be sprayed with another hallucinogenic. Both ideas were rejected after experiments with animals had failed. The Agency then turned to the idea of putting thallium salts into Castro's shoes in the hope that this strong depilatory agent would cause his beard to fall out. The operation was to be mounted when Castro was due to stay in a hotel and could be expected to place his shoes outside his room, but had to be abandoned when he failed to make the expected trip.

The first serious consideration of an assassination took place in July 1960, when a Cuban agent approached the CIA station in Havana and volunteered to arrange an accident for Fidel and his brother Raúl for $10,000. The offer was accepted, but the agent lost his opportunity. Then, the following year, a box of Castro's favourite cigars was contaminated with a botulinum toxin in a CIA laboratory and delivered to another agent in regular touch with him. Evidently, Castro never smoked one. Early in 1963, two imaginative schemes were considered: one was for a booby-trapped seashell to be placed in an area where Castro was known to go swimming; the other was for a diving suit to be dusted with a fungus that would produce a deadly skin disease, and for the aqualung equipment to be impregnated with a tuberculosis bacillus – and then for both to be sent to Castro as a gift. This plan was deemed 'cock-eyed' by the DCI, Dick Helms, and vetoed.[15] Later in the year, CIA technicians came up with a ballpoint pen concealing with a hypodermic needle so fine that the user would not notice he had been injected with a deadly, commercially available poison called Blackleaf-40. This was given to another local agent, Major Rolando Cubela, codenamed AM/LASH, who was in close touch with Castro, but he failed to follow through. He was also offered a consignment of grenades and a high-powered sniper's rifle fitted with a silencer, but nothing came of that idea either. Eventually, the CIA dropped Cubela because of his poor security and his history of mental problems.

Thereafter, three notorious underworld figures, Sam Giancana, Santos Trafficante and John Rosselli, were granted a $150,000 contract, with the cryptonym ZR/RIFLE, to carry out a classic 'Mafia hit.'. Giancana was a Chicago-based gangster, Trafficante was the Cosa Nostra boss in Cuba, and Rosselli a well-connected hoodlum from Las Vegas. Initially they objected to a gangland-style ambush, on the grounds that their gunmen would be unable to escape; instead, they opted for a lethal pill that was to be put into Castro's drink in a restaurant he was known to frequent. Rosselli knew a waiter there, who had agreed to administer the poison. However, the first pills failed to dissolve in water, so a second batch was delivered that seemed to work when tested on monkeys, but the entire operation was called off before they could be administered.

The CIA's plans for Castro eventually floundered, but partial success was achieved in the case of General Rafael Trujillo, the brutal dictator of the Dominican Republic. Trujillo himself was not averse to the principle of assassination, for in June 1960 he was implicated in an attempt on the life of the Venezuelan President Betancourt. Both the Eisenhower and Kennedy administrations were keen to remove Trujillo from power, and, in April 1961, four M-3 machine-guns were delivered to the local CIA station for onward transmission to a group of well-organized dissidents. However, in the aftermath of the Bay of Pigs failure in the middle of that month, Langley had second thoughts about the wisdom of encouraging the rebels and decided against handing over the machine-guns. Undeterred, the dissidents ambushed Trujillo just outside San

Cristóbal late in the evening of 30 May and the coup went ahead, using carbines, handguns and shotguns, based on a plan that the CIA had helped draw up. As soon as the CIA Station Chief learned of Trujillo's death, he drafted the following cable to Washington and obtained permission to destroy all incriminating documents and to ship his entire station home:'HG AWARE EXTENT TO WHICH US GOVERNMENT ALREADY ASSOCIATED WITH ASSASSINATION. IF WE ARE AT LEAST TO COVER UP TRACKS, CIA PERSONNEL DIRECTLY INVOLVED IN ASSASSINATION PREPARATION MUST BE WITHDRAWN.'[16] Thus, although the CIA's objective of eliminating Trujillo had been achieved, it was not directly responsible for the murder itself, or so the Senate investigators concluded.

They reached a similar judgment when they looked into the background of President Ngo Dinh Diem's murder in Vietnam on 2 November 1963. Diem was toppled by a group of army generals who had already approached John Richardson, the CIA Station Chief in Saigon, for help; the request had been referred to the DCI, John McCone, but it had been rejected. McCone's directive asserted that the CIA 'cannot be in the position of stimulating, approving or supporting assassination, but, on the other hand, we are in no way responsible for stopping every such threat of which we might receive even partial knowledge'.[17] It was McCone's oft-quoted view that 'Diem may be a sonofabitch, but he's our sonofabitch.'[18] Nevertheless, the coup went ahead successfully, but the CIA only got four minutes' advance warning of it. Exactly how Diem and his brother Ngo Dinh Nhu were killed remains unknown.

Perhaps the most contentious assassination plot involving the CIA centred on Dr Salvador Allende of Chile, who won a plurality in the country's presidential elections of September 1970. Because no single candidate had won a clear majority, the Chilean constitution required a further election to be held by Congress two months later; and, during the run-up to this second ballot, the CIA made contact with no less than twenty-one key military and police officers to encourage them to launch a pre-emptive coup to prevent Allende, an avowed Marxist, from winning. The scheme received widespread support, but there was one steadfast opponent to it, the army's commander-in-chief, General Rene Schneider. On 22 October, two days before the election, Schneider was shot during what appeared to be a bungled kidnapping. In fact, during the previous three days Schneider had narrowly escaped no less than two attempts to abduct him. The problem for the CIA was that, when the news of Schneider's murder was made public, it looked as though the weapons used by the conspirators were identical with those supplied only hours earlier by Santiago's CIA station.

The Church Committee found that although the CIA had indeed plotted against Castro, Diem, Trujillo and Schneider, and may also have given consideration to the assassination of Colonel Abdel Kassem of Iraq, President Nasser of Egypt and Ho Chi Minh, there was no evidence to show that they had played a direct role in anyone's death. But just to be on the safe side, Dick Helms issued a formal order banning assassination in 1972, and Bill Colby did the same a year later. Colby told the Church Committee: 'With respect to assassination, my position is clear. I just think it is wrong.'[19]

Since the release of the Church Committee Report, the word 'assassination' and all its euphemisms have been utterly rejected by successive DCIs and presidents. So, too, has the concept of plausible deniability. However, in October 1984 it was disclosed that the CIA had distributed a ninety-page training manual, entitled *Psychological Warfare in Guerrilla Operations*, to a group of Nicaraguan Contras. The primer recommended the use of 'selective use of violence' to 'neutralize carefully selected and planned targets such as court judges, police and state security officials, etc.' It even suggested that, 'if possible, professional criminals will be hired to carry out selective "jobs"'.[20] It was almost as though the Mafia had been taken back on to the payroll after a gap of twenty-odd years.

In the event, the impact of the document, right in the midst of President Reagan's re-election campaign, caused a political row which ensured that the DCI, Bill Casey, quickly disciplined those responsible for issuing the booklet. Only a few copies had been released, Casey assured everyone, and the storm passed.

The fact that the CIA is now obliged to operate under strict rules governing its behaviour, with tight restrictions requiring congressional consultations before it can embark upon risky undertakings, cannot diminish its record in the field of covert action and black propaganda. Although assassination may not have been contemplated, the CIA has played a part in an impressive number of *coups d'état*: Mohammed Mussadeq was overthrown (with British help) in Iran in 1953; Jacobo Arbenz was removed in Guatemala in 1954; Kwame Nkrumah was toppled in Ghana in 1966; Medibo Keita was dismissed from Mali in 1968; Salvador Allende was ousted in Chile in 1973; and Maurice Bishop's successor was dispossessed in Grenada in 1983. However, the CIA was less successful against Sukarno in Indonesia in 1958, Duvalier in Haiti and Castro, but not for want of trying.

The political climate in which the CIA exists, and what influences its relationship with Congress and the president, is also partly influenced by what might be termed an embarrassment quotient. Revelations about mind-control experiments, the payment of compensation to unwilling participants of bizarre research programmes and similar events create an aura of suspicion. It is not the disclosure itself that undermines confidence, but rather the regime or atmosphere which allowed the development to happen in the first place. Is the Agency living up to its obligations? The law requires Committee clearance for any new covert action and any significant expenditure. Doubts about whether the Reagan administration accepted these constraints were cast when it was disclosed, in April 1984, that the CIA had sponsored a clandestine operation in which underwater mines had been sown around three Nicaraguan harbours. Seven ships had been damaged, including a British registered vessel. Casey responded by showing that he had briefed the Intelligence Committee about the mining operation more than a month earlier. He had described how seventy-five mines would be placed outside Corinto on the Pacific and El Bluff on the Atlantic, as well as at the oil depot at Puerto Sandino. Apparently, the Committee had either been unable to grasp the implications of what the DCI had told it, or had not caught what he said.

The mining incident demonstrated that consultation and oversight were not foolproof safeguards against political discomfort, and was reminiscent of the early episodes which had created the original unease about the CIA among elected officials. Back in May 1960, one of the CIA's U-2 planes had gone missing on a routine aerial reconnaissance mission over the Soviet Union. President Eisenhower's spokesmen, having been assured that there was no chance of the pilot being alive, had been persuaded to gloss over the incident by describing the U-2 as a civilian weather research aircraft. It was only after the White House statement had been made public that the Kremlin chose to reveal that Francis Gary Powers had survived and had already admitted to working for the CIA. Far from being employed on a meteorological task, Powers had been engaged in espionage. This had been a severe blow for Eisenhower. So had the Bay of Pigs invasion for President Kennedy, who was taunted with its abject failure by Khrushchev. More embarrassment was to follow in later years when unpalatable details of the PHOENIX 'rural pacification' programme in Vietnam were revealed, and the CIA's illegal domestic surveillance of anti-war protestors was divulged.

Politicians are often quick to take the credit for operations that go well, yet failure is not just an orphan, but more akin to a leper. The gains on offer from the American intelligence community come at a high risk with an unbridled media and an unforgiving public. The proof is the synonymity between the initials 'CIA' in the mid-1970s and Watergate, dirty tricks and Vietnam. When it was subsequently learned that a CIA proprietary company, Air America, had been immersed in the drug trade in South-East Asia, few were surprised. Unethical conduct was recognized as a feature of CIA behaviour, but not tolerated. When the so-called 'family jewels' began to haemorrhage, and the darkest secrets of the Counterintelligence Staff appeared in daily print, CIA morale plummeted. President Carter responded to the crisis by appointing an old classmate, Admiral Stansfield Turner, to the post of DCI and, in so doing, turned disaster into a catastrophe. In just three years some 2,800 career intelligence officers were given retirement, many prematurely. Some, like Theodore Shackley, a thirty-year veteran of the Agency and one-time Station Chief in Vientiane, contended that 'the CIA was accused of a shocking variety of ugly deeds. It was a shadow government run amok; a nest of fascists existed at Langley. Its people were assassins, and worse. Under the harsh glare of public scrutiny, they were undressed, item by item, until they stood naked.'[21]

Public accountability of an effective intelligence apparatus in a democratic society is the key issue right at the heart of the trauma experienced by the CIA. Some old hands maintain that the circle simply cannot be squared. There is an essential contradiction here which implies a straight choice between an impotent, possibly ineffective organization and an efficient but ruthless service. The modern pragmatists take a more sanguine view: chancy enterprises with low returns are no substitute for the natural confidence that flows from legal initiatives. Act with the full authority of Congress and the Company's status will be enhanced; stray into freewheeling and there is immediate jeopardy. A balance has been struck, but it is one that the cold warriors find hard to come to terms with. This is especially true in that most perilous of territories, the refugee community. As Bill Hood, Piotr Popov's case officer remarked, 'deal with émigrés, and you look death in the face'.

Although the debriefing of a defector does not boast the same public profile as the arming of a guerrilla army in, say, Angola, or the creation of a powerful wireless station in Latin America, or even the secret subsidy of an anti-Communist trade union in Europe, there are enormous risks taken every day by the CIA's Operations Directorate and, in particular, the Counterintelligence Staff. After all, this was the fulcrum of the 'family jewels' scandal that precipitated many of the Agency's woes in the mid-1970s The criteria for judging the CIA's operational prowess must include the sensitive, but largely unpublicized, human dimension of intelligence-gathering which encompasses defector handling, the treatment of walk-ins, the planting of moles, the management of double agents and the less exotic occupation of émigré debriefing.

This latter calling has been exceptionally profitable and has its basis in the gradual development of Soviet emigration. During the past two decades the numbers of Soviet citizens leaving for the West has escalated dramatically. Public attention usually focuses on the Jewish exodus, and the 200,000 or so émigrés who have left for Israel or the United States, in roughly equal proportions, since the current exodus began in 1970. However, in addition to that figure, there are the very large numbers of Armenians and ethnic Germans who have also left, totalling around 100,000. Of course, the Soviet authorities are well aware of the hazards of granting exit visas to individuals with useful information, and know that throughout the 1950s and 1960s the CIA conducted a highly productive screening programme to extract data from returnees, concentrating on the German scientists who had been shipped East, sometimes unwillingly, immediately after the war. These technicians made a vital contribution to the Soviet military–industrial complex and enabled Moscow's planners to make 'leapfrog developments' in specialist areas such as missile research, atomic energy, submarine construction and aircraft manufacture. In short, the borrowed German expertise enabled the Kremlin to keep pace with technological advances achieved in the West without having had to make the fundamental, but costly, investment in time and money that is conventionally associated with such undertakings. When the German scientists began to filter back to the West, three-man interrogation teams were assigned to each of them, sometimes for anything up to six months, in order to assess what advances had been accomplished in the Eastern Bloc. The results were lengthy technical reports, which have subsequently been demonstrated to be extraordinarily accurate. Twenty years later a similar project has been initiated that has also shown exceptional results: high-grade intelligence from low-cost, reliable sources, who have sometimes slipped past the Soviet émigré vetting system, which is designed to identify and exclude applicants who have worked in classified establishments.

There have been three recent examples of this phenomenon: Captain Mikhail Turatsky of the Red Navy, who had served in the Northern Fleet's test basin at Severomorsk and, none the less, was granted permission to emigrate. He later wrote a very instructive 150-page report entitled *The Introduction of Missile Systems into the Soviet Navy*.[22] Two key helicopter designers, Lev Chaiko and Valeri Weinstein, were allowed to move abroad, taking with them enough knowledge to produce a detailed study of the latest Soviet design procedures, including those used on the MI-26. Similarly, a leading chemist, Viktor Yevsikov, received consent to leave Moscow in spite of his lengthy service at the aerospace industry's main research facility in Podlipky. He subsequently wrote the standard work, *Re-Entry Technology and the Soviet Space Programme*.[23]

Monitoring of émigré skills is conducted by a research organization, Delphic Associates, which channels US government funds to narrow fields of academic interest such as cybernetic and computer sciences. By sponsoring studies from émigrés on the latest developments, Soviet progress in areas of special interest can be assessed.

Intensive debriefing is also a feature of the treatment given by the CIA to defectors with intelligence backgrounds. Few are willing to discuss their experiences, but Vladimir N. Sakharov, a regular Foreign Ministry diplomat co-opted by the KGB who was brought out of Kuwait in 1971, recalls that 'debriefings are not a very pleasant experience',[24] although he is full of praise for the CIA's resettlement programme: 'At first, I had my qualms and criticisms of the programme. It was not due to the programme itself, it was just due to the people who administered the programme, because we do deal with different individuals.... I went through eight, nine or even ten case officers. Some were great guys, some of them were not so great guys.'[25] Sakharov eventually obtained a PhD from the University of Southern California, but not before he had been forced to take a job as a taxi driver when the motel management course he attended in Los Angeles went bankrupt. Another accomplished Soviet defector with a fine academic record was reduced to washing dishes in a fast-food restaurant. Criticisms of the Agency's tactless handling of a valuable commodity is widespread. Nicolae Horodinca, who escaped from Romania, says that many of the promises made to him concerning a house, a job and even medical insurance were not kept. 'The CIA makes zombies of defectors,' he says.[26]

The basic problem presented by all defectors, and highlighted by the Yurchenko débâcle and the three-year incarceration of Yuri Nosenko (see page 97), is the establishment of their *bona fides*. The present DCI, William Webster, who until March 1987 had run the FBI, acknowledges the dilemma: 'If they are treated as potential double agents, they are not going to be very good defectors.'[27] Fortunately, following Yurchenko's redefection, there has been a public inquest into the CIA's modus operandi, and opinion is fairly unanimous in highlighting the Company's shortcomings in the field. Perhaps not surprisingly, the Agency is keen to recruit and run agents. It is not so enthusiastic to deal with the resettlement problems that invariably arise when long-term penetration agents reach that moment of decision to opt for a new life in the West. The Agency was reportedly eager for its best Polish source, Colonel Wladyslaw Kuklinski, to remain in position in the General Staff in Warsaw, but in December 1981 he was successfully exfiltrated, along with his wife and one of their sons. In consequence, the CIA was taken by surprise when martial law was imposed shortly afterwards. In Arkady N. Shevchenko's case, he was persuaded to travel to Havana, even though he feared that he was already under suspicion as a CIA source. In fact, he survived the ordeal and returned to his job at the UN in New York, from where he eventually defected in April 1978 after receiving a summons for an unscheduled visit to Moscow. On this occasion Shevchenko's CIA case officer made no attempt to persuade his agent to risk a return home.

Neither the CIA nor the FBI's record of managing double agents is particularly impressive. The two Soviet sources who operated in New York during the 1960s under the cryptonyms TOP HAT and FEDORA, were supposedly KGB and GRU officers at the UN. Both supplied quantities of information, but the cases eventually petered out. TOP HAT has been identified recently as the late

General Dmitri F. Polyakov, and FEDORA turned out to be Viktor M. Lessiovsky, U Thant's personal assistant between 1963 and 1966. Remarkably, his later career in Moscow seemed unaffected by his exposure as a long-term FBI source, a sure indication that his duplicity had been sanctioned by the KGB.

Several other lengthy Soviet double-agent operations are also known to have gone badly wrong. In the late 1950s, a GRU illegal named Fedorov had wasted considerable amounts of the CIA's time and money, without producing any useful information, before disappearing back to Moscow. And, in December 1985, Nicolai F. Artamonov vanished in Vienna while making contact with the KGB. This was a particularly serious blow for the CIA, for Artamonov was a Red Navy officer who had defected in Sweden in June 1959 and had been used as a double agent following an approach made to him by a Soviet diplomat in Washington. Artamonov, who had been resettled in the United States with the new identity of 'Nicholas Shadrin', had reported the KGB's bid to recruit him and had reluctantly agreed to play along with them. This led to the rendezvous in Austria from which he never returned. Had Artamonov been an authentic defector, or a sophisticated 'plant'?[28] The truth was only revealed in 1985, when Yurchenko described how Artamonov had been killed accidentally by the KGB while they were trying to chloroform him. What made the affair so disastrous was the loss of another agent associated with the naval officer. The CIA believed it had managed to 'turn' Artamonov's KGB controller in Washington, Igor R. Kozlov, who was assigned the cryptonym KITTY HAWK. Once he returned to Moscow, he was never heard of again either.

In spite of considerable efforts made on a worldwide basis to develop sources inside the KGB and GRU, very little has been achieved. The CIA and Allied services will go to considerable trouble to construct an accurate order-of-battle of intelligence personnel inside every Soviet diplomatic mission, and will certainly use any relevant information gained, such as a particular person's vulnerability because of an illicit love affair, to make an offer. The conventional approach is to hold out the possibility of asylum and a pension in return for supplying secrets. If all else fails, a 'gangplank pitch' will be made. This involves conveying a message to the target just as he is ending his tour of duty to return home. It will give an address or telephone number in a third country, recommending that contact be made. Gangplank pitches often crystallize into double-

or even triple-agent scenarios, when the opposition has anticipated the manoeuvre, but rarely develop into worthwhile cases.

The only real successes in dealing with double agents have been those run for short-term advantage by the FBI against Eastern Bloc intelligence personnel legally based in the United States. In short, they fall into two categories: members of the public or armed forces who report a suspicious approach from a foreigner and are subsequently persuaded by the FBI to pretend to co-operate. A variation on the same theme is the 'dangle', a tempting target who is deliberately placed close to an identified or suspected intelligence officer. Few professionals can resist cultivating a potentially profitable prospect, and even the most skilled performer can be duped by a plausible agent provocateur. The majority of silent PNGs and expulsions from the US can be attributed to this strategy, which has the advantage of exposing intelligence personnel under legal cover, thereby giving a 'window' into the opposition apparatus and diverting hostile capability into relatively harmless, supervised activity.

Perhaps the classic provocation was John L. Stine, an FBI double agent who volunteered his services to the Soviet military office in Washington on Thanksgiving Day, 1982. He was accepted as genuine by Lieutenant-Colonel Vyacheslav Pavlov, who ran him for some months before the FBI closed their trap in April the following year, catching Pavlov's superior in the GRU, Colonel Yevgenni N. Barmyantsev, at one of Stine's dead-letter drops. Barmyantsev was PNG'd, just as his predecessor, Major-General Vasily I. Chitov, had been in February 1982, when he had been ambushed in similar circumstances in northern Virginia.

In a parallel case a senior USAF officer, codenamed YOGI, reported an illicit request for classified material about Cruise missiles and Stealth technology from Colonel Vladimir M. Ismaylov in May 1985. The FBI provided YOGI with impressive-looking but worthless documents that, over a period of thirteen months, Ismaylov paid $41,000 for. He was eventually arrested in June 1986, digging up a package of secrets left for him in a Maryland field by YOGI. Coincidentally, his expulsion on 24 June 1986 followed that a month earlier of Eric Sites from the CIA's Moscow Station, which makes it likely that a high-level political decision had been taken to retaliate, even if that meant sacrificing a promising double-agent operation.

The second group can be equally advantageous: Eastern Bloc illegals who are apprehended and given a straight choice of uninterrupted service, under control, or a lengthy prison term. As the Soviets know to their cost, even the committed agents like 'Kaarlo Tuomi', who was turned by the FBI in 1959, or 'Anton', who was caught in Montreal in December 1971, will succumb when confronted with such a stark choice. Their meal-tickets can vary from knowledge about a single agent, as happened with Reino Hayhanen, who betrayed Rudolf Abel, or Ludek Zemenek, who gave the vital testimony needed to snare Professor Hambleton, to Michal Goleniewski's unsurpassed bag of traitors (see chart on page 125). Other illegals, deployed as 'sleepers' under deep cover to await an instruction to execute a particular task, may have little to offer beyond details of their own experience, disclosing aspects of their training and the personalities of those who assisted in their preparation. All useful data, but of no great consequence.

It has been argued that it is this dimension of the game of intelligence that is so wasteful, so unprofitable and so unnecessary. Summed up as 'counter-intelligence operations for the sake of them' by one old hand, it is true that none of the participants accomplish any lasting advantage. However, neither side can afford to give their opponents a free hand, so any suspension of operations would require bilateral agreement which, in turn, would depend upon a radical improvement in the relationship between the nations concerned.

It is perhaps remarkable that given the poor press received by the CIA over the years, and the publicity given to the hapless victims caught in the crossfire, that security and intelligence agencies like the CIA and the FBI still get offers of assistance from the public. In John Stine's case, his employers were unimpressed by his cooperation and he was fired from his job with a defence research institute. Armand B. Weiss, another volunteer double agent used by the FBI to relieve Yuri P. Leonov of large sums in return for specious classified material, was given a gentle brush-off after his usefulness had come to an end, which left him embittered. Nevertheless, the CIA's programme of debriefing businessmen who have travelled to interesting areas of the world garners useful intelligence and operates on an entirely voluntary basis. No corporation pressurizes its employees to participate, yet only a few actively discourage the practice. Several large companies willingly post CIA officers to their overseas offices under business cover, the only limitation being a legal restriction on the use of journalists for this purpose. In contrast, in France the role of the 'honourable correspondent' is considered a patriotic duty, one that is fulfilled by a very high proportion of French international traders, regardless of their political leanings.

The final area to be considered when assessing the overall performance of the CIA is in the adjacent field of product exploitation. Having acquired the data, does the Agency have the ability to assess it correctly and distribute it to the right quarters? The CIA's advantage over parallel organizations in other countries lies in the dual responsibilities of the DCI, who not only takes charge of the CIA, but holds the brief for the co-ordination of all intelligence, including the products of such diverse departments as Energy, State and the Treasury. Through his chairmanship of the National Foreign Intelligence Board the DCI exercises control over the entire US intelligence community and is, therefore, in a powerful position to examine and compare every facet of its product. As we shall see, this puts the DCI in a unique position in the world of intelligence. However, it also makes it more difficult for the observer to judge the quality of the product of a single component. Intelligence assessments going to the White House are likely to have been compiled from data originating from all the agencies, including the NSA, which in terms of personnel employed and budget is several times the size of the CIA.

Occasional glimpses of CIA participation in projects as diverse as PYRAMIDER and IVY BELLS are eloquent testimony to the vast scale of the Company's technical interests and resources. The first cryptonym referred to a highly secret communications satellite, which enabled the CIA to receive and transmit signals direct to their agents without risk of hostile interception. A scheme of gigantic cost, starting at $443 million, it was considered vital if the Agency was to run sources in denied areas. The objective was to produce a global, push-button system that would put case officers in Langley in direct contact with their assets, whatever their location, with only minimal field equipment and ground stations. In theory, PYRAMIDER would allow a spy in the Laotian jungle, or a suburb of Leningrad, to signal the CIA with a piece of kit the size of a pocket calculator. It would also operate sophisticated sensors, planted in strategic positions, to be activated by remote control.[29] When Christopher Boyce's KGB controller read the CIA's requirements, as compromised by Boyce who had betrayed the contractual correspondence, he would have been forgiven if he had gasped at its implications. The Agency's conditions stipulated a capacity of 100 separate, simultaneous channels, with a daily volume of fifty signals from the agents, with twenty messages of varying lengths returned from headquarters. Contact had to be instantaneous and undetectable, with a less than one per cent chance of interception, utilizing the very latest techniques of burst transmission, encryption and frequency jumping.

If PYRAMIDER demonstrated the importance the CIA attached to keeping in touch with its agents, its willingness to invest enormous sums in high-risk ventures was proved in 1975, when details of AZORIAN were leaked. This ambitious project was the location and recovery of a Soviet diesel-powered Golf II class submarine, equipped with three *Sark* SS-N-5 nuclear missiles, which had sunk in the Pacific in April 1968, about 750 miles north of Hawaii. Having pinpointed the wreck on the sea-bed 18,000 feet below, the CIA awarded a secret contract to the Howard Hughes organization to lift whatever could be brought to the surface using a specially-converted underwater dredger, the *Glomar Explorer*. More than 4,000 people were eventually indoctrinated into the plan, which probably cost over $200 million. Whether any cryptographic equipment or missiles were salvaged remains classified, but the bodies of several crewmen were found and reinterred during a filmed funeral service. Other prized objectives were the torpedoes, the internal navigation system and code books, but security considerations precluded the release of any statements to the public concerning the project's level of success.[30]

Reminiscent of AZORIAN was the disclosure, in January 1986, of the existence of IVY BELLS, another underwater venture, conducted by the CIA with assistance from the NSA and the US navy. The operation, which had been worked undetected for more than a decade until it was betrayed in 1981, required a sophisticated listening device being placed directly over a Soviet underwater cable. The waterproof pod recorded all the traffic and was replaced periodically, the tapes being sent for analysis to the NSA's headquarters at Fort Meade.

PYRAMIDER, AZORIAN and IVY BELLS show how the CIA is prepared to indulge in uniquely imaginative and complex technical operations, but then can be caught unawares by a popular revolution in a key region. Not only was the CIA unable to predict the fall of the Shah in 1979, but it actually sustained great damage, both through the exposure of Tom Ahern and the other CIA staff taken hostage along with the rest of the embassy employees, and the inadequate destruction of its documents, many of which were subsequently reconstructed by Iranian self-styled 'students', even though they had been shredded. One, which is alleged to have identified Mehdi Bazargan, the former prime minister, as a valued CIA source, led to his arrest and execution.

There is a paradox that, with all its resources, the CIA cannot match the British for political analysis. Even on the diplomatic front some quite elementary mistakes have been made. One of Ahern's predecessors as Station Chief in Tehran had been a Jew, which raised a few eyebrows in SAVAK and the royal court. When Nixon appointed his ex-DCI Dick Helms as his ambassador, he suggested Moscow as a suitable post; Helms tactfully pointed out that perhaps Tehran would be more appropriate.

Strangely, despite a long-standing relationship with President Sadat, the Agency had no warning of his sudden decision to make a peace visit to Israel. Of course, there have also been occasions when the CIA's advice has been rejected. Neither Mossad nor the White House believed that a war was imminent in the Middle East in 1973; nor would President Johnson accept the Company's gloomy predictions for Vietnam. There have also been examples of the CIA acquiring and disregarding intelligence of great significance, like the satellite reconnaissance photographs of the secret South African atomic research laboratories deep in the Kalahari Desert, which had been filed at Langley without being subjected to the usual interpretation process that should have revealed their true function.

Despite its congressional restraints the CIA is quite the most powerful and most impressive agency of its kind in the world. The popular belief is that it is too heavily committed to expensive technical gadgetry, and too gullible or naive to cope with the complexities of human sources. Of course, the restrictions can be taken too literally. Stansfield Turner is fond of recounting the dilemma posed by an American missionary in an unnamed African country, who habitually transmitted situation reports on a local trouble spot to his church. The CIA was inhibited from listening in to his short-wave broadcasts because he happened to be an American citizen, and to do so without a warrant would have been contrary to US law. The truth is that the CIA has access to the very latest technology and, over a long period of years, has developed a unique capability to photograph, monitor and analyse even the most obscure items of interest. The CIA recently demonstrated this by supplying the West German and Swiss governments with incredibly detailed dossiers, compiled from assets on the ground as well as overhead reconnaissance, that convinced them of the existence of an embryonic chemical weapons manufacturing plant deep in the Libyan desert.

Like other clandestine services engaged in the same field, the CIA cannot expect complete success in the management of human assets. No doubt the revelation by Florentino Lombard, the DGI officer who defected to the CIA in Vienna in June 1987, that virtually all its long-term agents in Cuba were either plants or had been turned, sapped the Agency's confidence. Some of those denounced by Lombard as double agents, such as Ignacio Rodriguez-Mena, a senior official of the State Planning Board in Havana, had been run as trusted sources for twenty years or so. Evidently, the entire operation had been staged by the DGI. Nicolas Sirgado Ros, the director-general for supplies in the Cuban Ministry of Construction, had been recruited by the CIA during a visit to London in 1966. Ten years later he revealed his true role as a DGI double agent. In a worse case, Sanaya L. Lipavsky, a Jewish neuro-surgeon and close friend of Anatoli Shcharansky, had been cultivated as a source by the CIA in Moscow. However, in 1977, he denounced his CIA contacts and proceeded to give evidence at Shcharansky's trial, thereby portraying the dissident movement in the Soviet Union as the Agency's willing pawns.

But such setbacks are the occupational hazards of every intelligence-gathering organization. The key is not to be overly reliant on a single source and to seek corroboration from as many as possible. This is where the CIA scores highly, but the judgment to be made here is its comparative standing in relation to its rivals. Of course, the American intelligence community, based as it is in a free society, operates at something of a disadvantage to the KGB and the GRU. After all, while the KGB has enjoyed literally hundreds of sources roaming the US embassy in Moscow for decades, the FBI would have appreciated just a single source in any of the Soviet establishments in Washington. The match is not an equal one, but worthwhile comparisons can be made. However, before proceeding to look at the Neighbours, we should take a case history of how the world's intelligence agencies responded, on the practical plane, to the specific need for data relating to strategic missile strengths in the early 1960s.

Soviet Intelligence Personnel Expelled from the US

(* indicates UN cover)

Date	Name		Post
1946	REDIN	Nikolai G.	New York*
	RYZHKOV	Konstantin P.	Washington
1948	LOMAKIN	Yakov I.	New York*
	SOKOLSKA	Yekatrina	New York*
1949	GUBICHEV	Valentin A.	New York*
1952	SKVORTSOV	Nikolai S.	New York*
1953	NOVIKOV	Yuri V.	Washington
1954	AMOSOV	Igor A.	Washington
	KONOVALEV	Ivan	New York* (GRU)
	KOVALEV	Aleksandr P.	New York*
	KOVALEV	Paul F.	Washington (GRU)
	PIVNEV	Leonid Y.	Washington
1955	MARTINOV	Maksim G.	New York*
1956	BUBCHIKOV	I.A.	Washington
	GLADKOV	Boris F.	New York*
	GURYANOV	Aleksandr K.	New York*
	PETROV	Viktor I.	New York*
	PETRUNIN	Viktor I.	New York (GRU)
	POPOV	Anatoli A.	Washington
	SHAPOVALOV	Rotislav Y.	New York*
	TURKIN	Nikolai F.	New York*
	YEKIMOV	Konstantin P.	New York*
1957	GRUSHA	Vladimir A.	New York*
	KRYLOV	Yuri P.	Washington
	MASHKANTSEV	Gennadi F.	Washington
	MOLEV	Vasili M.	Washington
1958	KUROCHKIN	Nikolai I.	Washington
1959	DORONKIN	Kirill S.	New York*
	DOVOLEV	Leonid A.	New York*
	ZAOSTROVTSEV	Yevgenni A.	New York*
1960	GLINSKY	Vladimir F.	Washington
	IVANOV	Valentin M.	Washington*

	KIRILYUK	Vadim A.	New York*
	SHATROV	Vadim A.	New York*
	YEZHOV	Petr Y.	Washington
1961	GOLUBOV	Sergei M.	New York*
	KALMYKOV	Grigori D.	Washington
	MALEKH	Igor Y.	New York*
1962	KLOKOV	Vladilen V.	New York*
	MISHUKOV	Yuri A.	New York*
	PAVLOV	Yevgenni V.	New York*
	PROKHOROV	Yevgenni M.	New York*
	SAVELEV	Mikhail S.	New York*
	SOROKIN	Vadim V.	New York*
	VAYGAUSKAS	Richardas K.	New York*
	VIRODOV	Ivan Y.	New York*
	ZAYTSEV	Yuri V.	New York*
1963	GALKIN	Alexei I.	New York* (GRU)
	KUDASHKIN	Fedor D.	New York*
	MASLENNIKOV	Petr E.	New York* (GRU)
	OLENEV	Vladimir I.	New York*
	PAVLOV	Gleb	New York*
	ROMASHIN	Yuri A.	New York*
	SEVASTYANOV	Gennadi G.	Washington
	SOKOLOV	Aleksandr	New York (GRU)
	SOKOLOVA	Joy Ann	New York (GRU)
	TATISHCHEV	Sergei I.	Washington
	YEGOROV	Ivan D.	New York* (GRU)
	YEGEROVA	Aleksandra	New York* (GRU)
1964	GRECHANIN	Vladimir P.	Washington (GRU)
	IVANOV	Igor A.	New York
	MOLCHANOV	Valentin M.	Washington
	UDALOV	Aleksandr V.	Washington
	ZADVINSKY	Vasili V.	Washington
1965	BEREZIN	Viktor V.	Washington
	KARPOVICH	Boris V.	New York*
	KIRSANOV	Stefan M.	Washington
	PIGOROV	Yuri A.	Washington
	VAKULA	Vladimir	New York*
	VELIKANOV	Avenir A.	Washington
1966	ISAKOV	Vadim A.	New York*
	MALININ	Aleksei R.	Washington

	REVIN	Valentin A.	Washington
1967	KALINKIN	Georgi	New York*
	KIREYEV	Anatoli T.	New York*
1969	ANDREYEV	Igor I.	New York*
	POPOV	Nikolai	Washington
1970	FILIPOV	Yuri V.	New York*
	OREKHOV	Boris M.	Washington
	TIKHOMIROV	Aleksandr V.	New York*
	ZHEGALOV	Leonid N.	Washington
1972	MARKELOV	Valeri I.	New York*
1973	CHERNYCHEV	Viktor A.	Washington
1975	ANDREYEV	Anatoli V.	Washington
	CHARCHYAN	Eduard B.	New York*
	GADZHIYEV	Abdulkhalik M.	New York*
	PETROSYAN	Petros A.	New York*
	YAKOLEV	Aleksandr A.	New York*
1976	STEPANOV	Svyatoslav A.	New York*
1977	ALEKSEYEV	Vladimir I.	
	DZHASHI	Enriko A.	
	KARPOV	Yevgenni P.	New York
1978	CHERYAYEV	Rudolf P.	New York*
	ENGER	Valdik A.	New York*
	ZINYAKIN	Vladimir P.	New York*
1979	KUKHAR	Aleksandr A.	Washington
1980	POPOV	Vladimir V.	Washington
1981	MARAKHOVSKY	Yuri N.	Washington
1982	CHITOV	Vasily I.	Washington (GRU)
1983	BARMYANTSEV	Yevgenni N.	Washington (GRU)
	KONSTANTINOV	Oleg V.	New York*
	LEONOV	Yuri P.	Washington (GRU)
	MIKHEYEV	Aleksandr N.	New York*
	SKRIPKO	Anatoli Y.	Washington
1984	ZHIMZHIN	Vladimir	New York*
1986	ISMAYLOV	Vladimir M.	Washington
	ZAKHAROV	Gennadi F.	New York*
1988	KATKOV	Mikhail	New York
1989	PAKHTUSOV	Yuri	Washington

US Espionage Cases

Name		Service/Agency	Date of Arrest	Date of Conviction	Sentence	Conclusion
JAFFE	Philip J.		6 June 1945	29 Sept. 1945	$2,500 Fine	
LARSEN	Emanuel	State	6 June 1945	29 Sept. 1945	$500 Fine	
ROTH	Andrew		6 June 1945	29 Sept. 1945	Acquitted	
WEISBAND	William	AFSA	1948	Unknown	Unknown	
ZLATOVSKY	Lt George	OSS				Extradition refused
FOSTER	Jane	OSS				Extradition refused
HISS	Alger	State	15 Dec. 1948	25 Jan. 1950	4 yrs	
COPLON	Judith	Justice	4 March 1949	9 March 1950	15 yrs	Quashed on appeal
GUBITCHEV	Valentin A.		4 March 1949	9 March 1950	15 yrs	Deported on conviction
GOLD	Harry		22 May 1950	7 Dec. 1950	30 yrs	
SLACK	Alfred D.		15 June 1950	18 Sept. 1950	15 yrs	
GREENGLASS	David		16 June 1950	5 April 1951	15 yrs	
ROSENBERG	Julius	Army	17 July 1950	5 April 1951	Death	Executed 19 June 1953
MOSCOWITZ	Miriam		29 July 1950	8 Nov. 1950	2 yrs	
BROTHMAN	Abraham		29 July 1950	8 Nov. 1950	2 yrs	
ROSENBERG	Ethel		11 Aug. 1950	5 April 1951	Death	Executed 19 June 1953
SOBELL	Morton		18 Aug. 1950	5 April 1951	30 yrs	
VERBER	Otto	Army	14 Jan. 1953	8 June 1953	5–15 yrs	Deported 1960
PONGER	Kurt L.	Army	14 Jan. 1953	8 June 1953	3–10 yrs	Deported 1962
REMINGTON	William W.	Navy	7 Feb. 1951	27 Jan. 1953	3 yrs	Murdered in prison
PETERSEN	Joseph S.	NSA	1 Oct. 1954	22 Dec. 1954	7 yrs	
RHODES	Sgt Roy A.	Army	June 1957	21 Feb. 1958	5 yrs	
ROTHKRUG	Michael R.	Army		Jan. 1953		
ZBOROWSKY	Mark			Aug. 1957		Convicted of perjury
FRENCH	Capt. George H.	USAF	6 April 1957	20 Sept. 1957	Life	
ABEL	Rudolf I.	Illegal	21 June 1957	23 Oct. 1957	30 yrs	Swapped in Feb. 1962 for Powers
HIRSCH	Willi		27 Oct. 1960			Deported July 1961
MARTIN	William H.	NSA				Defected June 1960
MITCHELL	Bernon F.	NSA				Defected June 1960
SKARBECK	Irwin C.	State	1961	1961	10 yrs	Released 1966, died 1970
KAUFFMAN	Capt. Joseph P.	USAF	June 1961			
GESSNER	Capt. C.J.	Army		1961	2 yrs	Defected 1962
HAMILTON	Victor N.	NSA		1962		Defected July 1963

Name		Service/Agency	Date of Arrest	Date of Conviction	Sentence	Conclusion
DRUMMOND	Sgt Nelson C.	Navy	29 Sept. 1962	23 May 1963	Life	Deported 15 Oct. 1963
SOKOLOV	Aleksandre	Illegal	3 July 1963	2 Oct. 1963		Deported 15 Oct. 1963
SOKOLOVA	Joy Ann	Illegal	3 July 1963	2 Oct. 1963		
BUTENKO	John W.	USAF	29 Oct. 1963	Nov. 1964	30 yrs	
THOMPSON	Robert G.	USAF	7 Jan. 1965	13 May 1965	30 yrs	Swapped 1978
ROHRER	Sgt Glen	Army				Defected August 1965
MITKENBAUGH	Sgt Herbert W.	Army	Nov. 1965	31 July 1966	25 yrs	
JOHNSON	Sgt Robert L.	Army	25 Nov. 1965	31 July 1966	25 yrs	Murdered by son 1972
WHALEN	Col William H.	Army	12 July 1966	2 March 1967	15 yrs	
DUNLAP	Sgt Jack F.	NSA				Suicide July 1963
BOECKENHAUPT	Sgt Herbert W.	USAF	24 Oct. 1966	11 June 1967	30 yrs	
SMITH	John D.	State	1970			Defected November 1967
ATTARDI	Sgt		2 July 1971	2 Nov. 1971	3 yrs	
DECHAMPLAIN	Sgt Raymond G.	USAF	18 Oct. 1971	April 1972	7 yrs	
PERKINS	Sgt Walter T.	USAF	21 July 1975		2 yrs	
WOOD	Sgt James D.	USAF	27 June 1975		3 yrs	
DEDEYAN	Sadag K.	Univ.	27 June 1975		3 yrs	
PASKALIAN	Sarkis O.	Illegal	Dec. 1976	May 1977	22 yrs	
MOORE	Edwin G.	CIA	7 Jan. 1977		15 yrs	Paroled 1979
ROGALSKY	Ivan	RCA				Insane
BOYCE	Christopher J.	TRW	10 Jan. 1977	14 May 1977	40 yrs	
LEE	A. Daulton		17 Jan. 1977	14 May 1977	Life	
HUMPHREY	Ronald L.	State	20 May 1977	1978	15 yrs	
TRUONG	David	State	20 May 1977	1978	15 yrs	
YAGER	Cpl Joel	Marine	Sept. 1977			
CHERYAYEV	Rudolf P.	UN	20 May 1978	31 Oct. 1978	50 yrs	Swapped 27 April 1979
ENGER	Vladik A.	UN	20 May 1978	31 Oct. 1978	50 yrs	Swapped 27 April 1979
KAMPILES	William P.	CIA	17 Aug. 1978	22 Dec. 1978	40 yrs	
MADSEN	Ymn Eugene L.	Navy	14 Aug. 1979	26 Oct. 1979	8 yrs	
BARNETT	David H.	CIA	April 1980	24 Oct. 1980	18 yrs	
COOKE	Lt Christopher	USAF	21 May 1980	Feb. 1982	Discharged	
HELMICH	W/O Joseph G.	Army	15 July 1980	15 July 1981	Life	
MURPHY	Michael R.	Navy	June 1981	Aug. 81	Discharged	

Name		Service/Agency	Date of Arrest	Date of Conviction	Sentence	Conclusion
BELL	William H.	Hughes	23 June 1981	14 Dec. 1981	8 yrs	Swapped 1985
ZACHARSKY	Marian W.	Illegal	28 June 1981	21 Nov. 1981	Life	
BABA	Ens. Stephen A.	Navy	1 Oct. 1981	20 Jan. 1982	2 yrs	
HEDIGER	David A.	Navy	1982		Discharged	
HORTON	Brian P.	Navy	1982	12 Jan. 1983	6 yrs	
PUGH	Ernest C.	Navy	1982		Discharged	
GILBERT	Otto A.	Illegal	17 April 1982		15 yrs	
SLAVENS	PFC Brian E.	Marine	Aug. 1982		2 yrs	
COBERLY	Alan D.	Marine	1983		18 months	
HUGHES	Capt. William H.	USAF				Deserter
PICKERING	W/O Jeffery L.	Navy	1983	June 1983	5 yrs	
ELLIS	P/O Robert W.	USAF	Feb. 1983		3 yrs	
WOLD	Hans P.	Navy	1983		4 yrs	
DUBBERSTEIN	Walter H.	CIA	29 April 1983			Suicide on arrest
HARPER	James D.	Engineer	15 Oct. 1983	14 May 1984	Life	
ZEHE	Prof. Alfred	Illegal	4 Nov. 1983	21 Feb. 1985	8 yrs	Swapped 1985
DAI KIEM TRAN		Navy	1983		Discharged	
KOSTADINOV	Penyu B.	Illegal	Dec. 1983			Swapped June 1985
CORDREY	Pte Robert E.	Marine	Jan. 1984	13 Aug. 1984	2 yrs	
MOORE	Michael R.	Marine	Feb. 1984		Discharged	
MIRA	Francisco de A.	USAF	April 1984	Aug. 1984	7 yrs	
KEARN	Bruce L.	Navy	March 1984		18 months	
FORBRICH	Ernst	Illegal	19 March 1984	June 1985	15 yrs	
SMITH	Richard C.	CIA	4 April 1984	11 April 1986	Acquitted	
MITCHELSON	Alice	CIA	1 Oct. 1984	21 May 1985		Swapped 1985
MORISON	Samuel L.	Navy	1 Oct. 1984	4 Dec. 1984	2 yrs	
KOECHER	Karl F.	CIA	27 Nov. 1984	3 Feb. 1986		Swapped 11 Feb. 1986
OGORODNIKOVA	Svetlana	Illegal	2 Oct. 1984	25 June 1985	18 yrs	
OGORODNIKOV	Nikolai	Illegal	2 Oct. 1984	25 June 1985	8 yrs	
MILLER	Richard W.	FBI	2 Oct. 1984	14 July 1985	Life	
WOLFF	Jay C.	Navy	17 Dec. 1984	28 June 1985	5 yrs	
CAVANAGH	Thomas P.	Northrop	18 Dec. 1984	23 May 1985	Life	
WALKER	Arthur J.	Navy	19 May 1985	28 Oct. 1985	Life	

Name		Service/Agency	Date of Arrest	Date of Conviction	Sentence	Conclusion
WALKER	John A.	Navy	20 May 1985	28 Oct. 1985	Life	
WALKER	Michael L.	Navy	24 May 1985	28 Oct. 1985	25 yrs	
WHITWORTH	Jerry A.	Navy	20 May 1985	28 Aug. 1986	365 yrs	
SCRANAGE	Sharon M.	CIA	June 1985	26 Nov. 1985	2 yrs	
SOUSSOUDIS	Michael A.	CIA	June 1985	26 Nov. 1985	20 yrs	Swapped
TOBIAS	P/O Michael T.	Navy	13 Aug. 1985	12 Nov. 1985	20 yrs	
PIZZO	Francis X.	Navy	13 Aug. 1985	7 Oct. 1985	10 yrs	
TOBIAS	Bruce	Navy	Aug. 1985	7 Oct. 1985	Unknown	
IRENE	Dale	Navy	Aug. 1985	7 Oct. 1985	Unknown	
HOWARD	Edward L.	CIA				Defected Sept. 1985
PELTON	Ronald W.	NSA	24 Nov. 1985	5 June 1986	Life	
WU TAI CHIN	Larry	CIA	22 Nov. 1985	8 Feb. 1986	Life	Suicide 21 Feb. 1986
POLLARD	Jonathan J.	Navy	21 Nov. 1985	4 March 1986	Life	
POLLARD	Anne H.	Navy	22 Nov. 1985	4 March 1986	5 yrs	
JEFFRIES	Randy M.	Congress	20 Dec. 1985	13 March 1986	10 yrs	
OTT	Bruce D.	USAF	22 Jan. 1986	7 Aug. 1986.	25 yrs	
HAGUEWOOD	Robert D.	Navy	4 March 1986	20 June 1986	2 yrs	
SOUTHER	Glenn M.	Navy				Suicide 22 June 1989
BRACEY	Cpl Arnold	Marine	23 Aug. 1986	9 Sept. 1986	Demoted	Swapped
ZAKHAROV	Gennadi F.	UN	27 Oct. 1986	30 Sept. 1986	Deportation	
DAVIES	Sgt Allen J.	USAF	4 Dec. 1986	27 Aug. 1987	5 yrs	
ALLEN	Michael H.	Navy	2 Jan. 1987	14 Aug. 1987	8 yrs	
LONETREE	Sgt Clayton J.	Marine	Oct. 1987	21 Aug. 1987	25 yrs	
FLEMING	CPO David	Navy	1987	4 Oct. 1988	4 yrs	
GARCIA	Wildredo	Navy	7 Jan. 1988	22 Jan. 1988	12 yrs	
RICHARDSON	Sgt Daniel W.	Army	23 Aug. 1988	26 Aug. 1988	10 yrs	
CONRAD	Sgt Clyde L.	Army	17 Nov. 1988			
SPADE	Henry O.	Navy				
DOLCE	Thomas J.	Army	21 Dec. 1988	11 Oct. 1988		
HALL	W/O James	Army	21 Dec. 1988	1989	40yrs	
YILDIRIM	Huseyin	NSA	10 Jan. 1989	July 1989		
KUNKLE	Craig D	Navy	16 March 1989			
PERI	Michael	Army				
WOLF	Ronald C.	Army	4 May 1989	24 June 1989	30 yrs	

3

A Cuban Game of Bluff

'A major factor in restoring the CIA to a place of prestige and active participation in the policy process was the services it performed during the Cuba missile crisis of 1962.'[1]

Dr Ray Cline

Later in *Games of Intelligence* we shall turn to examine the relative structure and performance of other intelligence agencies, but before doing so it would be worth taking a detailed look at the case history of a particular intelligence event that had implications for practically all the agencies to be studied here.

Few such cases offer themselves for analysis in terms of intelligence because, in most instances, the few component parts in the public domain are necessarily incomplete. Nor can the political implications be discerned, sometimes for many years after the incident itself, but there is one particular occurrence that, because of its unique nature, lends itself to our purpose. Indeed, what makes the Cuban missile crisis so appropriate and relevant to this undertaking is the direct involvement of practically every intelligence agency described here. The French took an active role through the agents in situ run by Philippe Thyraud de Vosjoli, SDECE's representative in Washington, who actually travelled down to Havana to supervise them personally.[2] The British made an unacknowledged, but none the less vital, contribution by monitoring the movement and radio traffic of all the Soviet ships moving missiles from Odessa; and even Mossad played a part by participating in the debriefing of scientists who had emigrated from the Soviet Union.

What makes the dissection of this episode so germane is that virtually every facet of modern intelligence can be seen to have subscribed to it. Satellites and U-2 aerial reconnaissance photographed the suspected missile sites; human agents reported the movement of military *matériel*; two seaborne signals intercept ships, the *Oxford* and the *Joseph E. Muller*, were on station to relay wireless traffic to the NSA; the GRU was present in Havana in the person of Sergei M. Kudriavtsev,[3] who prepared the ground for the installation of the missiles; and the KGB was engaged in a molehunt in Moscow to track down the leakage of vital strategic information to the British.

Before turning to the various different pieces of this intelligence jigsaw, we should first examine the background to the crisis. It would not be unreasonable to trace the origins back to Grigori A. Tokaev, the GRU defector in 1948 who gave the West the first detailed insight into the Kremlin's determination to develop a long-range rocket capable of delivering a warhead to the West. From that disclosure onwards, there followed a concentrated effort to trace and interview every scientist who had been press-ganged into service by the Russians and transported to their two research facilities at Ostashkov, on Lake Seliger and near Gagra, on Lake Ritsa. Interrogation centres were set up in Germany and linked to the huge CIA station located in the old I.G. Farben building at Frankfurt. Refugees from the East underwent a discreet filtering process to identify those who might have acquired knowledge of what progress had been achieved by the Soviets. More detailed interviews were then conducted in a requisitioned mansion at Niederrad, just outside Frankfurt. Of course, the KGB was quickly aware of what was happening and took counter-measures to minimize the risk of leakage. In particular, it limited access to the main rocket assembly building to Soviet personnel only. It also embarked upon an ill-advised deception campaign to mislead the West, a consequence of which was the much-vaunted missile gap that hugely exaggerated Soviet missile strengths.

Despite the KGB's counter-measures, the West was able to gauge what was happening deep inside Soviet territory, thanks largely to the U-2 overflights of the Soviet Union, which began in June 1956 and allowed vast tracts of land to be photographed with unprecedented clarity from heights of 90,000 feet. These missions enabled the CIA's National Reconnaissance Office to monitor Russian experiments with booster rockets and focus on Kapustin Yar, the location in the Ukraine seventy-five miles east of Stalingrad, which had been confirmed as the Soviets' principal test site as early as 1947.

Interviews with German scientists who had previously worked on the V-2 rockets at Peenumünde before being transported East, combined with evidence obtained from the American intercept stations at Trabzon, in the Turkish Kuzey Anadolu Daĝlari mountains close to the Russian frontier, and at the Black Sea resort of Samsun, which kept a watch on all the flights, gave the CIA a fairly comprehensive picture of what was taking place.[4] During this period the Soviets did not possess a single deployed missile capable of intercontinental range, and had only perfected some short-range versions and some fairly low-altitude surface-to-air missiles. Fortunately for the U-2 pilots, none was effective at the normal operating heights of the reconnaissance aircraft, which continued their overflights with impunity, concentrating on possible missile development complexes and the warhead manufacturing plant at Alma Ata.

The first moment of concern for the Pentagon was the discovery, in 1957, of a ninety-five-foot-long ICBM, designated an SS-6 *Sapwood*, on a launchpad at Kaputsin Yar. When it was tested, on 15 May, it flew for just under a minute before disintegrating. Although this was an unpromising start, the Soviets had evidently made great technical progress. There was, therefore, additional pressure on the CIA to maintain vigilance. Indeed, the rival US programme was not in a much better condition: only one Atlas ICBM had been fired, which also exploded soon after lift-off. The CIA reckoned that, because the huge unwieldy Russian rocket required railway rolling stock to carry it into position, good warning could be given of the construction of any new ICBM base by comparing pictures of the Soviet rail network with captured German Wehrmacht maps based on aerial photography conducted during the war. Any new spur or branch line would be subjected to intensive analysis to determine whether it had a strategic significance. It was just such a comparative exercise that led to the discovery of a new 'cosmodrome' built in a disused quarry near Tyuratam, in the remote desert thirty miles east of the Aral Sea at the end of a fifteen-mile railway spur from the main Moscow to Tashkent line. On 3 August, an SS-6 flew the 3,500 nautical miles from Tyuratam to the Kamchatka Peninsula; this was followed two months later, on 4 October, by the successful launch of the first Sputnik. These two developments were proof that something of a breakthrough had been achieved by the Russians, and this view was confirmed two years later when the rate of ICBM test firings reached an average of four a month. All were monitored from vast new antenna arrays built by the Americans in Iran[5] and Turkey (see Map 1), and on Shemya Island in the Aleutians. By the end of 1959, about forty test missiles had been fired, and their telemetry signals had been monitored from the NSA's secret listening-posts located close to the Soviet border.[6] During these experimental shots each rocket routinely transmitted a steady stream of data describing its altitude, heading, speed, fuel consumption and engine thrust. All this crucial intelligence had been recorded on tape, but it was evident that as yet not a single missile had been deployed operationally. The first evidence of a non-experimental ICBM base came early in April 1960, when a U-2 investigated a suspicious construction site at Plesetsk, 600 miles north of Moscow, and photographed what appeared to be four ICBMs. Cloud had obscured some of the detail, so hurried arrangements were made for a further U-2 overflight, the twentieth authorized by the President, to get better pictures as soon as the weather improved.

The second key incident was the loss of a U-2 near Sverdlovsk on 1 May 1960, en route to the Plesetsk site. It was brought down by the detonation of an SA-2 *Guideline* anti-aircraft missile, one of fourteen fired. It had not been a direct hit, but the explosion had been sufficiently close for the pilot, Francis Gary Powers, to lose control of the fragile plastic and plywood plane, and be forced to eject. Powers's survival,[7] and his subsequent show trial in Moscow, proved a grave political embarrassment to President Eisenhower, who suspended permission for further overflights, so that confirmation of Plesetsk's purpose was not obtained for three months, soon after the launch of a surveillance satellite, *Discoverer* 14. It was not until a year later, on 30 August 1961, when *Discoverer* 29 obtained clear pictures of the ICBMs at Plesetsk, that an accurate estimate could be made of Soviet missile strength. By that time Oleg V. Penkovsky, a GRU colonel who had volunteered his services to the British as a spy, had made two visits to London. He had been contacted by his SIS cut-out, Greville Wynne, and had been debriefed by a combined SIS–CIA team at his London hotel, the Mount Royal, during a two-week visit by a Soviet trade delegation to England in April, followed by a repeat performance in July. During these sessions Penkovsky had supplied a wealth of data relating to

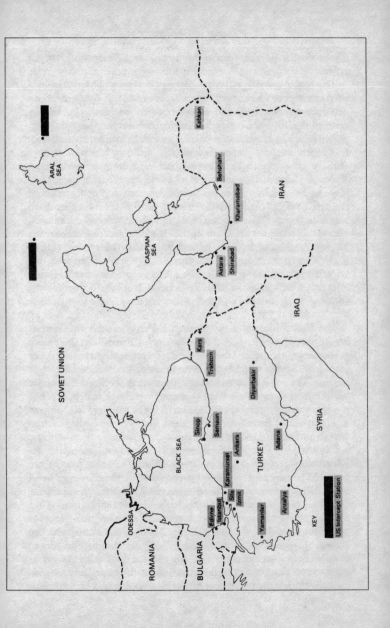

Soviet missile development to his British and American interrogators.

The final American estimate, based primarily on observation but corroborated by Penkovsky, was a figure of ten to fourteen SS-6s deployed operationally and equipped with warheads. Penkovsky claimed that his information had been gleaned from Marshal Sergei S. Varentsov, a close family friend, and said that 'not more than a few dozen' of the big missiles had been built, of which most were anyway either in the prototype stage or still undergoing tests. Varentsov happened to command all Soviet missile troops and artillery, so he was in a position to retail authentic intelligence and not the Kremlin's propaganda. Penkovsky's figures were in sharp contradiction to Khrushchev's own pronouncements on the subject, which had caused great alarm in the Pentagon and perpetuated the 'missile gap' myth. In 1959, he had stated that mass production of ICBMs had already begun, at a rate of 250 a year. Faced with this uncertainty, and in response to the Plesetsk base, another huge US intercept base was established at Bodö in Norway to monitor the anticipated ICBM deployment in the north. Later more stations were opened at Vardö, Vadsö and Viksjöfjellet.

The U-2 débâcle and the disastrous Paris Summit with Eisenhower proved a watershed in relations with Khrushchev; these were no better at Vienna in June the next year, when Khrushchev met President Kennedy and began issuing ultimatums on the future of Berlin. When Soviet troops suddenly started work on the Berlin Wall in August 1961, the Cold War got several degrees chillier, but it was not until November, and the arrival of two senior GRU officers in Havana, that there were signs that Cuba had suddenly acquired a strategic significance for the Soviets.

Colonel V. V. Meshcheryakov[8] and Lieutenant-Colonel N. K. Khlebnikov arrived in Cuba shortly before the show trial of the captured Cuban exiles who had participated in the CIA-sponsored Bay of Pigs invasion the previous April. Whatever the reason for their unexpected presence, it heralded a distinct build-up in Soviet military personnel on the island, many of whom were technicians of much the same age wearing very similar civilian clothes, and the arrival of some controversial *matériel*. All aspects of shipments to Cuba were already the subject of study by the CIA, with individual agents reporting activity in the docks, and Allied intelligence agencies monitoring the movement of Soviet shipping and the exchange of wireless traffic.[9] Over the years a pattern had emerged, and any deviation from the established routine drew attention to the phenomenon. Thus, the transfer of forty-two MiG-21 *Fishbed* jet fighters, forty Ilyushin-28 twin-engined *Beagle* bombers and a couple of fast motor torpedo-boats to Cuba during the spring of 1962 caused some anxiety in Washington. The number of Soviet vessels making the journey to Cuba doubled during this critical period, and then doubled again between July and September 1962. In consequence, surveillance of Cuba was intensified: two NSA intercept ships, the *Oxford* and the *Joseph E. Muller*,[10] sailed from Port Everglades for a leisurely cruise off the Cuban coast, and several U-2 flights were made by the CIA operating from a clandestine field at McCoy in Florida. In addition, 7,000 marines were drafted into the US base at Guantánamo Bay, a move that was bound to be reported instantly.

As the US embassy in Havana had been closed following the Bay of Pigs incident, SDECE's man in Washington flew down to Cuba to service his contacts, and he relayed several stories of SAM missiles being carried across the country. However, the first firm evidence of the deployment of any missiles in Cuba came on 29 August, when eight unmistakable SAM sites, with the characteristic trapezoid configuration seen at Plesetsk and elsewhere in the Soviet Union, were photographed for the first time.[11] Curiously, the SAM batteries had been placed in the western end of the island, where there were no known military installations worthy of this level of protection, closest to the Florida coastline and furthest from the US base at Guantánamo Bay. The only question remaining was, if they were to defend Soviet ballistic missiles, where were they?

That question was answered when the *Omsk* arrived from Odessa on 8 September, and the *Poltava* docked a week later. Radio communications intercepted by GCHQ indicated that exceptional arrangements had been made for these two freighters, and visual inspection at Istanbul and Gibraltar showed that the cargo was unusual, even for these ships which were normally timber carriers. Most of the bulky military hardware that had been transported across the Atlantic, like the disassembled *Beagle* bombers, had been boxed and carried on deck, giving the 'crate-ologists', who had perfected the art of judging their contents, an opportunity to exercise their skills. Yet these two ships rode high in the water, with no cargo on deck, suggesting that some very large, low-weight, space-consuming objects had been hidden in the hold. Furthermore, they were unloaded at night by Russians in conditions of unprecedented secrecy at Mariel. Shortly afterwards, an agent in Havana reported having seen a shrouded missile transporter heading towards San Cristóbal, and gave an estimate of its length. As he was a professional accountant, the agent's message was given added weight, and it was noted that his figure coincided with that of a Soviet MRBM, codenamed *Sandal* by NATO, which had been measured by a military attaché during the annual May Day parade in Red Square.

There was an immediate need for a further U-2 mission over San Cristóbal, which had not been the subject of aerial reconnaissance since 5 September, but it was at this moment that the CIA was prevented from undertaking any further sorties. The reason was the loss, on 9 September, of a Taiwanese U-2 near Nanchang in mainland China. Two years earlier, the CIA had supplied Chiang Kai-Shek's nationalist government with a pair of U-2s, which had been based at Taoyuan, close to the capital Taipei. Six Taiwanese pilots had been trained in Texas to fly the aircraft and had made regular flights over the Chinese nuclear test site at Lop Nor and the MRBM ranges near Chuang-Cheng-Tzu in Gansu Province. However, just as the crisis in Cuba was unfolding, one of the Taiwanese planes failed to return and an announcement was made in Peking that it had been shot down by a unit of the Red Air Force. Five days later, the Chinese delivered a strongly worded protest about American-sponsored espionage, which caused acute embarrassment in Washington. There the Defense Department expressed the view in private that, if the experience were repeated and a plane was brought down over Cuba, it would be imperative for the pilot to be a regular USAF officer in uniform and not a civilian employed on a transparent CIA contract. Accordingly, there was a ten-day delay while air-force pilots at Laughlin and McDill air-force bases in Texas were hurriedly introduced to the U-2 programme.

Finally, on 14 October, the mystery of what the accountant had reported seeing ended when Major Richard Heyser flew his U-2 over the San Cristóbal area and took 928 pictures, which, upon his return, were rushed to Washington. Photo interpretation by experienced analysts revealed four SS-4 erector launchers in a grove of palm trees, together with all the ancillary equipment such as fuel trailers, transporters and long rectangular tents that had been listed in a Soviet MRBM deployment manual supplied to the CIA by Penkovsky the previous year.

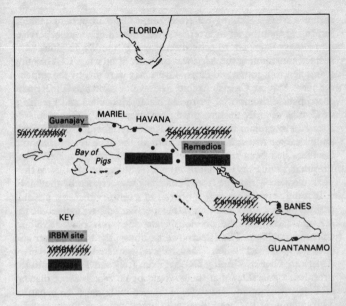

The strategic significance of the deployment of these medium-range missiles, which had a range of 1,100 nautical miles, was that it altered the balance of power. Whereas the Soviets were known to possess less than fifty operational ICBMs, a number regarded as insufficient to launch a surprise attack on the North American continent, the MRBMs and IRBMs (with a range of 2,200 nautical miles) brought Washington within striking distance of their four-to-six megaton warheads. If the missiles were made operational, the whole global equation would be changed.

Following the discovery of the four SS-4s in Heyser's pictures, further low-level sorties were flown from 14 October and revealed two MRBM sites near Sagua la Grande, IRBMs at Remedios and Guanajay, and a combined radar and communications centre at Camaguey. These locations were defended by a total of sixteen separate SAM batteries, and on 18 October a U-2 pilot described seeing a MiG-21 taking off from Santa Clara in pursuit of him, indicating that the jet interceptors had entered operational service. Three days later, after hectic discussions in the White House, the secrecy surrounding the crisis was partially lifted when CIA briefing teams flew to London and Paris. There they were met by the respective local Station Chiefs, Archie Roosevelt [12] and Al Ulmer, who accompanied them to see Prime Minister Macmillan and President de Gaulle, in order to show them photographs of the Cuban missile sites and to explain that President Kennedy intended to announce an immediate maritime blockade until all the offensive missiles and bombers had been removed. By coincidence, within hours of the President giving his ultimatum, the CIA officer in Moscow scheduled to collect a message from Penkovsky was arrested by the KGB.

It is only after more than a quarter of a century that it is possible to put these events into some perspective and to gather all the relevant facts, like the previously classified role played by surveillance satellites. The superpowers came to the brink of war and only stepped back when Khrushchev negotiated the removal of American Thor and Jupiter IRBMs from Italy and Turkey, plus the President's guarantee that there would be no repetition of the Bay of Pigs invasion, in return for a Soviet withdrawal from Cuba. Throughout, as has been illustrated, intelligence performed a vital function, on both sides. Writing long after these events, Dr Ray Cline, then the CIA's Deputy Director for Intelligence, said that he could 'not imagine a more intimate linking of intelligence in all functional categories with the highest level policy decision-making'.[13] All human and technical sources were exploited by the Americans to clarify what was taking place in Cuba, while the Russians were engaged upon a molehunt to find the traitor responsible for haemorrhaging strategic secrets to the West. The Kremlin's strategy to deploy offensive missiles in Cuba was a well-kept secret,[14] but it was utterly dependent on the maintenance of absolute silence until the missiles were completely operational. Any premature disclosure would surely wreck the scheme because, without a warhead and technical support, a rocket is simply an expensive piece of useless hardware, worthless even as a bargaining counter. Certainly, the West had no inkling of Khrushchev's intentions until it was almost too late, as is clear from a declassified Special National Intelligence Estimate,[15] dated 19 September 1962, which considered, and specifically ruled out, the likelihood of Soviet IRBM deployment in the Caribbean. This report, commissioned by the DCI, John McCone, from his honeymoon villa in Cap d'Antibes the previous week, cited 'serious problems of command and control' and suggested that the large number of Soviet military personnel required to oversee 'a significant strike capability with ballistic weapons' would be 'a political liability in Latin America'. In short, it was the CIA's view (but one not shared by the DCI) that political and logistical considerations would deter Khrushchev from behaving rashly. The scale of this miscalculation is highlighted by the report's omission to note the recent arrival of some 22,000 Soviet 'advisers' in Cuba,[16] and the knowledge in hindsight that this assessment was written after the missiles had been unloaded at Mariel and while they were being readied for transport to their launchpads.

What remains unexplained is exactly why no attempt was made to camouflage the Cuban sites, since Khrushchev's gamble was wholly reliant on concealing the true nature of his scheme.[17] The sudden appearance of the SAM batteries in August 1962 heightened American suspicions and alerted Washington's intelligence community to the possible installation of offensive weapons. When these fears were confirmed by Major Heyser, not even the most rudimentary steps had been taken to hide the conspicuous rockets and their trailers.

Altogether twenty-four SS-4 MRBMs at six sites, and eighteen IRBMs at four sites, were discovered, photographed and then dismantled for shipment back to Odessa. On the journey home the Russian merchantmen obligingly left the crated *matériel* open so that the contents could be photographed by low-flying reconnaissance aircraft.

As events turned out, the direct victims of this historic confrontation were Major Rudolf Anderson, shot down in his U-2 while overflying the Cuban naval centre of Banes on 28 October 1962, the day the Soviets announced their climbdown;[18] and Colonel Oleg Penkovsky, who was executed by a firing squad immediately after his conviction for treachery in May 1963, having tendered information that 'proved invaluable to US intelligence analysts'[19] during the crisis. The affair brought the superpowers to the brink of war, and it is now wellknown that some of the options put to President Kennedy to restore the status quo were of a drastic nature, involving an air strike against Cuba, followed by occupation. During the vital hours that the West waited for Khrushchev's response to the imposition of the quarantine, the military balance continued to shift. More SAM batteries were put into action and more MiG-21s achieved operational readiness; but, paradoxically, while these developments had a conventional significance, there was no reason to suppose that a single nuclear warhead had ever been delivered to Cuba. The photographic evidence suggested that the distinctive underground bunkers, then still under construction, were not ready to accommodate the devices. Although there was an outside chance that atomic weapons had been supplied with the *Beagle* bombers, which were certainly capable of delivering them, there was no sign of the special storage facilities they would require on any of the U-2 photos.[20]

If it were not for the global implications of the crisis, this episode might well be described as a microcosm of the intelligence game, with vital contributions made by each of the services studied here. Certainly, all the major political decisions in the West were based on intelligence, in the first instance through analysis of the Soviet ICBM development programme and the monitoring of Soviet and Cuban wireless traffic, and thereafter on clandestine photographs obtained by U-2s. In between were the vital pieces of the jigsaw added by Penkovsky and SDECE's agents in the field. Thus, on this occasion at least, the whole spectrum of intelligence activities was exploited, and the game ran its course.

At its conclusion, one is bound to ask who won? Who conceded the least? The answer is not as clear-cut as might be supposed. The Soviets had to endure a humiliating climbdown, with sixteen ships executing 180 degree turns in mid-Atlantic to return home as soon as the blockade had been declared, but achieved the removal of American MRBMs from Europe as well as a pledge that Cuba would not be invaded. Americans would retort that the Jupiters were obsolete, scheduled to be dismantled anyway, and that the political climate in the US after the Bay of Pigs fiasco virtually precluded any overt military intervention. One significant point, acknowledged by those who analysed the Russian telemetry signals intercepted in Turkey and Iran, was the implication of the entire episode for the disastrous Soviet ICBM programme. The Kremlin's range missile project had been an abject failure and, according to Penkovsky's testimony, had stalled in October 1960, when Chief Marshal of Artillery Nedelin and some 300 of his colleagues had been killed in an accidental launchpad explosion. At the time, Nedelin's death had been attributed by the authorities to an aircrash, but Penkovsky gave a different version, describing how the Chief Marshal and his guests had emerged from a viewing bunker prematurely, after a rocket had failed to lift off. They had waited twenty minutes for the missile to be declared safe, but as soon as they had stepped into the open, it had detonated, taking an appalling toll among those assembled.[21]

The need to place shorter-range weapons nearer to their targets amounted to a damning indictment of Soviet rocketry skills. Subsequent events proved that this was, indeed, a valid interpretation of Khrushchev's motive. Apparently alarmed by the speed with which the US had drawn ahead in the race to develop reliable ICBMs, he had opted for the most expedient solution possible and had simply positioned his weapons closer to their objectives.

There was throughout an element of bluff used by both sides. Originally Khrushchev, through his ambassador in Washington, had emphatically denied any intention of positioning offensive weapons outside Soviet borders. Then, when the naval quarantine had been imposed, US forces had been deliberately moved into the region. Instead of dispersing aircraft to pre-selected airfields, or concealing them in protected hangars, hundreds of bombers had been lined up in the open on bases in Florida, Texas, Louisiana and Puerto Rico, to demonstrate Kennedy's resolve. Coincidentally, the very first Soviet reconnaissance satellite, *Cosmos* 10, was launched from Tyuratam on 17 October and spent four days in unusually low orbit surveying the southern United States, before being recovered and its exposed film developed. No doubt the impressive display of military hardware at Homestead, McDill and Jacksonville airbases, in plain sight, had the desired impact on the Soviet photointerpreters. A second surveillance satellite, *Cosmos* 11, had followed on 20 October, in an unprecedented flurry of activity at the Tyuratam cosmodrome.

Apart from Anderson[22] and Penkovsky, Khrushchev himself was to pay a heavy price for his adventurism. He clung to power for a further two years before being forced into an isolated retirement, having lost the support of that most valued of Soviet institutions, the KGB.

The KGB *Rezident* in Havana since 1959, Aleksandr I. Shitov, who used the alias Aleksandr I. Alekseev, was promoted to ambassador in 1962 following the recall of Kudryavtsev. Shitov remained in

Cuba until 1968 and in 1970, turned up in Peru and Chile under journalistic cover.

Chronology of the Crisis

1956

June — First U-2 overflight of Soviet Union

1957

15 May — First SS-6 launched

3 August — SS-6 flies 3,500 miles to Kamchatka

4 October — First Sputnik launched

1960

9 April — Plesetsk ICBM site under construction

1 May — Powers' U-2 shot down near Sverdlovsk

6 July — Sergei Kudriavtsev appointed ambassador in Cuba

1961

April — Bay of Pigs invasion

20 April–6 May — Oleg Penkovsky debriefed in London

18 July–10 August — Oleg Penkovsky's second visit to London

6 August — Construction of Berlin Wall commenced

20 September–16 October — Oleg Penkovsky debriefed in Paris

1962

30 May — Sergei Kudryavtsev replacd by Aleksandr Shitov

August — SDECE reports SA-2 missiles in Cuba

29 August — U-2 photographs eight SAM sites

5 September — U-2 flight over west Cuba confirms SAMs

8 September — *Omsk* docks at Mariel

9 September — U-2 shot down over China

15 September — *Poltava* docks at Mariel
U-2 flight over west Cuba reports SAMs only

4 October — Last U-2 flight over west Cuba for ten days because of cloud cover

10 October — Kennedy authorizes USAF U-2 missions over Cuba

14 October — Major Richard Heyser overflies San Cristóbal

17 October — IRBM sites found at Remedios and Guanajay
Cosmos 10 launched

18 October	MiG-21s operational at Santa Clara
20 October	*Cosmos* 11 launched
21 October	Macmillan and de Gaulle briefed
	Cosmos 10 recovered
22 October	Kennedy imposes maritime blockade
	Penkovsky's case officer arrested in Moscow
27 October	Khrushchev agrees to withdraw missiles
	Il–28s spotted uncrated at San Julian
28 October	Major Rudolf Anderson's U-2 shot down
29 October	U-2 accidentally overflies Chukot Peninsula

4

The Neighbours

'The KGB is not a super-human, omnipotent
organization. If our counter-measures are to
be based on false evidence and wrong assump-
tions, they are doomed to failure.'

Ladislav Bittman, giving evidence to the
Senate Permanent Sub-committee on Investigations, October 1987

How much is known in the West about the KGB? The answer is
surprisingly little, and much of what has become widely accepted
about the organization is based on exaggerated accounts written by
journalists who may have allowed political opinion to colour their
perception. According to Tom Polgar, a veteran of thirty-five years'
experience in the CIA, having been Chief of Station in Berlin,
Hamburg, Vienna, Buenos Aires, Saigon and Mexico City,
'our knowledge about the KGB is limited in both substance and
specifics'.[1]

The present KGB was constituted in March 1954, just a few
months after the trial and execution of Lavrenti Beria, the main
instrument of Stalin's terror. Beria had controlled the Soviet state's
vast security bureaucracy in its various successive guises, as the
NKVD, MVD, NKGB and MGB, since 1938, but his ill-judged bid
for power within days of Stalin's death from a stroke early in March
1953 left him isolated within the Kremlin. It was even rumoured
that he had actually murdered Stalin himself. Whatever the truth,
Beria and his acolytes were not to survive. Outmanoeuvred by his

Directors of the First Chief Directorate

Evgenni Petrovich Pitovranov	1944–52
Sergei Romanovich Savchenko	1952–3
Vasili Semenovich Ryasnov	1953
Aleksandr Semenovich Panyushkin	1953–65
Aleksandr Mikhailovich Sakharovsky	1965–72
Vladimir Aleksandrovich Kryuchkov	1972–88
L. V. Shebarshin	1988–

own deputy, Sergei Kruglov, who acted in concert with the influential Nikita Khrushchev, the Ministry of Internal Affairs (the MVD) underwent a dramatic purge, with many of Beria's loyal supporters facing the firing squad after having been convicted of conspiring to betray the motherland. Beria himself was shot on 23 December 1953, having been found guilty of spying for British intelligence. The official announcement cited his 'treason by working as a secret agent for. . .the British Intelligence network' since 1919. No less than two of his predecessors, Vyacheslav R. Menzhinsky and Genrikh G. Yagoda, had suffered the same fate. Menzhinsky was reported to have died suddenly of heart failure in 1934, having fallen under suspicion; and Yagoda had been dismissed from his post in September 1936 and shot in March 1938 for espionage. Even Beria's immediate predecessor, Nikolai I. Yezhov, had fared little better. He had hanged himself in a mental institution in 1938. Ever since the demise of the Czar's secret police, the *Ochrana*, in the 1917 Revolution, Russia had experienced a series of variously titled state security organs. Over the years the GPU had given way to the OGPU, which had been followed by the GUGB, NKGB and the MVD. All the different Commissariats had acquired a well-earned reputation for the ruthless treatment of those opposing (or even suspected of opposing) the regime.

The reorganization of March 1954 left the Ministry of Security in charge of internal matters, under Kruglov, with his deputy, Ivan Serov, administering the Committee for State Security, the KGB, which had responsibility for state security and foreign operations. Since that date the KGB's internal structure has changed in response to particular events, but when the new body was formed few people in the West had any knowledge of what had taken place. Indeed, the standard textbook used by Western intelligence agencies at that time, *Soviet Espionage* by David Dallin (Yale University Press), had been published the following year, too soon to mention the KGB at all.

Information about the inner workings of the Soviet intelligence and security apparatus has filtered through to the West mainly via defectors. Although it was to be revealed much later that certain Russian wireless traffic during the 1940s had been intercepted and deciphered in a joint research project run by GCHQ and the NSA, this only served to whet the appetite of those seeking to understand Moscow's worldwide intelligence strategy. The decrypted signals, codenamed VENONA, gave tantalizing glimpses of the NKVD's operations on a global basis and demonstrated that it was running well-maintained networks of spies on every continent, but there were few clues to the actual personalities involved. And of the occasional examples of Soviet espionage that did surface in the immediate post-war period, like those of Allan Nunn May and Klaus Fuchs, most had been run by the GRU, the Soviet military intelligence service, and had, therefore, been of limited value in terms of exposing the NKVD. Nor was there any co-ordinated attempt to monitor the movements of suspected Soviet diplomats, or to keep them under prolonged surveillance. In the complete absence of reliable agents inside Beria's monolith, the role of the defector became crucial to the West's perception of what was happening behind the Iron Curtain. Some, like Walter Krivitsky before the war, had given lurid accounts of their first-hand experiences in the foreign intelligence division of the OGPU and its successor, the NKVD. This was the branch of Soviet intelligence that masterminded espionage and subversion overseas, and was of prime concern to the West's security authorities. However, reliable, up-to-date data was extremely hard to come by, and knowledge was limited to the handful of pre-war espionage cases that had surfaced. As Tom Polgar has pointed out,

> however valuable the information from a defector may be, both objectivity and veracity of the information may often be questionable. The defector has an obvious motive to exaggerate the significance of the information he provides and to try to enhance his own position in the eyes of the interrogators.[2]

The single individual who did more to alert the West to the Soviet post-war espionage threat was, ironically, a member of the GRU. Igor Gouzenko defected from the Soviet embassy in Ottawa in September 1945, bringing with him a stack of 109 documents purloined from his coderoom. Gouzenko's haul revealed some of the operations of a sophisticated GRU network based in Canada, with links further afield, but he was unable to shed much light on another group active in the same field known as the *Smezhniki*, or 'the Neighbours'. Gouzenko's office was in a special suite of eight offices on the second floor of the embassy, at 285 Charlotte Street, and extraordinary precautions had been taken to seal off this particular wing from the rest of the building. A pair of huge steel doors guarded the entrance, and none of the GRU personnel was permitted to trespass into the NKVD's special rooms which were barred and shuttered. The Neighbours even boasted their own separate cipher arrangements and an incinerator to destroy secret communications.

The GRU's parallel organization was the NKVD, headed in Ottawa by Vitali G. Pavlov, whose official status was a diplomat with the rank of second secretary. Although Gouzenko could testify to the integrity of the security precautions taken by the Neighbours, he was unable to expose the organization's operations. Nevertheless, he did shed considerable light on the GRU's activities, and a number of networks were rolled up by the Royal Canadian Mounted Police's Special Branch and Britain's Security Service in consequence, including twenty Canadian Communists, of whom eleven were imprisoned. Similarly, Kirril M. Alexeev, the commercial attaché in Mexico who defected the following year, was able to identify Lev A. Tarasov as the local NKVD *Rezident*, but could not do much more in terms of naming individual agents.

Not long after Gouzenko's escape in Canada, another GRU defector surface in Turkey. In fact, Ismail G. Akhmedov had fled from the Soviet consulate in Ankara in May 1942, but had kept a low profile for some years so as to avoid the GRU's retribution. Thus it was not until 1948 that he was made available for debriefing at the hands of the CIA and the British SIS by the Turkish Security Inspectorate. While he could substantiate much of Gouzenko's general observations about the GRU, he had no direct detailed knowledge of the NKVD. The first post-war NKVD defector was Anatoli M. Granovsky, an NKVD captain who, in July 1946, had been assigned to the *Petrovorets*, a steamer under repair in Stockholm which was scheduled to sail to the Black Sea. Like all Soviet merchantmen, some of the ship's company were undercover NKVD agents, and Granovsky was one of three from the NKVD's Third Chief Directorate in the crew. His task was to monitor the behaviour of his shipmates and report any 'anti-Soviet' activity. He was also developing his credentials as a seaman for another as yet undetermined mission abroad on behalf of the foreign intelligence division, the First Chief Directorate, for whom he had previously worked in Czechoslovakia.

Granovsky approached the US military attaché in Sweden and secured his passage to America, where he was to settle and write his memoirs, *I Was an NKVD Agent* (Devin-Adair, New York, 1962). He was later to give valuable insights into the NKVD's methods, but, apart from the names of colleagues who had recently been posted to Germany, Japan and the United States, he was unable to supply the kind of detailed operational material that the West was anxious to acquire. In any event, the US still had no centralized system of dealing with useful intelligence defectors, for the CIA was not to be created for a further year.

Between 1947 and 1954 the Americans were to receive no less than three important Soviet defectors who were to add significantly to the West's knowledge of the NKVD. Captain Boris Bakhlanov escaped from Vienna in 1947, but was rejected by the US authorities, who failed to recognize him as an authentic source and passed him on to the British. He partly anglicized his name to 'Boris Haddon' and later wrote of his experiences in *Nights Are Longest There* (Hutchinson, London, 1971), under the pseudonym 'A. I. Romanov'. He died of drowning in London early in 1984.

It was only later, when two senior NKVD staffers defected, that the West first got a good glimpse of the Neighbours. Lieutenant-Colonel Grigori S. Burtulsky escaped in Berlin in June 1953, with Lieutenant-Colonel Yuri A. Rastvorov following early in January 1954 from Tokyo. Burtulsky was, in effect, a high-ranking secret policeman, who was to give evidence to Congress about Stalin's mass deportation to Siberia of disloyal populations, which he had overseen from his position within the NKVD's Fifth Chief Directorate. According to Burtulsky, the arrests were not limited to individual families suspected of having collaborated with the Nazis. The inhabitants of entire towns in the Chechen-Ingush Republic had been rounded up and sent to forced labour camps. He also described how Karachays, Balkars, Kalmyks and Crimean Tatars had suffered the

KGB Organization

FIRST CHIEF DIRECTORATE	SECOND CHIEF DIRECTORATE	THIRD CHIEF DIRECTORATE	FIFTH CHIEF DIRECTORATE
Foreign Intelligence	Counter-Intelligence	Cheka Joint Commission	Counter-Subversion
	Secret Political Section	Agents	
	Section for Extraordinary Matters	GRU Liaison	
	Records		

SEVENTH CHIEF DIRECTORATE	EIGHTH CHIEF DIRECTORATE	BORDER GUARDS	INTERNAL TROOPS	NINTH CHIEF DIRECTORATE
Surveillance	Investigations			Kremlin Security
	Prisons			Provincial Garrisons
	Economic			Registration
	Communications			Training
				Technical

same fate, sometimes within a few weeks of liberation from German occupation. For his part Rastvorov, who had spent four and a half years in the Toyko *Rezidentura*, was able to expose NKVD operations in the Far East and Japan, and to give a rare account of the first Chief Directorate. He also identified three members of the Japanese Foreign Office, Hiroshi Shoji, Shigeru Takamore and Nobunori Higurashi as Soviet sources. The latter was killed when he threw himself out of a window while under interrogation.

Ironically, one of the best possible sources of information about this particular division of the NKVD had been living quietly in Cleveland, Ohio, for the past fourteen years. 'Alexander Berg' was actually General Aleksandr M. Orlov, an NKVD veteran who had narrowly escaped Yezhov's purges by ignoring his orders, telegraphed to him in Barcelona at the height of the Spanish Civil War where he was the NKVD's senior adviser to the Nationalist side on counter-intelligence and guerrilla tactics, to return to Moscow. Instead of following his instructions, Orlov fled with his wife and daughter to Paris and used his diplomatic passport to obtain a visa to enter Canada. A month later he received a visitor's visa from the American legation in Ottawa and eventually settled in Cleveland under a false identity. Early in 1953 he sold his memoirs to *Life* magazine and, much to their embarrassment, it was not until the first instalment was published in April 1953 that either the CIA or the FBI realized that such a senior NKVD official was in their midst. Orlov co-operated with the authorities, but there was always a doubt about exactly how candid he had been about his own pre-war activities. He remained in Ohio until his death, from progressive heart disease, in April 1973.

While Orlov, and later Rastvorov, disclosed aspects of the First Chief Directorate's methods and activities, it was to be the sudden defection of four well-informed NKVD officers that was to supply the West with the data it really needed: the nuts and bolts of current operations. The West received this unexpected windfall in February 1954, when Piotr S. Deriabin turned up in Vienna and Nikolai E. Khokhlov surrendered to the American authorities in Frankfurt.

Major Deriabin had served in the NKVD's Guard Directorate, an independent unit within the NKVD's hierarchy which employed some 16,000 uniformed and plain-clothes guards to man the Kremlin's garrison and supply bodyguards to senior Party officials. According to Deriabin, Stalin's personal security team had consisted of 400 selected members of the Directorate. In 1952, Deriabin had been transferred from his counter-intelligence post within the Guard Directorate to the First Chief Directorate, then based in the old Comintern headquarters next to the Agricultural Fair grounds at 1a Tekstilshchikov Street in Moscow. His new role was that of a *operupolnomochenniy*, or case officer, in the Austro-German sub-section of the Directorate, running agents in Vienna and Berlin. In September 1953, he was moved from his office in NKVD head-quarters, at 2 Dzerzhinsky Square, to run security for the *Sovetskaya Kolonia* section of the *Rezidentura*, based in the old Imperial Hotel in Vienna. Here he had responsibility for keeping a watch on the rest of the Soviet intelligence apparatus, but in reality he was waiting for the right moment to defect. That opportunity arrived on 15 February 1954, when he walked into the American Kommandatura and offered his services to the CIA. He is still employed by the CIA as an expert on Soviet affairs to this day.

Captain Khokhlov surrendered to his intended murder victim, Georgi S. Okolovich, the feared leader of the NTS émigré opposition group based in Frankfurt. Instead of carrying out his orders and killing Okolovich, Khokhlov volunteered to tell everything he knew about his particular section of the First Chief Directorate, then known as the Ninth Section and later to be reorganized as Department 13. He also turned in two fellow assassins, Hans Kurkovich and Kurt Weber, both Germans who had been trained in Moscow by the KGB.

The picture painted by Orlov, Burtulsky, Deriabin and Khokhlov was grim. The First Chief Directorate was a huge structure, employing several thousand intelligence personnel, all gathering information about useful targets in the West. What was lacking, and was due to be supplied by a further defector, was the exact organization of a *Rezidentura* in a foreign country. Both MI5 and the FBI had developed a broad understanding of the inner machinations of the Soviet foreign intelligence arm of the NKVD and its successors, the MVD–MGB and the KGB, but no first-hand reports of how its overseas representatives operated in the field.

This vital information was to be supplied in April 1954 upon the long-expected defection of Lieutenant-Colonel Afanasy M. Shoro-khov, the *Rezident* in Canberra, who had been cultivated for the past three years by a Polish-born agent provocateur, Dr Michael Bialoguski, who happened to work for ASIO's counter-espionage branch, B2. Shorokhov had been posted to Canberra in February 1951 to replace the senior foreign intelligence directorate representative, Ivan Pakhomov, who had only been in Australia a short time, following the recall of Valentin M. Sadovnikov, the embassy's supposed second secretary, who had been reported for having spent the night in the home of an Australian without permission and, less seriously, for getting an embassy typist pregnant. Pakhomov, operating under TASS cover, had also been found wanting, so Shorokhov and his wife Evdokia, who doubled as an MVD–MGB cipher clerk, were transferred from Moscow to take control of the *Rezidentura*, using the names Vladimir and Evdokia Petrov. Their arrival was followed by the departure of the Sadovnikovs and the pregnant Iya Griazanova, and in February 1952 of Pakhomov. He was replaced by another TASS journalist, Viktor Antonov, to be based in Sydney, leaving the Petrovs with an MGB embassy complement of just five: Antonov, two co-opted Foreign Ministry officials, the commercial attaché, Nikolai G. Kovaliev, the press attaché, George I. Kharkovetz, and another stand-in from Moscow, Filip V. Kislitsyn. Janis E. Plaitkais was to follow later and take responsibility for dealing with émigrés.

As Bialoguski successfully wormed his way into Petrov's confidence, so ASIO took a greater interest in the developing scene. That the Canberra *Rezidentura* had been particularly active in recruiting spies was known from the VENONA traffic, and several espionage cases had been pursued as a result. However, it was Petrov's eventual decision to defect, which was in part prompted by his unwelcome recall to Moscow in 1954, that enabled ASIO to tie up the loose ends of its clandestine investigations. Petrov supplied damning material about two old suspects, Jim Hill and Ian Milner, who had both leaked documents from the government, and offered sufficient additional information to compromise four further well-placed Soviet sources.

Petrov's defection was soon followed by that of his wife, and together they built up the West's previously sketchy understanding of the structure and personalities of what was about to become the KGB's First Chief Directorate. In much the same way that Gouzenko and Akhmedov had not been very helpful about the work of the NKVD, so neither of the Petrovs could say much about the other organization's activities in Australia, which had been directed successively by Colonel Viktor Zaitsov and Anatoli Gordeev. Nevertheless, the Petrovs did confirm many of the conclusions reached by the analysts who had pored over the VENONA intercepts and tried to identify the cryptonyms of the individual sources mentioned. In short, the Petrovs had served to establish the scale of effort dedicated to foreign espionage by the KGB. If Australia, which incidentally did not even possess an overseas intelligence-gathering capability until ASIS's creation in 1952, had attracted so much attention from across the world, what was happening closer to London and Washington?

The evidence accumulated from Soviet defectors indicated that the KGB's First Chief Directorate employed some 15,000 officers globally, with around 3,000 based at its headquarters at Teplyystan, just outside Moscow's ring road, to the south-west of the capital. The organization was structured into functional directorates and geographical operational sub-sections, known as directions. Quite the largest of the three directorates was 'S', which handled the recruitment, training, maintenance and support of an astonishing number of illegals around the world. These illegals were agents deployed abroad under covers that did not enjoy diplomatic immunity, and varied from journalistic fronts, such as TASS and Novosti, to commercial enterprises like Aeroflot and the Moscow Narodny Bank, and the numerous opportunities provided by the UN.

As well as supervising the work of Soviet intelligence officers abroad, Directorate S also took charge of the recruitment of individual assets, usually the ideologically motivated volunteers who had been talent-spotted by well-placed locals. Each case would be assigned to the appropriate geographical department, where a case officer would act as a controller and make the necessary arrangements with subordinates to maintain clandestine communications with the case. The Directorate S controllers had two methods of servicing their sources: through the 'legal' channel, using specialist case officers attached to the KGB's nearest convenient *Rezidentura*, normally inside diplomatic premises; or via 'illegal support officers', whose sole function was to undertake the tasks that hostile surveillance prevented the 'legals' from risking. However committed the agent to his cause, he or she would need support, even if only on an intermittent basis. It might consist of an apparently innocuous postcard, simply to remind the source of the KGB's continuing interest in the case, or the more frequent necessity to supply funds and instructions and to exchange information. Where the host country's

First Chief Directorate

Directorate S Illegals (Line N)	Directorate T Scientific & Technical (Line X)	Directorate K Counter- Intelligence (Line KR)	Special Service I Information Dissemination	Service A Active Measures	Service R Planning & Analysis

*Operational
Departments*

(Line PR)
1 North America
2 Latin America
3 UK, Scandinavia,
  Australia, New Zealand
4 West Germany, Austria
5 Western Europe

6 China, Vietnam, Korea
7 Japan, Philippines,
  Indonesia, Singapore
8 Near & Middle East
9 Anglophone Africa
10 Francophone Africa

*Support
Departments*

11 Liaison with satellite services
12 Officers under cover
13 Communications
14 Documentation
15 Records
16 Cipher targets

security apparatus exercised vigilance, this important but routine tradecraft might be difficult to engage in without raising suspicions that could inadvertently compromise a valued agent. Accordingly, when the circumstances dictated caution, an illegal support officer would be dispatched to make contact with a source or even service him regularly.

Where the local environment was more favourable, which might be as a consequence of penetrating the host country's counter-intelligence structure, the essential business of surveying locations suitable for a covert rendezvous, and selecting dead-letter drops and sites for leaving clandestine signals, would be handled by staff from the 'legal' *Rezidentura*. Under the overall command of the *Rezident*, intelligence officers from the three principal directorates would take responsibility for cultivating their sources. Thus a 'Line N' expert from Directorate S would liaise with a standard illegal; a 'Line X' specialist on behalf of Directorate T would handle an agent with access to technical or scientific material, leaving the most sensitive area, *Kontrazvedka*, or counter-intelligence, to the counter-intelligence virtuosos in 'Line KR' from Directorate K, which concentrated on *Politicheskaye Razvedyvatel'noye*, or political secrets.

Case officers in the *Rezidentura* reported their progress up their chosen line to the relevant directorate at Moscow Centre, where three additional services disseminated the intelligence product ('Special Service I'); subjected the product to intensive analysis ('Service R'); or simply used it to develop predetermined strategies, such as disinformation campaigns (Service A').

The *Rezidents* in each country would in effect act as the field representative of whichever of Moscow Centre's operational 'directions' dealt with that particular territory, fulfilling a function roughly equivalent to a CIA Station Chief or an SIS Head of Station. Since the tradecraft practised by professionals is common the world over, knowledge of an opponent's internal arrangements is an essential prerequisite to taking preventive counter-measures or mounting penetration operations. Once the order-of-battle of a target agency has been determined, vulnerable case officers can be assessed as prospects, and recruitment and surveillance operations can be concentrated on identified intelligence personnel, instead of the more hit-and-miss process of keeping observation on diplomats chosen at random. Obviously the latter system is both time-consuming and potentially extremely wasteful. Furthermore, it tends to lower the morale of those engaged as watchers, because their target may well turn out to be completely innocent of espionage or, worse, a decoy deliberately deployed to distract the watcher teams from active case officers.

In physical terms knowledge of the exact location of the *referentura* inside a Soviet building is highly desirable so that audio surveillance, known to insiders by the euphemism 'technical coverage', can be attempted and the exterior monitored, so as to identify the intelligence professionals among the authentic diplomats, and the potential walk-in traitors among the regular *bona-fide* callers.

There may well have been an element of scepticism in Western security circles concerning the unusual emphasis made by the KGB on the use of illegals. This concept was virtually unknown to the KGB's opponents for two reasons. Firstly, no Soviet-trained illegal had ever been caught in the post-war era prior to the defection of the Petrovs, who confirmed Deriabin's analysis of the First Chief Directorate. There was, therefore, no independent corroboration of the claims made about the scale of effort, apart of course from the VENONA decrypts which simply indicated a large number of sources without disclosing exactly how they were being run. Secondly, the environment inside the Eastern Bloc precluded the Western agencies from even contemplating the infiltration of illegals.

Totalitarian regimes invariably retain control over subservient populations by imposing rigorous restrictions on movement. Unlike the West, where people are rarely challenged for a proof of identity, the necessity to carry certain essential documents is an accepted fact of life behind the Iron Curtain. The sheer number of separate items required by law is in itself a disincentive to even the most enterprising organization planning to embark on a programme of forgery so as to equip an illegal. For a start, every Soviet citizen is obliged to possess a small, drab, olive green, cloth-covered *pasporta* from the age of sixteen. This is the basic identity booklet bearing a photograph of the holder, which also contains various endorsements showing his marital status and his place of employment. However, an authentic *pasporta* cannot be granted without the production of a *svidetelstvo o rozhdenii*, the equivalent of a birth certificate, which can only be obtained from the regional document centre, known by the Russian acronym of ZAGS. Then there is his grey labour book, the *trudovaya knizhka*, filled with details of his job, and authority from the local labour office for any change in his post. At eighteen every male youth has to register with the *voyenkomat*, which will issue a red military service card, the *voyenny bilet*. This will describe the draft status of the holder. In addition, the average citizen will also carry a Party membership card, trade union booklets, certificates of various kinds, and probably some papers giving permission to travel to a particular destination. Every one of these documents can have its validity checked through a simple telephone call to the relevant issuing office. A second infraction of the regulations, such as possession of an expired *pasporta*, will result in immediate arrest on a criminal charge.

If all this were not daunting enough, Soviet citizens cannot travel freely, even within their own republic. It is a serious offence to stay overnight at an address where they are not registered, and all legitimate travellers are obliged to fill in the *domovaya kniga*, or housebook, with their full name and address whenever they leave home. This system is administered for each address by the *upravdom*, or house manager, who may be the head of the household. Enforcement is strict and every home is subject to inspection by the housing authority.

In the immediate post-war era the West did attempt to beat the system by infiltrating well-documented illegals into Soviet territory, but most eventually came unstuck. They were equipped with a coveted *belyy bilet*, which exempted them from military service, and carried a *listok netrudosposobnosti*, which certified the holder was somehow incapacitated for work. Unfortunately, the CIA discovered that their forgeries were of rather too good a quality. Genuine *pasporta* were manufactured from a poorly woven, coarse cotton and were held together by a pair of metal staples. While the CIA tried to duplicate the *pasporta*'s paper stock, the coloured underprinting, the characteristic watermarks and the elaborate stamps and embossed seals, they could never match the irregular cotton used on the covers. It was also realized, somewhat belatedly, that unlike Western staples, which are plated to prevent rusting, the Russian ones are uncoated and tended to rust within a few weeks, leaving distinctive stains on the surrounding paper. The CIA's replicas did not.

In short, there were plenty of obstacles to mounting 'black' operations to infiltrate illegals into Soviet territory. Several attempts were made, including a series utilizing documentary material from a secret store captured by the Abwehr from the Russians. Located in Oberstdorf, a small alpine village near the Austrian frontier, the cache provided the CIA with an opportunity to equip their agents with a plausible 'legend' complete with supporting papers, but few of the missions achieved their objective because of insufficient help available on the ground to establish the illegals with a long-term future. Reluctantly, the Western intelligence agencies accepted that the security environment created by the omniscient KGB precluded effective illegal operations.

In contrast, the challenges presented to the KGB mounting similar undertakings in the West were relatively insignificant, as was eloquently demonstrated in May 1957 when a disaffected KGB illegal, the first of his kind in the post-war era, requested asylum from the CIA station in Paris. Reino Hayhanen was a First Chief Directorate professional, who had been born in Finland but had adopted the identity of Eugene N. Maki, an American from Enaville, Idaho. Apparently, the real Maki had died in Finland, and the KGB had obtained a copy of his birth certificate and, with it, had applied for an American passport from the US embassy in Helsinki, using Hayhanen's photograph. Equipped with an authentic passport, Hayhanen had taken up residence in New York as an assistant to the KGB's illegal *Rezident*. Although he never learned his name, Hayhanen was able to give the FBI sufficient clues for them to track him down and arrest him in a Manhattan hotel on 21 June 1957.

The man caught by the FBI was using the name Mark Collins, but had previously lived under the alias Emil R. Goldfus and had entered the US from Canada in 1948 as Andrew Kayotis. Under interrogation he admitted to being Rudolf Ivanovich Abel, a Soviet citizen with the rank of colonel, but subsequent research showed that he was really William Fischer, born in Newcastle-upon-Tyne, where he had lived for the first eighteen years of his life before his left-leaning family had emigrated to the Soviet Union. Although much has been written about Abel's exploits during the war, very little is known about his activities between his arrival in Moscow in 1921 and his appearance in a German displaced persons camp in 1946 as Andrew Kayotis.[3]

Abel was sentenced to thirty years' imprisonment and in 1962 was swapped for the U-2 pilot Francis Gary Powers. Abel acquired a reputation as a master spy, but there was little justification for it. The only person that Hayhanen and Abel had attempted to run as an agent was Sergeant Roy Rhodes, a soldier who had been recruited by the KGB while assigned to the US embassy's car fleet as a mechanic in Moscow some years earlier. Rhodes had extracted some large sums from the KGB, but most of the information he had supplied was fictitious. In 1958, he was sentenced to a dishonourable discharge from the army and five years' hard labour.

Although Abel was found in possession of a lot of espionage paraphernalia, including one-time pads, a short-wave transmitter and a radio receiver, there was never any evidence to show that he had ever handled classified information. Although instructed by Moscow to trace Sergeant Rhodes, Abel and Hayhanen had failed to contact him. The case was therefore of only limited value, but it did substantiate the accounts given by Deriabin, Rastvorov and the Petrovs about how the First Chief Directorate conducted its business.

There was to be a curious sequel to the Abel case. One of the loose ends left by the FBI investigation was a pair of photographs found in Abel's briefcase attached to a bundle of notes worth $5,000. The photos were marked 'Shirley' and 'Morris', and the FBI suspected the two to be Lena and Morris Cohen, two Communist sympathizers of long standing. Morris, the son of Russian immigrants, had fought in the Spanish Civil War and had worked for Amtorg, the Soviet trading organization in New York. His wife, born in Massachusetts of Polish parents, was equally politically committed, and in the war had worked in a munitions factory as a trade union shop steward. Both had disappeared in the wake of the Rosenberg arrests in 1950. Four years later they turned up in Austria, where they applied to the New Zealand consulate in Paris for passports in the names of Peter and Helen Kroger. Their request had been supported by the genuine birth certificates of the real Krogers, who had died in the Soviet Union, and the passports had been issued.[4] Abel's tenuous connection with the Cohens was not to be tidied up until January 1961, when they were arrested in England for complicity in the Portland spy case, a KGB network supported by another Directorate S illegal, Konon Molody, alias Gordon Lonsdale.

In the meantime, three further KGB defectors had enhanced the West's knowledge of the First Chief Directorate. A man who later called himself Kaarlo R. Tuomi allowed himself to be used as a double agent by the FBI in 1959, and later in the same year Aleksandr Y. Kaznacheev defected from the Soviet embassy in Rangoon. Although not a KGB regular, Kaznacheev had been co-opted to work for the local *Rezident*, Ivan Vozny, and during the course of his duties had discovered the embassy's complete intelligence order-of-battle, which, of course, was of inestimable value.

Eighteen months after Kaznacheev's defection, the KGB suffered another grievous loss. Late in December 1960, a major in the Polish SB, who happened also to be a part-time informant for the KGB, escaped to West Berlin with his girlfriend. Michal Goleniewski had been in clandestine contact with the CIA for more than a year before his defection, and his meal-ticket led directly to the arrests of Harry Houghton, Ethel Gee and three KGB illegals: the Krogers and Konon Molody. He was also directly responsible for unmasking two spies in the West German intelligence structure, Heinz Felfe and Hans Klemens, of whom more will be said later.

The true identities of the Krogers were eventually established by the FBI, but Molody's background was rather more difficult to research. According to his own account, given under interrogation in prison, he had adopted the identity of a Canadian, who had moved to Finland with his mother and subsequently died in Karelia, which had been absorbed into the Soviet Union. Molody's command of English dated back to the five years he had spent in California, between 1933 and 1938, living with his aunt.[5] He had apparently slipped off a ship in Vancouver in 1954, acquired a passport in Lonsdale's name and then travelled to London, where he made contact with the Cohens, acting as a cut-out for Houghton and Gee.

By the middle of 19__ certain pattern had emerged in the uneasy relationship between the KGB and the West's security authorities. A dozen KGB officers had switched sides, and each had given another piece of the picture that had been outlined so incompletely by the original VENONA decrypts. Some, like Yuri Rastvorov, had been able to put a name to an individual agent, as happened with Takamore Shigeru of the Japanese Foreign Ministry, a long-term source of classified material for the KGB's *Rezident* in Tokyo. The trained assassin, Nikolai Khokhlov, had turned in his two German accomplices. With the Petrovs the situation had been rather more complicated as much of the information received by Vladimir Petrov and his predecessors had not been classified. Indeed, several of the documents removed from the embassy by Petrov and produced at the subsequent Royal Commission had actually been written or compiled by four people who were exposed as having given help to the KGB: Rupert Lockwood, a well-known journalist and Com-

Then there was the element of ruthlessness on the part of the KGB. Khokhlov had given a graphic account of his own murderous tasks and had backed up the chilling stories told by Orlov, Deriabin and Burtulsky. Clearly the KGB was an organization to be reckoned with. Indeed, if any further proof was needed, Khokhlov himself was to provide it. After his debriefing he went to live in Switzerland, but took a close interest in Russian émigré politics. In September 1957, he attended a NTS conference in Frankfurt and nearly died of a mysterious illness, apparently brought on by a powerful toxin. He had been administered a dose of radioactive thallium.

In spite of the setbacks represented by these defections, the KGB continued to run its operations unhindered, and the GRU went largely unnoticed. In fact, the GRU was not to experience a single defection between 1948 and 1971. That, of course, is not to say that Soviet intelligence did not sustain any serious damage during the fifteen years after the end of hostilities. By early 1960 the West's intelligence authorities were prepared, on the basis of information from defectors and their own experience of espionage cases, to believe virtually anything about the KGB. Goleniewski had prompted a spate of investigations across Europe, implicating suspects in Germany (Heinz Felfe), Sweden (Stig Wennerstrom) and Britain (George Blake and Harry Houghton). In the years that followed others appeared, some with harrowing stories. Bogdan Stashinsky confessed in 1961 to having murdered two Ukrainian émigrés, Lev Rebet and Stefan Bandera, on behalf of the KGB. He was tried in Karlsruhe and convicted, but was later offered resettlement in the US in return for his information. Anatoli Golitsyn, who defected from Helsinki with his wife and daughter in December 1961, was one of the few who had apparently planned his escape for years, carefully accumulating a meal-ticket that was to lead to the exposure of some 200 Soviet agents worldwide.[6] Although Golitsyn was not especially high-ranking, he possessed a well-developed political perspective and arrived in the West bearing a complex message about the KGB's conspiratorial machinations. His self-chosen task was to alert the counter-intelligence authorities to the scale of the forces ranged against them and to wake governments to the KGB's global subversion. While Golitsyn's data was used to good effect, rolling up KGB networks around the world, his interpretation of the Kremlin's arcane manoeuvres found only a limited audience and he was assigned the role of part-time consultant to the CIA's counter-intelligence branch, a small but powerful group within the Plans Division.

Golitsyn was to be followed by Evgeny Runge, an illegal based in West Germany with the KGB rank of lieutenant-colonel, who in 1967 traded jos network for a new life. It included Heinz and Leonore Sutterlin, a husband-and-wife team with access to sensitive Foreign Ministry papers, and the janitor of the French embassy in Bonn. That Runge's case was not a one-off, and the KGB had continued to deploy illegals in the West, was proved when Rupert Sigl, a Moscow-trained Austrian, defected to the Americans two years later.

However, not all the KGB's defectors received a warm welcome. Golitsyn had warned that he was likely to be discredited by false defectors, and two of those appearing soon afterwards were treated as hostile. A well-known Soviet playright, Yuri V. Krotkov, defected in September 1963 and disclosed his alleged involvement in numerous entrapment operations conducted by the Second Chief Directorate in Moscow against foreigners. Principal among his victims had been the French ambassador, Maurice Dejean, who was recalled as soon as Krotkov revealed the plot to compromise him and his wife. Krotkov was later allowed to settle in the US, although he was never to be trusted;[4] however, his treatment was fair, compared to Yuri Nosenko's experience.

Nosenko had indicated his wish to spy for the CIA in Geneva in June 1962 and had been instructed on how to earn his meal-ticket as a defector-in-place. Sixteen months later, in February 1964, he had suddenly demanded to be received and his debriefings had begun. Warned by Golitsyn and prepared by Krotkov, the CIA subjected Nosenko to a thorough interrogation, in which he was forced to admit that many of his claims were false. He had exaggerated his KGB rank, his length of service, his relationship with influential superiors and his involvement with cases of particular interest to the CIA, including that of Lee Harvey Oswald. Coincindentally, the Warren Commission started to take evidence concerning President Kennedy's assassination soon after Nosenko's appearance in the West, and he seemed remarkably well-informed about the KGB's file on Oswald, who had himself defected to the Soviet Union in 1959. According to Nosenko, Oswald had been considered of no value to the KGB and had been rejected. Some CIA insiders wondered why the KGB had gone to such elaborate lengths to convey the impression that they had absolutely no involvement with Oswald, when experience demonstrated that someone of Oswald's background, with service at sensitive marine bases, would have been of considerable interest to the Soviets. It was an issue that was never to be resolved fully.

Nosenko was kept in solitary confinement at a purpose-built facility inside a secure compound at Camp Peary, the CIA's training base in Williamsburg, Virginia, for three and a half years, and questioned on 292 separate occasions, only to be exonerated and then hired as a lecturer on counter-espionage techniques.

By the mid-1960s, the West had been conditioned by a continuous diet of defectors' tales and elaborate spy rings. Unlike the GRU, about which relatively little was known, the KGB had acquired an awe-inspiring reputation. The historical literature tended to concentrate on the pre-war purges and the ruthlessness with which the organization would pursue émigrés and renegades. The assassinations of Trotsky, Miller and Reiss were often cited to demonstrate the barbarous commitment of the foreign intelligence directorate's leadership and the political support enjoyed by it. It was a frightening example of institutionalized violence condoned by officialdom, and the testimony of former insiders like Khokhlov and Stashinsky showed that the KGB had retained its pre-war capability to hunt down the regime's opponents and murder them. Apparently, the mobile death squads, so vividly described by General Orlov, had become a permanent feature of Soviet tactics. The concept of *Smersh*, an abbreviation of the Russian for 'death to spies', was so captivating that the 'wet affairs' section received huge publicity over a prolonged period. Indeed, the KGB's notoriety was such that it was credited with performing executions that, in all probability, it had nothing to do with. Two early examples were the deaths of Valentin Markin and Walter Krivitsky. Both were on the run in America before the war, having denounced Stalin, and were found dead in unusual circumstances. Markin died in a bar brawl in New York in 1934, while Krivitsky appeared to have committed suicide in his Washington hotel room in February 1941. The main evidence of murder on both occasions was nothing more substantial than the knowledge that the victims had been sentenced to death in absentia. Nevertheless, there were plenty of commentators willing to see *Smersh*'s hand in the business.

While the KGB probably had no involvement in these particular cases, it did, however, indulge in widescale 'executive action', another popular euphemism for murder. Thousands died in the pre-war purges and an unknown number of people were abducted in Germany and Austria immediately after the war. It is this well-documented use of officially sanctioned violence that set the KGB apart from its opponents in the intelligence field. As William Hood, a long-serving CIA counter-intelligence expert, has commented, 'Except for the Soviet proclivity for murder, kidnapping and black-mail, there is not much difference in espionage methodology East or West.'[8]

The KGB also acquired a reputation for masterminding espionage networks on a gigantic scale. Ironically, this was in part due to Gouzenko's revelations, which, of course, had actually concerned the GRU and not the Neighbours. Nevertheless, the Hiss–Chambers controversy and the Rosenberg case heightened fears about the ease with which the KGB had systematically exploited Communist Party members and their sympathizers. Clearly the strategy used had not been limited to the US Communist Party. The Burgess and Maclean defections in 1951 had revealed a British dimension, and the Petrovs had provided documentary proof in Australia of the KGB's skill at recruiting local Communists to undertake espionage. Petrov had also supplied the first confirmation, regarding Burgess and Maclean, of Soviet prowess at running long-term moles. Combined with the VENONA material, which had still not been made public, the KGB presented a frightening challenge to the integrity of Western secur-ity.

And yet there was another aspect to the story. Few of the defectors had been ideological converts to the West, and most had been opportunists seeking to better their own circumstances in the face of the *nomenklatura*, the systemized corruption of the Soviet regime. Some, such as Khokhlov, Stashinsky and Burtulsky, had been genu-inely appalled by the nature of their missions and had rebelled. Others, like Petrov and Hayhanen, simply had feared their recall to Moscow and had opted for the safer alternative of asylum. Of the twenty-one intelligence defectors mentioned in this chapter, only Golitsyn showed any deep political appreciation of his situation, or could be said to have laid a careful, long-term plan which happened to include defection as a means of achieving a particular objective. In addition, only a handful of KGB defectors have been from outside the First Chief Directorate. As Tom Polgar has said:

There have been few if any defectors who could be considered as having had policy-level positions or positions from which they could have had access to a broad spectrum of normally well-compartmented KGB activities. I cannot recall any KGB defector of higher than field-grade rank. There have been very, very few defectors from outside the First Directorate. Thus it is inevitable that we should know more about some of the KGB's failures than about its successes.[9]

During the 1970s the number and quality of KGB defectors diminished noticeably, and some did not have very useful access. For example, Artush S. Hovanesian and Alekei Myagkov were relatively junior 'line crossers', opportunists who saw a chance of escaping a hated system. Raya Kiselnikova, a co-opted Ministry of Foreign Affairs secretary, and K.G. Nadirashvili, who defected from Vienna in June 1975, also fall into this category. Only Vladimir N. Sakharov, who had been recruited initially by the CIA in Moscow in 1963, Oleg A. Lyalin and Stanislav A. Levchenko, who defected in Tokyo in October 1979, supplied information that could be described as really important. Lyalin had been a trade delegation official, without diplomatic immunity, who, early in 1971, was discovered to be conducting an illicit affair with his attractive blonde secretary, Irina Teplyakova. They were both compromised in a classic honeytrap and Lyalin supplied the British with a mass of useful information for six months until August 1971, when he was arrested by the police in London on a drunk driving charge. He was taken out of circulation and the British government used the excuse to expel 105 known Soviet intelligence officers from the capital. Lyalin had served in a highly secret KGB sabotage unit, known as Section V, and produced his very revealing wartime contingency plans.

Of this group, Sakharov was unique. He was a long-term agent recruited while still undergoing his studies at the Ministry of Foreign Affairs, who had maintained clandestine contact with his case officers until his successful exfiltration from Kuwait in 1971. His other overseas posting had been to Cairo, and in both places he used good tradecraft to exchange covert messages with his handlers, which effectively blew the complete order-of-battle of the two *Rezidenturas*. It was also the first time that the KGB had been penetrated by a recruited agent, as opposed to a walk-in, like Nosenko, who had been sent back as a defector-in-place. In terms of the sophistication of the CIA's tradecraft, the Sakharov case only proved that the CIA had the ability to develop and run an agent in a 'denied area', hostile territory. In fact, there had been two similar cases, as we shall see, involving the GRU, but for the KGB Sakharov's defection must have held profound implications. It was the first of its kind, and the KGB would have been unable to know the full background of his recruitment by the CIA until the publication of his memoirs, *High Treason*, a full decade after his defection. Apart fom the two GRU traitors, the KGB believed that there had only been one example of a KGB walk-in: a Second Chief Directorate officer named Chere-panov, who had approached the British in Belgrade in 1958 and offered to spy for SIS. On that occasion he had been rebuffed as a rather crude agent provocateur, but he had made a second attempt to the Americans in Moscow in October 1963. The case had died when Cherepanov disappeared, presumably entrapped by ubiqui-tous Soviet surveillance.

The Cherepanov incident received wide circulation within the KGB *pour encourager les autres*, as did another of the same kind, involving a certain Lieutenant Vladimir A. Skripkin who had been entrapped in Moscow following a tentative discussion with the British in Japan. Upon his return home Skripkin had betrayed himself to two plausible KGB men, who had masqueraded as SIS officers on a follow-up mission. Skripkin had promptly been taken out of circulation.

Since the 1970s there is growing evidence that the First Chief Directorate has experienced a veritable haemorrhage of its secrets (see chart on pages 122–3). The French DST ran a highly successful penetration, codenamed FAREWELL, from the end of 1980 until his arrest on a murder charge two years later. Meanwhile, the British had managed a parallel case, that of Vladimir A. Kuzichkin, who successfully extricated himself from a Soviet consulate in Iran late in October 1982, having spent at least eighteen months earning his meal-ticket for SIS. Similarly, Oleg A. Gordievsky, the KGB's acting *Rezident* in London, was exfiltrated from Moscow in August 1985 after an estimated twelve years' work as a spy for SIS. These three penetrations, combined with the defection of Ilya G. Dzirk-velov from Geneva in March 1980 and Igor Gezha from New Delhi in March 1985, must have shaken the organization to its very foun-dations. Certainly, no Western equivalent could have hoped to sustain such a series of operational catastrophes and survive intact.

Yet, in spite of these disasters, the KGB's standing within the Kremlin was actually enhanced during this period, with Yuri Andropov, who had been Chairman since 1967, taking over as General Secretary of the CPSU in 1982, and one of his successors, Vitaly Fedorchuk, attaining an unprecedented membership of the Politburo. However, by 1988, the situation had deteriorated, with Viktor Chebrikov being removed unceremoniously from office and his replacement, Colonel-General Vladimir Kryuchkov, losing the KGB's seat in the Politburo.

One reason for the KGB's perceptible decline in relative status within the Soviet power structure may well be the gradual (and belated) comprehension by the West's security authorities of its purpose, methodology and size. As we have seen, there were probably rather fewer defectors overall from the KGB than most people suppose, a total of just thirty-three over a period of forty years, of which only twenty could be considered to have supplied really worthwhile information. Of the group Yuri Krotkov and Yuri Nosenko proved to be of doubtful value, and Vitali S. Yurchenko redefected. Although in retrospect some defectors have proved invaluable and ensured the capture of a large number of agents who would otherwise have gone undetected, a major factor in the equation is the counter-measures taken by the West, having been alerted to the scale of the challenge.

Some of the precautions taken have been relatively simple initiatives. For example, the development of Movement Analysis has enabled individual Soviet intelligence personnel to be monitored wherever they appear in the world. The project was largely the creation of Terry Guernsey, the long-serving Director of the RCMP Security Service's 'E' (counter-espionage) Branch, who had been trained by SIS in London. The task itself is not always quite as easy as it sounds, given the input of seven million separate movements per annum, but the benefits are considerable. Unusual promotions, demotions, postings and work names become highlighted against a backdrop of mundane appointments around the world. In 1963, Robespier N. Filatov was posted to Rio de Janeiro as second secretary, previously having served as a lowly interpreter in Ottawa. Similarly, Pavel I. Lomakin was accredited in 1964 to the Soviet ambassy in Cyprus as an assistant military attaché with the rank of lieutenant-colonel. Yet four years earlier he had been a civilian chauffeur at the military attache's office in Rome. In 1961, Evgenny

A. Zaostrovtsev, the second secretary at the Soviet embassy in East Berlin, was implicated in an espionage case and was recognized as the diplomat who, two years earlier, had been the cultural attaché in Washington expelled for spying. By cross-referring with Allied security agencies, a massive amount of useful data was accumulated which assisted in that most basic of counter-intelligence tasks: the construction of an accurate KGB order-of-battle for each Soviet mission.

It was information from defectors that originally revealed the variety of covers available to Soviet intelligence staff posted abroad. According to a secret CIA analysis dated July 1968,

> the overseas deployment of Soviet intelligence officers, whether located within or outside official installations, comes reasonably close to saturating the available accredited cover positions. The majority of Soviet news media personnel abroad are intelligence officers. Overall, more than 60 per cent have been so identified and this is considered a minimal figure. Included in this category are correspondents for the newspapers *Pravda* and *Izvestia* and representatives of the TASS and Novosti news agencies. Aeroflot, the world-wide and still expanding civilian airline, provides both cover and support to Soviet Intelligence, particularly the GRU, and surveys in recent years have established that 70 per cent of its overseas representatives are staff officers of that service.[10]

The same document demonstrated that the Soviet mission to the UN, the internationally staffed UN secretariat itself and other UN offices were exploited as cover by the KGB.[11] At UNESCO's head-quarters in Paris the French DST estimated that a minimum of sixteen out of the Soviet complement of sixty were confirmed intelligence professionals. At the International Atomic Energy Authority headquarters in Vienna about half the fifty-five resident Soviets were regarded as spy suspects. In Geneva the picture was considered roughly the same, with heavy KGB representation in the UN European Office, the Economic Commission for Europe, the World Health Organization, the World Meteorological Organization, the International Labour Organization, the International Telecommunications Union and others. Cord Meyer, another senior CIA officer and a former Chief of Station in London, agrees with this assessment: 'Intelligence personnel occupy on average 30 per cent of the official positions in Soviet embassies worldwide; but in some strategic underdeveloped countries the figure can go as high as 70 per cent.'[12]

Movement Analysis also demonstrated that the KGB routinely took advantage of student exchange programmes to acclimatize KGB graduates before their first operational posting abroad. Nikolai G. Korotkikh studied at London University in 1965 and then appeared in Copenhagen the following year as a third secretary. Similarly, Valentin I. Ilyintsev attended Yale before going to New Delhi as cultural attaché, where he seemed to spend most of his time cultivating American contacts, taking a particular interest in clerks working in the US embassy's cipher room.

Of the many books written about the KGB since David Dallin's[13] seminal work, no less than seven have been written by former US intelligence officers. Harry Rositzke, Lyman Kirkpatrick, Raymond G. Rocca, John Barron, Robert T. Crowley and John J. Dziak have all studied the KGB from inside the US intelligence community and offer a broad spectrum of opinion. There is also a healthy internal debate about which of the retirees offer the most valid opinions. Rocca, a long-time associate of Jim Angleton in the CIA's counterintelligence division, criticizes Rositske, for example, for suggesting that the KGB 'is a straightforward secret service, even in its more devious and deceptive practices',[14] while George C. Constantinides, once the CIA Station Chief in Athens, refers to *KGB: The Secret Work of Soviet Secret Agents*, the first of Barron's two studies of the KGB, as 'very nearly a textbook'.[15] Even the defectors have a view on such matters, with Stanislav Levchenko calling Dziak's *Chekisty* 'the most comprehensive study of the KGB ever published in the West'.[16] No less than thirteen post-war defectors from the KGB have written their own stories, but in general they are of limited value.

In contrast to the impressive literature on the KGB, and the above list does not include the many worthwhile histories written by journalists and academics, the GRU remains something of an enigma. Just a handful of defectors have switched sides, and only Vladimir B. Rezun has given an authoritative account from the inside.[17] Igor Gouzenko was to write several books during his lifetime, albeit with substantial editorial help, but because he had never been more than a coding clerk he was unable to give an authentic, first-hand description of the GRU's activities in the field.

In fact, it was not until October 1971, with the defection of Anatoli K. Chebotarev from the Soviet trade delegation in Brussels, that the West was to gain access to a GRU defector again. Unfortunately, Major Chebotarev later changed his mind and returned to Moscow the following Christmas, having first disclosed details of how he and his GRU colleagues had habitually tapped indiscreet radio-telephone conversations at NATO's headquarters. A little later two other of his GRU contemporaries, Nikolai G. Petrov and Evgeny G. Sorokin, underwent similar experiences. Captain Petrov was offered asylum by the CIA after his involvement in a motor accident in Jakarta in June 1972, but redefected in November the following year. Lieutenant Sorokin was another drunk driver who defected in Vientiane, only to have difficulty with his resettlement in the US and opt to go home in October 1973. More recently, in 1985, Sergei Bokhan, under first secretary cover at the Soviet embassy in Athens, has been granted asylum in the US, having traded resettlement in return for a bout of intensive debriefings about his activities as the GRU's deputy *Rezident* in Greece.

It is largely due to him and Rezun that anything at all is known about the modern GRU. The West's two prized walk-in sources, Major Pyotr S. Popov and Lieutenant-Colonel Oleg V. Penkovsky, were both arrested and executed in 1959 and 1963 respectively. Rezun cautiously worked his meal-ticket for the British over nearly a year and was eventually extricated in June 1978 from Geneva, where he was working under UN cover. Rezun's subsequent debriefing revealed a wealth of detail concerning his organization, including the facts that it operates quite separately from the KGB, drawing on selected military personnel, and that its headquarters, known as 'the aquarium', are accommodated inside a large secure compound at the edge of the Khodinka military airfield near Moscow. Rezun, writing under the pseudonym Viktor Suvorov, provided a chart showing that the organization's internal structure is markedly different to that of the Neighbours. However, its overseas representation is not dissimilar, with a GRU *Rezident* attached to each Soviet embassy and known as a 'navigator'.

5

Navigators from the Aquarium

'Naturally people remember the KGB.
But never the GRU.'[1]

Vladimir Rezun

Although the GRU is considerably more adept than its 'neighbours'
at keeping its secrets and deterring defectors, rather more was known
about its activities at the end of the war than about those of the
NKVD. Although somewhat dated, a vast quantity of authentic
information about the Red Army's intelligence work had fallen into
Allied hands when Brussels was liberated in 1944. Both the Abwehr
and the Gestapo had undertaken lengthy investigations into the
Soviet network they called the 'Rote Kapelle', an enormous spy
system boasting branches in practically every country in Europe,
and even a few connections in Canada and the USA. The Nazis had
been very successful in penetrating the ring and even managed to
'turn' several of its members into double agents.

The German counter-intelligence experts responsible for breaking
up the Rote Kapelle were themselves interrogated at the end of
the war, and their records, all captured intact, were to become an
extremely useful database for identifying other Soviet spy suspects.
One series of compromised signals, for example, which dated back
to March 1941, betrayed the identity and location of a senior agent
in London codenamed JEAN. This turned out to be a piano player
from Breslau named Ernest D. Weiss, who was calling himself
Walter Lock and living in the Paddington district of London. Weiss
was questioned by the British Security Service and revealed a further

six GRU agents who had been active before and during the war.[2] None was prosecuted, but one was already well known to MI5 for entirely different reasons. Major Wilfred Vernon had been a Communist Party activist who, since 1924, had happened to work for the Air Ministry. Since 1929, he had been in the technical publication section of the Royal Aircraft Establishment at Farnborough. He had visited the Soviet Union in May 1932 with a group of colleagues and had been approached by Weiss upon his return. Vernon and another RAE worker, Frederick Meredith, had supplied Weiss with information until August 1937, when Vernon's bungalow in Farnham had been broken into while he had been away on holiday. Police investigating the burglary had found a quantity of classified papers in two of Vernon's suitcases and he had been charged with the unlawful retention of official documents upon his return. When the case was heard by magistrates in October, Vernon had been fined £30 and dismissed from his post.

At the time of the prosecution, which had been regarded as a relatively minor disciplinary matter, there had been no suggestion of spying; but when the matter was investigated much later, Meredith confirmed Vernon's true role. He also alleged that Vernon had given a full account of his dealings with Weiss to his barrister, Denis Pritt, then the Socialist Member of Parliament for Hammersmith. Pritt had a long track record of being pro-Soviet, but this was the first evidence of his involvement with espionage.

Pritt had concealed the part played by Weiss in the Vernon affair and thus had enabled him to continue his activities in England unhindered for several more years. When he was eventually interrogated after the war, Weiss had given an account of his recruitment by his Soviet controller, a mysterious spy of German origin from Frankfurt who had often used the name Henri Robinson. He had been arrested by the Paris Gestapo in December 1942, in possession of many hundreds of compromising documents, including dozens of secret messages from his sub-agents which, for the sake of his network's security, really ought to have been destroyed. These became known as the Robinson Papers and were still in active use by the British Security Service's counter-espionage branch in 1966,[3] twenty-two years after the owner's execution by the Gestapo. What made them unique was Robinson's exalted status within the Soviet intelligence system. He had operated as an agent for nearly two decades, directing clandestine operations in France, Switzerland and

Britain at different times. According to the CIA, 'Robinson was a member of the Comintern apparatus'[4] as well as being a key figure in the GRU's Rote Kapelle, thus making him a doubly important catch for the Nazis. In 1968, the French DST confirmed that it possessed information indicating 'that Robinson had once been Kim Philby's case officer'.[5] Thus Robinson may have played a vital role for both the KGB and the GRU.

Weiss was not the only member of the Rote Kapelle to co-operate with Western security authorities. Another important member of the network, Alexander Foote, defected to the British in Berlin in March 1947 and described his own part, as a wireless opertor, for the Swiss branch of the same organization. A British subject, Foote had spent much of the war in Geneva, but had been arrested by the *Bundespolizei* in November 1943. After his release in September the following year, he had been recalled to Moscow for training in preparation for a new assignment: an espionage mission to the United States. It was while he was en route to his new post that he had switched sides and volunteered a detailed (and somewhat exaggerated) confession to MI5. He was to be used as a human encyclopaedia of Soviet undercover activities in Europe until his death in 1958.

Together Foote, Weiss, the Robinson Papers and the German files recovered from Belgium gave a fairly complete picture of the Red Army's intelligence apparatus in Europe during the 1930s and 1940s. Names of those that appeared prominently in the Robinson Papers, and had escaped capture by the Nazis, were to crop up later in many of the more notorious post-war spy cases: Jurgen Kuczynski was revealed to have acted as Klaus Fuchs's cut-out in England and moved to East Berlin; his sister Ursula had operated as Fuchs's courier and also fled to East Germany; Hermina Rabinowitch was mentioned in Gouzenko's purloined documents as having delivered money from the Soviet consulate in New York to a contact in Geneva; Mrs Lubszynski, a Swiss resident and mother of Hans Lubszynski, a radio engineer and German Communist who was listed as one of Weiss's main sub-agents in England, gave Melinda Maclean instructions for her defection to Moscow in September 1953; Rudolf Roessler and Xavier Schnieper were both charged with espionage in March 1953 in Switzerland, having previously escaped imprisonment when their first network was rounded up in 1943; Hans Voelkner, convicted of espionage in Paris in February 1970 and sentenced to twelve years' imprisonment for running a spy named Marthe Danilo inside the Quai d'Orsay's cipher office, turned out to be Kathe Voelkner's son – she had been a veteran GRU agent, who had been arrested by the Paris Gestapo in January 1943 and executed; in 1949 Eugene Gruber was arrested in Frankfurt for possession of forged American passports; his mother, Malvina Gruber, had been sentenced in February the same year to ten years' imprisonment by a military court in Brussels for espionage; and Sergei M. Kudriavtsev, appointed Soviet ambassador to Cambodia in 1969, was actually Alexander Erdberg, another veteran GRU case officer who played a key role in the Rote Kapelle in Europe and featured in several of Gouzenko's documents when he was running agents under first secretary cover at the Ottawa legation (he later turned up in Vienna, Paris and Cuba, all under diplomatic cover).

Although the material captured by the Allies in 1944 (and apparently 'lost' by the British until 1947) chiefly concerned networks that had been destroyed by the Germans, there was a core of individuals who had been able to avoid arrest. Some were in Britain, while others had operated in neutral Switzerland and had only been inconvenienced by the *Bundespolizei*. As the above list demonstrates, a number of those who did survive the Rote Kapelle continued their undercover work for 'the Centre'.

In sharp contrast to the high number of defectors from the KGB received in the West, the GRU suffered only a tiny handful of such losses. Indeed, of the total eleven listed, three can be discounted straightaway as being of only minor significance even if, at the time, their information was considered useful. Ismail Akhmedov had gone to ground during the war and surfaced much later, so he had little to offer in terms of current intelligence. Grigori A. Tokaev, who escaped from Berlin in 1948, proved to be important, but in an entirely different field. After his bebriefing in England, he changed his name to Tokaty and was later appointed Emeritus Professor of Aeronautics at the City University in London. Igor Gouzenko also made a profound contribution to the West's understanding of the post-war Soviet espionage offensive, but not with direct knowledge. He will be remembered for the 109 documents he removed from the Ottawa embassy's closely guarded *referentura* shortly before his defection. This authentic collection of original papers effectively 'blew' a complete GRU network of international proportions and led to the prosecution of twenty spy suspects. The conviction of thirteen defendants (two of whom were subsequently acquitted on appeal) was due to this material, which served to alert the world to the scale of Soviet undercover work. It also prompted a Royal Commission and, judging by the VENONA decrypts for the relevant period, a state of panic in Soviet *Rezidenturas* around the world. Individual agents were warned to suspend operations and new security procedures were introduced to protect those sources that survived Gouzenko's revelations. In fact, the ramifications of the defection were much greater than even the RCMP's Special Branch suspected at the time. For example, Klaus Fuchs's name was discovered in Israel Halperin's address book, but the clue was not followed up, thus allowing Fuchs to continue undisturbed until his arrest more than four years later, in January 1950. Codenamed BACON, Halperin had been born in Canada of Russian parents and was an assistant professor of mathematics at Queen's University, Kingston, Ontario, then engaged on classified artillery research for the Canadian army. He was also a member of the Communist Party and his address book was found to contain 436 names, including Fuchs (listed at his temporary wartime home in Edinburgh) and his sister, Kristel, who had married an American. Halperin denied ever having met Fuchs, who confirmed Halperin's recollection, and said that he had simply mailed a few magazines to Fuchs at Kristel's request when her brother had been interned in Canada in 1940. There was no evidence of a closer relationship than that, and when Halperin was tried in March 1947 he was one of the seven individuals mentioned in Gouzenko's papers to be acquitted. One of those found guilty of espionage was Allan Nunn May, who received ten years' imprisonment, the longest sentence of all.

Of the remaining eight GRU defectors, three returned to Moscow quite quickly, leaving only Rezun and Bokhan known to describe the GRU from the inside. Hence its enduring reputation as the most secret Soviet intelligence service. Although much is known about the KGB's successive chairmen, practically nothing has been published about General Grigori F. Krivoscheiev, who took over from the long-serving General Piotr I. Ivaschutin at the end of 1986. Even Ivaschutin, who remained in his post for twenty-three years and outranked Yuri Andropov when the latter headed the KGB, is almost completely unknown outside his own circle. His reputation is that of a man with an unenviable past. He is supposed to have commanded

GRU Organization

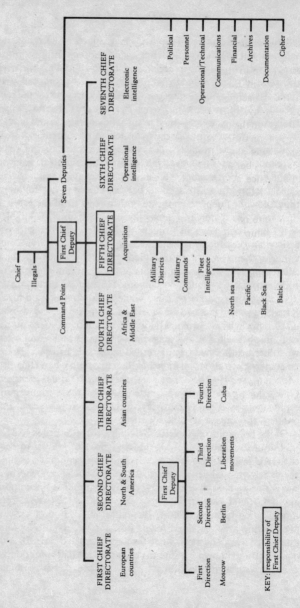

the notorious *Smersh* units during the bloody Ukrainian campaign in 1943 and then operated in Romania, Hungary and Bulgaria, ending up in Austria where he was based at the Red Army's headquarters in Baden and Vienna. Krivoscheiev is believed to have played an active part in the invasion of Afghanistan, but the details are sketchy. There is, therefore, a greater mystique surrounding the GRU than the Neighbours, but none the less it is perfectly possible to draw upon the criteria already established to make a few comparative judgments about the relative performance of Soviet intelligence. However, before doing so we should take a brief look at the satellite intelligence agencies which, to a greater or lesser extent, can be termed KGB surrogates.

There are no less than eight satellite services which enjoy a close relationship with the KGB: the Bulgarian *Drzaven Sigurnost* (DS); the Cuban *Direccion General de Inteligencia* (DGI); the Czech *Statni Tajna Bezpecnost* (STB); the East German *Hauptverwaltung für Aufklärung* (HVA); the Hungarian *Allami Vedelmi Batosag* (AVB); the Polish *Sluzba Bezpieczenstwa* (SB); the Romanian *Departmentul de Informatii Externe* (DIE); and the Vietnamese *Bo Cong An* (BCA). Western knowledge about these organizations varies considerably, as does the amount of direct liaison each conducts with the KGB, so it is worth examining each in turn. In much the same way that defectors played a critical role in opening up the KGB and the GRU to the outside world, each of these organizations has experienced revelations from their own disenchanted.

For the past thirty years Bulgaria has been ruled by Todor Zhivkov, and his feared security apparatus, the DS, has until quite recently limited its activities to the intimidation and murder of troublesome exiles. The DS has been responsible for several political assassinations, including that of the prominent Bulgarian émigré Georgi Markov in September 1978. Another attempt on a former DS officer using an identical method, a clandestine injection of ricin, had been made on Vladimir Kostov in Paris ten days earlier, but proved unsuccessful. Kostov, who worked for Radio Free Europe, suffered a cardio-vascular collapse but narrowly escaped death.[6] The DS is also thought to have had a hand in the murder of a Bulgarian rocket technician in Vienna and the editor of an émigré newspaper. The DS probably played a murky role in the arming of Mehmet Ali Agca, the Turkish terrorist who shot Pope John Paul II in May

1981. Agca implicated the DS and its local representative, Sergei Antonov, the Bulgarian state airline manager in Rome, but his evidence was judged inconclusive. Nevertheless, the suspicion remains that the DS is dominated by the KGB and is apparently willing to undertake risky but deniable missions on its behalf. This, at least, if the view of Colonel Stefan Svredlev, a high-ranking Bulgarian police officer who defected in 1971. The most recent defection of note was that of Iordan Mantarov from the Bulgarian embassy in Paris in 1981.

In contrast, the Cuban DGI maintains a high profile and is well represented around the world. Although it was originally created, in 1961, as a part of the Ministry of the Interior, principally to monitor and infiltrate counter-revolutionary movements, it has since expanded and turned its interest further afield, especially to Europe and Africa. Much is known about its structure and organization, which was initially developed under the guidance of a KGB adviser, General Viktor Simenov, because of several key defectors. Among them are Orlando Castro Hidalgo, who defected from the Cuban embassy in Paris in March 1970 (and later wrote *A Spy for Fidel* in 1971, in which he gave a detailed breakdown of the DGI and boasted of having compromised more than 150 DGI agents), and Major Florentino Azpillaga Lombard, who escaped from Prague in June 1987. Another useful source has been General Raphael del Pino, one of Castro's most trusted aides, who has supplied the CIA with a detailed, up-to-date analysis of the DGI's order-of-battle and objectives, when he suddenly materialized in Florida in May 1987.

The DGI's current Director is Luis Barreiro, who succeeded José Mendez Cominches. His predecessor, Manuel Pineiro Losada, fell victim to a purge conducted by Cástro's brother Raúl, who was largely responsible for transforming the DGI from a minor, Third World security apparatus to a highly motived cadre of 2,000 trained operatives posted across the world to Cuban diplomatic missions.

According to the most recent information, the DGI consists of two branches: 'ML', dealing with political intelligence and headed by Colonel Ramón Oroza, and 'MZ', handling the management of illegals and headed by Lieutenant-Colonel Enrique Cicard. Operations are directed from the DGI's headquarters in Havana, known as the *Centro Principal*, and three training schools are maintained in Prague, East Germany and the Soviet Union.

Like the DGI, the Czech STB has also suffered grievously from defectors. One of the first was an STB cipher clerk, František Tisler, who was based at the Czech embassy in Washington and was run for two years by the FBI before he finally left (with the contents of a complete filing cabinet containing classified material) in 1958. Rather better known are Ladislav Bittman, who deserted his post in the Czech embassy in Vienna in 1968, and Jozef Frolik and František August, who defected the following year. Together they have described a potent organization, based in a former monastery on the Vltava River, orchestrated entirely by the KGB, and compromised several of the STB's most useful sources in Britain and West Germany. Among those arrested as a consequence of the 'invasion defections', which were prompted by the Russian takeover in Prague in 1968, were a British MP, Will Owen, an RAF technician, Nicholas Prager, and Dr Harald Gottfried, a nuclear physicist at the Karlsruhe atomic research centre. As news of the STB defections spread in the Federal Republic, a string of suicides was reported. Admiral Hermann Luedke, SHAPE's logistics chief, shot himself, as did Horst Wendland, deputy chief of the BND. Hans Schenke of the Ministry of Economics and Colonel Johann Grimm of the Defence Ministry hanged themselves, and Gerhard Boehm, another Defence Ministry official, was found drowned. Recent STB successes include penetration of the CIA through a contract employee, Karl Koecher, and the resettlement in 1987 of Edward L. Howard, the CIA defector. Perhaps the most significant Czech defector in recent years has been General Jan Sejna, the Deputy Foreign Minister who, although unable to identify individual STB sources, has provided the West with a unique overview of his country's war contingency plans. Sejna was followed in May 1985 by Colonel Milan Svec, from the Czech embassy in Washington.

The East German HVA is the foreign intelligence arm of the Ministry of State Security and has been headed since its inception in 1956 by Markus Wolf, the legendary agent-runner who has masterminded literally thousands of penetrations into the Federal Republic. Based at 22 Normannenstrasse, Berlin-Lichtenberg, the HVA has pulled off many coups, including the penetration of the BfV, the BND, through Hans Clemens and Heinz Felfe, and Chancellor Willi Brandt's private office in the person of Gunter Guillaume. There have been numerous defectors from the HVA, including Werner Stiller in 1979, Lieutenant-Colonel Siegfried Dombrowski and Martin Winkler, who switched sides in Argentina in 1985.

The Hungarian AVB is understood to have resisted KGB blandishments to engage in hostile intelligence-gathering abroad, and is apparently limited to keeping dissidents under surveillance in conjunction with a special branch of the regular police. Laszlo Szabó, the most senior AVB officer known to have defected, operated under second secretary cover in London until 1965.

The Polish SB has been an open book to the West following the defection in December 1960 of Michal Goleniewski, a career SB officer and a part-time KGB informer. But apart from him, the SB has experienced several important losses, including Zdzislaw M. Rurarz, the Polish ambassador in Japan who defected in December 1981 as a consequence of the imposition of martial law, to reveal a twenty-five year 'association' with the SB; Colonel Pawel Monat, who sought asylum in Vienna in June 1959; and the anonymous lieutenant-colonel who defected in Copenhagen in February 1967 and subsequently wrote his autobiography, *Double Eagle*.[7]

The Romanian DIE is unique in that it is the only one of the Soviet Bloc intelligence agencies to have had its own chief defect. Lieutenant-General Ion Pacepa did exactly that on 26 July 1978, when he walked into the US embassy in Bonn seeking political asylum. Twenty-four hours later he was flown to Andrews Air Force Base near Washington DC to begin three years of detailed debriefings, which effectively invalidated much of the DIE's activities around the world. Its operations had already been severely handicapped by a series of embarrassing defections: Ion Iacobescu in Paris in 1969; the DIE station chief in Tel Aviv, Constantin Dumitrachescu, to Mossad in 1972; Colonel Ion Marcu, A DIE officer under commercial cover in Tehran who moved his whole family to Canada; and engineer Constantin Rauta, a lower-level DIE defector who was received by the CIA in 1973. Two years later, in June 1975, there was another loss, that of Virgil Tipanudt, a DIE officer masquerading as a third secretary in the Romanian embassy in Copenhagen. Together these intelligence disasters transformed the DIE from a worthwhile asset of the KGB into a positive liability.

The Vietnamese BCA is also a KGB surrogate, but little of its activities are known in the West and it is believed to confine itself to counter-revolutionary surveillance.

All of these agencies are regarded by Western security services as mere adjuncts of the KGB's First Chief Directorate, convenient vehicles to undertake particular missions that they might specialize in. For example, the Czech STB has demonstrated considerable success in recruiting in Britain, and the Cubans have built up an impressive infrastructure in Africa. Similarly, the Bulgarian DS has provided useful training facilities to terrorist groups from which the Kremlin would be keen to distance itself publicly. In emergencies, such as the unexpected expulsion of a large group of Soviets, the Czech STB has supplied stand-by accommodation and personnel to service agents who would otherwise be abandoned. In short, these satellite organizations should be considered as occasionally useful Soviet assets.

In the opinion of insiders, both the GRU and the KGB score high marks for professionalism, which is not entirely surprising given the level of resources devoted to intelligence-gathering and the manpower and covers available. The joint KGB–GRU expenditure can only be guessed at, and comparisons with the CIA and the FBI would not be equating like with like, but it is certainly fair to say that their budgets must dwarf the combined efforts of the West's five principal agencies studied here. Both Soviet services are ruthless, dedicated, determined and broadly successful, if overly bureaucratic and subject to petty corruption. On the basis of defector evidence the *nomenklatura* wields greater influence over the KGB than the GRU, which is wholly staffed by military personnel. Although very few of the defectors reviewed here enjoyed an overview of their organizations, their opinions do tend to conform. Other professionals have also testified to the professionalism of the Soviets and their rigorous control of their surrogates. Ladislav Bittman, for example, has confirmed that 'all Socialist intelligence services are, of course, under the supervision and command of Soviet intelligence operat-. ives. There is not a single operation that would be unnoticed by the Soviets. They control the whole process of initiating, conducting intelligence operations, and getting the results.'[8] Laszlo Szabó has verified this in testimony to a House Committee:

> The Soviets call conferences with the Bloc services in the USSR
> for discussion of intelligence objectives and problems. The work
> between Soviet and Bloc intelligence and security services is a
> direct result of the co-operation between the national Communist
> parties and the Communist Party of the Soviet Union.... Each
> Bloc service has agreed with the Soviet service to achieve certain

broad objectives in its own interest and in the interests of other Bloc services.[9]

As well as exercising control over the satellite agencies, the KGB has acquired, probably unjustifiably, a reputation for ruthless professionalism. Melvin Beck recalls 'the attitude of seasoned counter-intelligence case officers to regard the Russian Intelligence Services not only as a tough elite organization but one composed of officers "nine feet tall".' However, a study of defections from both the KGB and the GRU exposes the myth of KGB supermen for exactly what it is. Almost by convention intelligence literature has dwelt upon the Soviet predilection for eliminating traitors wherever they hide. Numerous examples are cited, and the testimony of two defecting assassins, Khokhlov and Stashinsky, is usually mentioned to emphasize the KGB's endorsement of institutionalized homicide. However, it is also fair to observe that the KGB is equally content to take the credit for deaths over which it probably had no control. Valentin Markin's death started the syndrome, and rumours abounded when Walter Krivitsky was found shot dead in the locked room of his Washington Hotel; these may have had an influence when commentators came to consider the death of Reino Hayhanen in a car accident in 1961, and the suicide of Viktor Kravchenko in his New York apartment in August 1966.[10] In all of these incidents the KGB had a direct interest in propagating belief in its omniscience, but sheer opportunism may be a more rational explanation.

The Achilles' heel of the Soviet apparatus, which is particularly relevant to the KGB's First Chief Directorate, is the haemorrhage of vital data through the activities of defectors. It is worth repeating again that no Western agency could hope to bear the momentous losses sustained by the KGB in recent years. In 1985 alone the KGB lost four key players, and although it may be argued that Yurchenko did eventually find his way back to Moscow, there can be no disguising the impact he had. Since that time there have been other defectors, with as many as four, as yet unannounced, received by the CIA.

In counter-intelligence terms the KGB has an entirely different perspective to the West. It has few ideologically motivated defectors to resettle and take care of, and those that have made the change have hardly fared well. Guy Burgess hated the petty restrictions of life in the East, which inhibited his promiscuous homosexuality;

Maclean was given a menial clerical post that he felt underestimated his intellectual status; Kim Philby revealed shortly before his death that, despite reports of his rank as a KGB major-general, he had only been allowed to visit the KGB's headquarters at Dzrzhinsky Square twice in twenty-five years;[11] Bernon Mitchell, one of three defectors from the NSA, has tried to negotiate a return home several times; and George Blake must have found Soviet anti-Semitism disagreeable. In short, the Soviets do not trust defectors to their cause, although they recognize the need to avoid the propaganda consequences of redefection. Most low-level defections take place unnoticed, so that the number is rather larger than most people believe. Major Richard Squires vanished in Germany in 1947,[12] and was followed by Corporal Brian Patchett, a signals intercept operator with the Intelligence Corps who went missing from RAF Gatow in Berlin in July 1956. The US has suffered similar, unsung losses, like Captain C.J. Gessner, who defected in 1962, and Victor Hamilton, another NSA defector who turned up in the Soviet Union in July 1963. There was also the mysterious case of John Smith, a cipher clerk from the US embassy in New Delhi, who was interviewed by *Izvestia* on 11 November 1967 and described as a CIA defector.[13]

The KGB can easily get away unchallenged with ploys like this: another advantage is its inheritance of an impressive system of state-controlled documentation. It is not burdened by legalistic concerns about weight of evidence and there are no juries to persuade or open courts to contend with. Nor is there any anxiety about failing to achieve a conviction because of the retention of sensitive material for fear of it leaking. Press reports of operational matters are scarce, and whatever material released is usually done so for a specific purpose. Statistics relating to espionage are virtually impossible to obtain, and, for more than a decade after the execution of Oleg Penkovsky in 1963, there was no mention of any Soviet traitor. Even when V.G. Kalinin's death sentence was announced in February 1975, there was no explanation of exactly which foreign intelligence service had been responsible for his recruitment, and nothing was said of his background. The disclosure in March 1980 that an engineer named A.B. Nilov had been executed, after he had confessed to having spied for the CIA since his recruitment in 1974, was a remarkable departure from the norm. Firstly, that the statement, which was released seven months after Nilov's trial and attributed to General Semyon K. Tsvigun, one of the KGB's six Deputy

Chairmen, had been made at all; and, secondly, that the CIA had been identified as the hostile foreign concerned.

Suspects like Kalinin and Nilov can be placed under Second Chief Directorate surveillance with the minimum of effort, and its blanket coverage of the few cities where Westerners can visit enable the KGB to make it virtually impossible for foreign intelligence organizations to operate. Indeed, for a considerable period, until 1972, the local environment was regarded as so repressive that all the CIA's Moscow station operations were conducted from Langley with individual case officers flying in to perform specific missions. Even the most elementary of tasks, such as finding a Moscow telephone number, can be a major undertaking. Until recently there were no telephone directories and obtaining a number required a visit to a directory booth, which meant registering the request with the authorities. Similarly, no accurate street maps of Moscow were published, so the CIA was obliged to do its own cartographic experiments.

If life was not difficult enough for Western intelligence officers attempting to mount operations in denied areas, the geography seems to conspire against them as well. The Soviet Union's coastline is short and inhospitable. The international frontiers are well patrolled by an elite force and there are only a limited number of border crossing-points, which are strictly monitored. In addition, most of those are to other Eastern Bloc countries, where conditions are equally as strict. Nor is the single road crossing to the West, at Vybourg-Vaalimaa, viewed as a viable proposition for smuggling because many Western intelligence agencies look upon Finland as a Soviet client state. Security at airports is tight, and even the usual ruses of switching passports or substituting documentation is difficult to pull off because of the Soviet preoccupation with height. All departing passengers have their passports inspected while standing against a backdrop marked with graded heights, so that details in travel documents can be checked visually. Accordingly, the opportunities for clandestine infiltrations or illicit exits are few and far between. Faced with these daunting challenges, it is not surprising that so few assets have been recruited and run inside the Soviet Union.

Whatever the scale of the KGB's operational advantage in the Soviet Union and Eastern Europe, it is clear that the First Chief Directorate has always been willing to take risks in the hope of cultivating useful sources. Even though it has experienced numerous provocations with double agents supervised by the West, particularly by the FBI in the United States, it appears to have accepted the downside because of the potential returns from the authentic walk-ins, of whom there have been a consistently large number, especially from the non-commissioned officer level of the military where relatively lowly staff enjoy considerable access to secret material. The KGB certainly recognized the dangers to its own personnel of exposure by responding positively to all offers from volunteers, and its pool of uncompromised staff used to be sufficiently large to refill every post suffering a PNG. However, the recently introduced policy of permanently terminating each diplomatic position in Britain and the US that has been the subject of a formal PNG has imposed a severe strain on the Ministry of Foreign Affairs, which had previously been perfectly tolerant of the KGB's manipulation of its overseas representation. As each post has been eliminated, the burden borne by the host ministry granting legal cover has escalated. The consequence, as predicted by the CAZAB countries, is the imposition of a greater discipline on members of the legal *Rezidenturas* and a reduction in co-operation between the intelligence organs and their hosts.

In 1961, Aleksandr N. Shelepin, then Chairman of the KGB, circulated a directive to all *Rezidenturas* demanding a concentration of efforts 'to recruit cipher clerks' where 'the most fruitful results' could be obtained.[14] Events such as the long-running Walker family spy case show that Shelepin's instructions were obeyed and successes of great magnitude followed. KGB doctrine, as revealed by instruction manuals delivered by defectors, accepts that most walk-in volunteers will be motivated by greed:

> The successful use of financial motivation in recruitment requires an understanding of the psychological makeup of the average American. He seriously thinks of money as the only thing which can ensure his personal freedom and independence and fulfil his material and spiritual needs. The typical American attitude toward money creates indifference to the means by which it is obtained, even if there is some risk involved.[15]

This somewhat cynical attitude has been fostered by the KGB's long experience of receiving unsolicited advances of classified material. The US security authorities have also analysed this phenomenon and scrutinized every post-war case of Soviet espionage. The 1966 report *Motivations to Treason* concluded that it had 'found no evidence in any espionage case studied of an Army serviceman having been recruited on the basis of foreign birth, ideological preference for communism or threats based on the presence of relatives in communist controlled areas'. However, it did find that

> military personnel who are maladjusted and have 'gone sour' are the ones most susceptible to Soviet and other hostile recruitment. Present in some degree as common denominators in virtually all cases of both espionage and defection have been factors of sex, liquor, marital problems, personal immaturity and debt. The greatest single inducement to espionage has been greed for money.[16]

The only really effective method of countering the Soviet passive attitude of waiting to be approached by walk-ins, apart from increased surveillance and publicity to deter those contemplating treachery, is the deployment of large numbers of agents provocateur. This is precisely what has occurred in the United States. The other development of significance, directly linked to the pressure on the legal *Rezidenturas* from defections and heightened counter-intelligence activity, is a perceptible switch to the use of trusted old hands, particularly scholars, brought back from retirement to participate in political operations, often under academic covers. It is the belief of some CAZAB experts that the game of intelligence as played by the Soviet Union has undergone a sea-change of tremendous importance. The First Chief Directorate, crippled by a series of damaging blows, has lost both status and influence. New, political tasks have been assigned to a super-elite operating outside the Line K structure, and the initial manifestation of this extraordinary change in accepted practice is the widespread introduction of a technique known as 'selective pairing'. This involves skilled agents being allocated particular individuals as targets on a one-to-one basis. Whereas emphasis had previously been placed on active recruitment, in the hope of developing a formal agent–controller relationship, the objective of pairing is limited to exercising political influence to achieve specific goals. This approach, more subtle than previous efforts to acquire agents of influence, can be undertaken with minimal risk of exposure. Only time will tell whether it will have the impact required by Mikhail Gorbachov. Perhaps the final irony is that the most devastating blows dealt to the modern KGB have originated from the one organization in the West that for years it had little fear of – 'the Friends'.

Soviet Defectors to the West

Name		Service	Date of Defection	Place Defection	Cover/Status	Country of Resettlement	Autobiographies (References)*
AKHMEDOV	Ismail G	GRU	May 1942	Turkey	Press Attaché	USA	In and Out of Stalin's GRU
GOUZENKO	Igor S.	GRU	5 Sept. 1945	Ottawa	Cipher Clerk	Canada	This Was My Choice
GRANOVSKY	Anatoli M.	KGB	21 Sept. 1946	Stockholm	Diplomat	USA	I Was an NKVD Agent
BAKHLANOV	Boris I.	KGB	July 1947	Vienna	Captain	UK	Nights Are Longest There
TOKAEV	Grigori A.	GRU	1948	Berlin	Scientist	UK	Comrade X
RASTVOROV	Yuri A.	KGB	23 Jan. 1954	Tokyo	Diplomat	USA	(Life, 29 Nov. 1954)[1]
BURTULSKY	Grigori S.	KGB	June 1953	Berlin	Lt-Colonel	USA	(Hingley, p. 194)[1]
DERIABIN	Piotr S.	KGB	15 Feb. 1954	Vienna	Major	USA	The Secret World
KHOKHLOV	Nikolai E.	KGB	18 Feb. 1954	Frankfurt	Captain	UK	In the Name of Conscience
PETROV	Vladimir	KGB	3 April 1954	Canberra	Diplomat	Australia	Empire of Fear
PETROVA	Evdokia	KGB	18 April 1954	Darwin	Cipher Clerk	Australia	Empire of Fear
HAYHANEN	Reino	KGB	6 May 1957	Paris	Illegal	USA	(Bernikow)[2]
'TUOMI'	Kaarlo R.	KGB	March 1959	Milwaukee	Illegal	USA	(Barron)[3]
KAZNACHEEV	Aleksandr R.	KGB	23 June 1959	Rangoon	Diplomat	USA	Inside a Soviet Embassy
GOLENIEWSKI	Michal	KGB	Dec. 1960	Berlin	Major	USA	(Imperial Agent)[4]
STASHINSKY	Bogdan	KGB	8 Dec. 1961	Berlin	Captain	USA	(Anders)[5]
GOLITSYN	Anatoli M.	KGB	22 Dec. 1961	Helsinki	Diplomat	USA	New Lies for Old
KROTKOV	Yuri V.	KGB	13 Sept. 1963	London	Journalist	USA	The Angry Exile
NOSENKO	Yuri I.	KGB	4 Feb. 1964	Geneva	Diplomat	USA	(Epstein)[6]
FARMAKOVSKY	Olga	KGB	16 Oct 1966	Beirut	Translator	Canada	(For Services Rendered, p. 215)[7]
RUNGE	Evgeny E.	KGB	Oct. 1967	Berlin	Lt-Colonel	USA	(Rositzke)[8]
SIGL	Rupert	KGB	12 April 1969	Berlin	Illegal	USA	In the Claws of the KGB
KISELNIKOVA	Raya	KGB	4 Feb. 1970	Mexico City	Secretary	USA	(Barron)[9]
SAKHAROV	Vladimir N.	KGB	11 July 1971	Kuwait	Diplomat	USA	High Treason
LYALIN	Oleg A.	KGB	31 Aug. 1971	London	Diplomat	UK	(Wright)[10]

Name		Service	Date of Deflection	Place Deflection	Cover/ Status	Country of Resettlement	Autobiographies (References)*
CHEBOTAREV	Anatoli K.	GRU	2 Oct. 1971	Brussels	Engineer	Canada	[Redefected 26 Dec. 1971]
	'Anton'	GRU	Dec. 1971	Canada	Illegal		(News of the World, 26 March 1972)
PETROV	Nikolai G.	GRU	12 June 1972	Jakarta	Diplomat		[Redefected 12 Nov. 1973]
HOVANESIAN	Artush S.	KGB	July 1972	Turkey	Lieutenant		[Redefected Sept. 1973]
SOROKIN	Evgenny G.	GRU	10 Sept. 1972	Vientiane	Diplomat	USA	[Redefected 26 Oct. 1973]
MYAGKOV	Aleksei	KGB	2 Feb. 1974	Berlin	Captain	USA	Inside the KGB
NADIRASHVILI	Konstantin G.	KGB	June 1975	Vienna			(Krasnov)[11]
ZEMENEK	Ludek	KGB	4 May 1977	New York	Illegal	USA	(Barron)[12]
REZUN	Vladimir B.	GRU	10 June 1978	Geneva	UN Official	UK	The Aquarium
LEVCHENKO	Stanislav A.	KGB	25 Oct. 1979	Tokyo	Diplomat	USA	On the Wrong Side
DZIRKVELOV	Ilya G.	KGB	3 March 1980	Geneva	Journalist	UK	Secret Servant
KUZICHKIN	Vladimir A.	KGB	25 Oct. 1982	Tehran	Diplomat		(Dobson)[13]
BOGATY	Anatoli	KGB	22 Sept. 1982	Morocco	Diplomat	USA	(Washington Post, 3 Oct. 1987)
	'Boris'	KGB	1983				(Dobson)[14]
FEN	Chang	KGB	12 Dec. 1983	New York	Illegal	USA	(Readers Digest, June 1988)
GEZHA	Igor A.	KGB	17 March 1985	Delhi	Journalist	USA	(West)[15]
BOKHAN	Sergei	GRU	May 1985	Athens	Diplomat		(West)[16]
YURCHENKO	Vitali S.	KGB	1 Aug. 1985	Rome	Diplomat		[Redefected 2 Nov. 1985]
GORDIEVSKY	Oleg A.	KGB	3 Aug. 1985	London	Diplomat	UK	(West)[17]
GUDAREV	Viktor P.	KGB	14 Feb. 1986	Athens	Colonel	USA	(Washington Times, 10 July 1986)
AGRANYANTS	Oleg	KGB	June 1986	Tunis	Diplomat	USA	(Washington Post, 10 June 1986)
REMENCHUK	Andrei A.	GRU	Dec. 1987	Montreal	Translator	Canada	[Redefected 21 June 1988]
SMUROV	Yuri	GRU	May 1988	Montreal	Translator	Canada	(Toronto Star, 14 Sept. 1988)
IGNASTE	Vladimir A.	KGB		Manila			(Barron)[18]
			1983		Trade Del.		(Wise)[19]

* For notes, see pages 226–8.

Defector Meal-tickets

Defector	Agent	Codename	Position	Conclusion
GOUZENKO	May, Dr Allan Nunn	ALEK	Atomic Energy research	10 yrs
	Wilshire, Kay	ELLI	British High Commission	3 yrs
	Carr, Sam	FRANZ	Leader of Communist Party	6 yrs
	Rose, Fred	DEBOUZ	Member of Parliament	6 yrs
	Lunan, Capt. David G	BACK		5 yrs
	Halperin, Prof. Israel	BACON	Army Research and Development Establishment	Acquitted
	Smith, Philip Durnford	BADEAU	National Research Council	5 yrs
	Poland, Sqdn-Ldr Fred	ERIC	Canadian Air Force	Acquitted
	Adams, Eric	LEADER	Bank of Canada	Acquitted
	Nightingale, Sqdn-Ldr Matt	PROMETHEUS	Canadian Air Force	Acquitted
	Shugar, Lt David	GRAY	Radar expert	Acquitted
	Gerson, Harold	BURMAN	Munitions Dept.	5 yrs
	Burman, Maj. Sol			Not charged
	Pappin, W. M.			Acquitted
	Mazerall, Edward	BAGLEY	National Research Council	4 yrs
	Boyer, Prof. Raymond	PROFESSOR	Explosives expert	2 yrs
	Soboloff, John			Fined $500
	Benning, James	FOSTER	Munitions Dept	Quashed on appeal
	Harris, Henry		Optometrist	Quashed on appeal
	Chapman, Agatha		Bank of Canada	Acquitted
	Linton, Freda	FREDA	International Labor Office	Charges withdrawn
	Woikin, Emma	NORA	External Affairs Dept.	2 yrs
	Veall, Norman			Not charged
	Gottheil, Capt. Jack	KINGSTON		Not charged
RASTVOROV	Takamore, Shigeru		Japanese Foreign Ministry	
	Shoji, Hiroshi		Japanese Foreign Ministry	
	Higurashi, Nobunori		Japanese Foreign Ministry	Committed suicide

Defector	Agent	Codename	Position	Conclusion	
PETROV	Clayton, Walter		CP functionary		
	Throssell, Ric	KLOD	External Affairs Dept		
	O'Sullivan, Fergan	FERRO	Journalist		
	Christiansen, Wilbur		Physicist		
	Lockwood, Rupert	MASTER	Journalist		
	Hill, Jim	TOURIST	External Affairs Dept	Moved to Prague	
	Milner, Ian	BUR	External Affairs Dept	Granted immunity	
	Bernie, Frances	SESTRA	External Affairs Dept		
	Legge, George	BIBAK	External Affairs Dept		
HAYHANEN	Abel, Rudolf		Illegal	30 yrs	Swapped
	Rhodes, Roy		US Army Sgt	5 yrs	
GOLENIEWSKI	Houghton, Harry		Royal Navy research	15 yrs	
	Gee, Ethel		Royal Navy research	15 yrs	
	Lonsdale, Gordon		Illegal	20 yrs	Swapped
	Kroger, Peter		Illegal	20 yrs	Swapped
	Kroger, Helen		Illegal	20 yrs	Swapped
	Wennerstrom, Stig		Swedish Air Force Col	Life	
	Felfe, Heinz	PAUL	German BND	14 yrs	Swapped
	Clemens, Hans	PETER	German BND		
	Tiebel, Erwin		German lawyer		
	Blake, George	DIAMONT	British SIS	42 yrs	Escaped
	Skarbeck, Irwin		US diplomat	10 yrs	
	Beer, Israel		Israeli Col	10 yrs	
GOLITSYN	Paques, Georges	COLUMBINE	NATO official	20 years	
	Foccart, Jacques		French Intelligence	Cleared	
	Watkins, John		Canadian diplomat	Heart attack	
	Philby, Kim		British SIS	Defected	
	Fell, Barbara		British civil servant	2 yrs	

Defector	Agent	Codename	Position	Conclusion
NOSENKO	Vassall, John		British Admiralty clerk	18 yrs
RUNGE	Johnson, Robert		US Army Sgt	25 yrs
	Sutterlin, Leonore		German Foreign Ministry	Suicide
	Sutterlin, Heinz		Illegal	
BITTMAN	Frenzel, Alfred		German Foreign Ministry	17 yrs
	Luedke, Hermann		German Admiral	Suicide
	Wendland, Horst		German BND General	Suicide
	Schenke, Hans		German Economics Ministry	Suicide
	Grimm, Johann		German Col, Defence Ministry	Suicide
	Boehm, Gerhard		German Defence Ministry	Drowned
LYALIN	Abdoolcader, Sirioj		Clerk, London Motor Dept	3 yrs
	Costi, Kyriacos		Illegal	6 yrs
	Martianon, Costantinos		Illegal	4 yrs
ZEMENEK	Hambleton, Hugh		Canadian professor	10 yrs
LEVCHENKO	Miyanaga, Yukihisa		Japanese Maj.-General	20 yrs
YURCHENKO	Howard, Edward		CIA	Defected
	Pelton, Ronald		NSA	Life
GORDIEVSKI	Bergling, Stig		Col, Swedish Intelligence	Heart attack
	Haavik, Gunvor		Norwegian Foreign Ministry	15 yrs
	Treholt, Arne		Norwegian Foreign Ministry	8 yrs
	Weibel, Bent		Danish businessman	
	Petersen, Arne		Danish journalist	
	Bettaney, Michael		British Security Service	23 yrs
GUDAREV	Bothwell, John		CIA	Cleared

6

The Friends

'The British get by with a minimum of red
tape, but at the same time their SIS is
endowed with a high degree of confidence by
both government and Parliament.'[1]

Reinhard Gehlen, Chief of the West German
Bundesnachrichtendienst 1945–68 .

In recent years the British Secret Intelligence Service has acquired
a contradictory reputation. According to *Time*'s survey published in
1978, SIS 'is tops at analytical work and political judgments. Good
on the Middle East, less impressive on Africa.'[2] Yet four years later
the British Cabinet was to be taken completely by surprise when
the Argentine military junta launched an invasion of the Falkland
Islands. This particularly costly intelligence failure was to be the
subject of an intensive study undertaken by a special committee
headed by Lord Franks, which recommended widespread reforms,
not in SIS's methods of intelligence collection, but in Whitehall's
assessment machinery.

Attempting to judge the performance of Britain's intelligence
service on the basis of the formula described in the introduction is
uniquely difficult because of the inhibitions of insiders. Unlike its
French or American equivalents, SIS has actively discouraged its
personnel from writing about their experiences. Accordingly, none
of the most senior SIS staff has ever been published, and only a
relative handful of junior officers have actually gone into print. The
full list is sufficiently short to be given here in full. Probably the

Chiefs of the Secret Intelligence Service

Sir Stewart Menzies	1939–51
Sir John Sinclair	1952–6
Sir Dick White	1956–68
Sir John Rennie	1968–73
Sir Maurice Oldfield	1973–8
Sir Dickie Franks	1978–81
Sir Colin Figures	1981–5
Sir Christopher Curwen	1985–9
Colin McColl	1989–

most notorious were Kim Philby, who wrote his memoirs *My Silent War* in 1968 from the safety of Moscow, and George Blake, whose *No Abiding City* was never released outside the Soviet Union. Apart from those wartime SIS officers who have produced books about their duties during the hostilities, such as Fred Winterbotham, R.V. Jones, Philip Johns, Leslie Nicholson, A. J. Ayer, Graham Greene, Malcolm Muggeridge and Hugh Trevor Roper, there are a few who wrote on other, not necessarily related, subjects. These include such scholars as Robert Carew-Hunt, Hugh Seton-Watson and David Footman, who all penned tracts for a chiefly academic readership.

Post-war SIS officers who have described their adventures, or proffered opinions on international relations, are few and far between. David Smiley has inserted some interesting and revealing references into his wartime recollections, *Albanian Assignment*, and Nigel Clive's *A Greek Experience* recalls his service in SOE before he joined SIS. Sir Douglas Dodds-Parker makes a couple of worthwhile asides in *Political Eunuch*, and Monty Woodhouse, another SOE veteran, reminisced discreetly in *Something Ventured* about his key role in the joint CIA–SIS operations to overthrow the Iranian Prime Minister Mussadeq in 1953. Thereafter, the field is really very limited. Charles Ransom joined Professor Harry Hinsley's team of historians to compile *British Intelligence in the Second World War*, but only after he had retired from Century House, SIS's modern headquarters in the Westminster Bridge Road. George K. Young, SIS's Vice Chief until 1961, wrote *Masters of Indecision: An Inquiry into the Political Process* upon his retirement and, in 1972, published *Who is my Liege? A Study of Loyalty and Betrayal in our Time.* (He also completed a book on merchant banking, his latter occupation, and two political commentaries, *Finance and World Power*, and a tract on British immigration policies, *Who Goes Home?*)

Rather more relevant to our subject is the impressive editorial work undertaken by Stephen de Mowbray on Anatoli Golitsyn's analysis of Communist deception and disinformation, in *New Lies for Old*. This was a joint effort with a veteran CIA officer, Scott Miler, and MI5's celebrated molehunter, Arthur Martin.

The only two significant literary endeavours by SIS insiders during the post-war era, apart from an article written in an obscure specialist journal, *World War II Investigator*, by Theodore (Bunny) Pantcheff about atrocities committed by the Nazis during their wartime occupation of the Channel Islands, are the chapters written by John Bruce Lockhart and Robert Cecil in *British and American Approaches to Intelligence*. Lockhart, who was described as having been 'actively involved with intelligence at a senior level' until 1965, had originally made his comments during a lecture at the Royal United Services Institute for Defence Studies in November 1973. Cecil, on the other hand, who contributed a detailed study of the Falklands campaign, had served as the SIS Chief's personal assistant during the last years of the war.

In addition to the above, certain SIS officers have written on unrelated topics and ought to be mentioned. Three years after his retirement in 1970, Brian Montgomery wrote his brother's biography, *A Field Marshal in the Family*. Brian Stewart, on the other hand, produced his anthology of Chinese proverbs, *All Men's Wisdom*, just before he joined SIS in 1957. Donald Prater took up writing after his premature departure from the SIS station in Stockholm in 1968 and subsequently wrote a biography of Stefan Zweig, *European of Yesterday*, and *A Ringing Glass: The Life of Rainer Maria Rilke*. Since works of non-fiction have been included here, perhaps the contribution made by SIS personnel to fiction should be recorded briefly. Three novelists stand out: David Cornwell, alias John le Carré, who opted to be a full-time author in 1964 after his success with *The Spy Who Came in from the Cold;* Kenneth Benton, who followed his example in 1968 and left the SIS station in Rio de Janeiro to write a series of best-selling thrillers; and Alec Waugh, who wrote *The Sunlit Caribbean* and a string of other successes after leaving one of SIS's German stations in 1947.

This effectively concludes the printed material publicly available for those seeking to discern the views of insiders on the subject of the post-war performance of British intelligence. Privileged researchers with good contacts can probably find an illicit copy of Anthony Cavendish's *Inside Intelligence*. This was injuncted by the British authorities in 1987, but the civil law did not prevent the author from privately distributing free copies of his book. Cavendish subsequently won his case in the Scottish courts, leaving a ban on the book only in England. Now he has been commissioned to write a biography of his old friend and former Chief of SIS, Sir Maurice Oldfield.

It is curious that SIS and the KGB have something in common in the literary field: they are the only two major intelligence services in the world not to have had their respective heads write their own accounts of their work. Several DCIs, as we have seen, have gone into print; the German BND Chief Reinhard Gehlen has written *The Service*; the Comte de Marenches has released *The Evil Empire*; and Isser Harel has told his version of Mossad's abduction of Adolf Eichmann in *The House on Garibaldi Street*. However, lack of encouragement for literary endeavour is about the limit of the similarities between the KGB and SIS.

Considering the handicaps that SIS has to endure, even though they are admittedly largely self-inflicted, it is remarkable that the organization retains its high standing in the Allied intelligence community. Of course, it is often the subject of ridicule, as is demonstrated by this account by Chester L. Cooper, a senior CIA officer attending a Joint Intelligence Committee conference, shortly before the Suez crisis:

> British intelligence officers do not have to be seven feet tall, but when I walked into the meeting room on this my first working day in London, it did seem that height was a primary qualification for employment. As if to emphasize the point my new colleagues rose as I made my maiden entrance. I was passed from giraffe to giraffe.[3]

Perhaps as a consequence of the historical departmental guilt felt by SIS because of Kim Philby and George Blake, the only two Soviet spies ever detected in the service, the CIA have been given a remarkable degree of access, even beyond the CAZAB limits. This has not always been reciprocated, as can be seen from this recollection of Anglo–American co-operation in Singapore from the then Deputy Chief of the CIA station, Joseph Smith:

> There are two schools of thought about liaison with the British.
> One was that it was a rare and beautiful thing to be nurtured
> with every care, because the British were the more sagacious in
> the business, with a long and remarkable tradition of success.
> The other was that it was a waste of time, the British officers were
> a bunch of supercilious snobs toward whom we should show an
> equivalent disdain ... as a result of being briefed by both schools
> of thought however, I arrived at my post with a formula for
> guiding my conduct that went something like this: our liaison
> with the British is one of our greatest assets; don't tell the
> bastards anything important.[4]

In fact, a close relationship does exist between SIS and the CIA, in much the same way that the NSA and GCHQ co-operate in each other's interests and mount joint operations. Among the numerous examples of bilateral undertaking targeted against the Soviets are the Berlin tunnel project, financed by the CIA and serviced by SIS, and the Penkovsky case, initiated by the British but shared with the Americans.

Although it may be argued that congressional oversight has had a restraining effect on the CIA, it is actually SIS that suffers operationally from a lack of political supervision. Ever since the Buster Crabb fiasco in 1956, when an SIS contract agent severely embarrassed Sir Anthony Eden by getting caught in a scheme that had been expressly prohibited, the service has had to live with severe restrictions which require political sanctioning at ministerial level for virtually every risky project. In recent years Vladimir Kuzichkin, a walk-in of tremendous value, had his approach rebuffed because of the potential implications of receiving a Soviet defector in post-revolutionary Iran.[5] It was only on the intervention of a senior minister, who saw the probable advantages of accepting Kuzichkin's offer, that the KGB officer was wooed back into the British fold. However, leaving responsibility for granting authority for operations to a single individual, and a politician at that, is hardly a formula for imaginative decision-making in the intelligence field, even if on this memorable occasion the objections of the ever-cautious Foreign Office were overruled.

SIS is acutely conscious of its own none-too-impressive history, which dates back to 1909, and is forever tainted with the duplicity of some of its wartime intake. Soviet penetration is a constant anxiety, but the successful completion of Major Kuzichkin's defection in October 1982, and the brilliant exfiltration from Moscow of Oleg Gordievsky in August 1985, after a hazardous career as an SIS source lasting twelve years, bear testimony to an effective counter-intelligence regime.

The political environment in which SIS operates is certainly very inhibiting, and for good reasons. Perhaps naively, politicians are shocked to learn of past unsavoury incidents. For example, immediately after the war SIS embarked upon a plan to limit illegal Jewish immigration to Palestine by sabotaging the Haganah's refugee ships. The best documented episode to be disclosed concerns the *Pan Crescent*, a steamer blown up with a limpet mine in Venice shortly before it was scheduled to carry a cargo of desperate Holocaust victims to Tel Aviv.[6] Whilst there is no evidence that SIS ever resorted to assassination, allegations that it seriously contemplated the murder of President Nasser and General Grivas also sparked off political rows. Similarly, suggestions in 1972 that a pair of criminals, the Littlejohn brothers Kenneth and Keith, had been given carte blanche to rob banks in return for information about the Provisional IRA, or that SIS had turned a blind eye to Howard Marks's drug smuggling because his tips about terrorists were so useful,[7] were also received poorly by a public reluctant to accept SIS denials at face value.

The root of SIS's poor standing is based on a traditionally tangled relationship between politicians and Britain's domestic security apparatus. It is now known that on several occasions the Security Service, MI5, deliberately misled the Prime Minister in order to protect itself from criticism. In one instance Clement Attlee was assured that there had been no delay in apprehending Klaus Fuchs. In reality, it was discovered that a suspicious investigating officer had recommended more enquiries into Fuchs's background, which would have revealed the extent of his past Communist connections, but the request was filed instead of being acted upon. In another example of gross misconduct MI5 concealed its own bungled pursuit of Burgess and Maclean, and then sanitized its files before passing them to the Americans. Neither event inspired confidence.

Whilst it is perfectly true that these embarrassments, and others such as the Profumo affair, the Anthony Blunt scandal and the inconclusive Hollis molehunt, had little to do with SIS, they did contribute to the political climate in which politicians and the public alike are reluctant to accept official assurances on intelligence matters. Nor is SIS entirely free of blame in this regard. When George Blake was sentenced to a record term of imprisonment in 1961 for betraying every secret that passed over his desk, an orchestrated attempt was made to prevent his role as an SIS professional from leaking. He was presented as a regular Foreign Service diplomat, and even after the truth had been revealed, stories were planted in the press suggesting that his recruitment into SIS had occurred some years after he really had joined.

Once SIS realized the scale of Soviet penetration of the British establishment, which only became apparent after the defections of Burgess and Maclean in 1951, a series of debilitating molehunts were conducted to root out the contamination. In the event, the innocent were penalized along with the guilty. Kim Philby was fired swiftly from SIS because he had been implicated by Burgess. John Cairncross, who had served in SIS at the end of the war, was also interrogated, and he too was allowed to live abroad. In later years four other senior SIS officers were investigated as possible long-term Soviet sources: Dick Ellis, who admitted to having sold SIS secrets before the war; Professor Robin Zaehner, a homosexual SIS case officer who had recruited the Shah of Iran's tutor as a valuable agent; Andrew King, who had been an underground member of the Communist Party at Cambridge with Philby; and Donald Prater, another former CPGB activist. However, no evidence of espionage activities was found against these officers.

It will be noted that none of the investigations cited above, apart from that of George Blake, resulted in any formal prosecutions. The cynics believe this to be proof that SIS looks after its own and is reluctant to wash its dirty linen in public. The reality is that even where there is some evidence of espionage activities, convictions are notoriously difficult to achieve under British law, which requires a spy to be caught in the act of passing classified secrets to a foreign power. Furthermore, the spy ought to sign (and resist retracting) a detailed, admissible confession in the presence of a police officer who has cautioned him. In these circumstances it is hardly surprising that the government found itself in the awkward position in 1955 of having to exonerate Philby publicly when he had been accused, with no evidence whatever, of playing the role of the 'third man' in the Burgess and Maclean defections four years earlier.

In 1963, an atomic scientist, Dr Giuseppe Martelli, was acquitted on all charges after he had admitted being in clandestine contact with Nikolai Karpekov, a known Soviet intelligence officer. The jury found Dr Martelli innocent, accepting that he had been trying to dupe his Russian contact in order to entrap him. Amongst the reasons for Martelli's prosecution were that a search of his house had revealed the paraphernalia of espionage and, at the time of his arrest, one of his shoes was found to have a false heel; his suitcase also contained a rendezvous map and radio schedule. In another case seven years later, a Labour Member of Parliament, Will Owen, was accused of having sold confidential defence papers to a Czech intelligence officer, who had later defected and was on hand to accuse his old accomplice. Owen was acquitted after he had successfully shown that the charges against him were unfounded.[8] In a more recent case a former CIA officer, Commander John Bothwell, was released from custody in London without charge after it was discovered that the testimony of Viktor P. Gudarev, the KGB defector who had compromised him, was flawed and, in fact, there was no evidence at all that Bothwell was guilty of espionage.

The difficulty of obtaining enough evidence to achieve a conviction is partly the reason why there have only been thirty-three returned since the end of the war. And of that number, only twenty-five can be described as serious cases of Soviet Bloc espionage. A much larger number of suspects, such as Leo Long, John Cairncross, Alister Watson, John Stonehouse and Anthony Blunt, were never prosecuted, even though most made incriminating admissions.

It is shaking off the past that has proved to be one of SIS's greatest challenges. While still subject to the geographical carve-up of the world in 1909, which left the Security Service with responsibility for defence intelligence within the Empire, SIS has had to come to terms with a declining overseas presence and successive governments constricted by economic crises, which saw little merit in funding an intelligence apparatus that seemed to boast a high embarrassment factor but was not conspicuously adept in producing the timely data needed to prevent costly wars and undermine international terrorists. SIS did not anticipate the Falklands invasion in 1982, nor did the economic blockade imposed on Rhodesia bring the dispute with that country to a swift end as predicted by SIS. But before describing SIS's modern role one must return to the immediate post-war era to put the organization into its international perspective.

SIS's preoccupations at the end of the Second World War were dominated by the onset of the Cold War and the government's determination to limit the spread of Soviet hegemony. This led to involvement in disastrous covert actions in the Ukraine and Albania, which were doomed to failure, partly due to Soviet penetration of SIS, but mainly because of inadequate assessment of the support available locally for partisan resistance movements. The preparatory surveys conducted were minimal, and the groups infiltrated into denied areas to foment counter-revolutionary unrest were either promptly eliminated by the local security apparatus or actually 'turned' and run against the organizers. In short, the experience was unsuccessful, and numerous lives were lost in the Baltic republic, the Ukraine and the Balkans before the operations were terminated.

The other undertakings targeted against the Soviets met with similar failure. While the Americans were receiving a fairly steady stream of important intelligence defectors from the KGB and the GRU, the British received none of any significance. The first, Colonel J.D. Tasoev, plucked from US jurisdiction in Bremen in May 1948, announced his desire to be repatriated almost as soon as he had arrived in London. He was followed by Grigori A. Tokaev, who switched sides in Berlin and proved to be the only authentic Soviet intelligence defector received in England until 1971. If reception of defectors is to be regarded as an indication of an agency's integrity, this must surely be a matter of some gravity. It should be noted that during this same period, the British authorities only apprehended a single Soviet agent on its own initiative, William M. Marshall. When all the defector meal-ticket cases supplied by the CIA, such as the Portland spy ring, John Vassall, Brian Linney and Douglas Britten, are eliminated, just one case remains. It so happens that this single example, of a Diplomatic Wireless Service operator who sold out to Pavel Kuznetsov in 1952, was entirely fortuitous. Far from being an epic of counter-intelligence, or a coup resulting from a prolonged study of Soviet espionage techniques, the Marshall case was initiated after a Security Service watcher had, quite by accident, spotted Kuznetsov behaving suspiciously. Instead of returning home to have lunch, as the watcher had intended to do, he kept the Soviet under observation and saw him rendezvous with a young man. All that remained was for Marshall to be identified and prosecuted. Apart from this unique investigation which proceeded without interference or mishap, as Peter Wright has confirmed, 'up to the end of 1965, every case for twenty years or more was tainted by Russian "sticky fingers" '.[9]

The molehunts that effectively paralysed MI5 and SIS during the 1960s were brought to an end by the recruitment in 1971 of Oleg Lyalin by a team consisting of an old SIS hand, Tony Brooks, and Harry Wharton, who caught the Soviet trade official in a classic honeytrap. They continued to run Lyalin for six months until his defection was forced when he was arrested for drunk driving in August 1971, by which time MI5 and SIS had developed greater confidence about their respective abilities to operate without fear of contamination of betrayal by a well-concealed mole. Nevertheless, as a result of Lyalin's information MI5 and SIS went ahead with a well-planned show of strength to PNG every identified member of the KGB and the GRU in London. Implementation was delayed while Lyalin added further data and, once he had formally requested political asylum, the announcement was made that ninety Soviet officials had been expelled and a further fifteen had been refused re-entry.

Not long after these events the SIS station in Copenhagen recruited Oleg Gordievsky as a source, and his uninterrupted work, over a span of twelve years, was further evidence that the British had shaken off the spectre of hostile penetration that had dogged them for so long. His transfer to the London *Rezidentura* in June 1982 was a coup of some magnitude, matched only by his eventual exfiltration from Moscow, right from under the noses of KGB counter-intelligence teams who, Yurchenko is said to have reported, were closing in for a final confrontation. Since Gordievsky is rightly regarded as the proof that SIS can keep secrets and run good cases, the circumstances of his ultimate exposure are significant. Allegedly, it was Arne Treholt's arrest in Norway on 20 January 1984, just as he was about to fly to Vienna for a rendezvous with his controller, Gennadi T. Titov, that raised the KGB's suspicions about the existence of a Western source in its own ranks. Treholt was found to be carrying a briefcase containing sixty-five classified Foreign Ministry documents and received a prison sentence of fifteen years. Titov himself was an experienced case officer, having served in London before his eventual expulsion from Oslo in January 1977 with five other Russians. On that occasion he had been implicated in the espionage of Fru Gunvor Haavik, an elderly clerk in the Norwegian Ministry of Foreign Affairs and a Soviet spy of long standing. Combined with the arrest of Colonel Stig Bergling, the spy in Sweden's military intelligence service and the detention of Michael Bettaney in London, it is not surprising that the ever-vigilant Second Chief Directorate called the newly appointed KGB *Rezident* back from London to face an investigation. Evidently, the KGB had not swallowed the stories deliberately circulated in Norway that Treholt had been apprehended due to a complicated double-agent operation run against his Soviet controller, Leonid Makarov, who also happened to be the KGB *Rezident* in Oslo.[10] During Gordievsky's second tour of duty in Copenhagen, which lasted from October 1972 to July 1978, no less than seven Soviet diplomats had been expelled and two Danes had been caught spying. Bent Weibel received eight years for smuggling advanced technology to the Soviet Union,[11] and Arne Petersen was convicted of penetrating the Danish peace movement for the KGB.

While expulsions do not tell the whole story, it should be recorded that between 1970 and Gordievsky's exfiltration, the Soviets experienced an unprecedented number of expulsions in Europe and an unknown number of silent PNGs. Norway kicked out a total of twenty-five, France fifty-one (of whom forty-seven were removed in April 1983), Portugal twelve, Spain fourteen, Holland and Switzerland eleven and Canada twenty. No wonder the Second Chief Directorate had grounds for thinking that something had gone badly wrong. Once Gordievsky had been received safely, a further twenty-five Russians were PNG'd from London, bringing the total removed from London since Lyalin to thirty-nine.

As to whether SIS's own internal security has really improved, it must be noted that there has been little effort to conceal its present headquarters at Century House in the Westminster Bridge Road, or its other premises in London that have received widespread publicity. Indeed, SIS only moved out of its completely compromised old wartime offices, at Broadway Buildings, in 1967. Nor has SIS taken any step to introduce polygraph testing to screen employees.

The criteria for assessing relative performance, as applied to the CIA and the KGB, are rather simpler to judge in SIS's case. As for the opinion of insiders, it is invariably derogatory, little of it that there is. Other professionals are struck by the purely British characteristics of behaviour, rather than any striking regard for dedication, loyalty or other traits, praiseworthy or otherwise. Indeed, by treaty with the United States, the principal source of literature on this subject, references to British intelligence are automatically deleted whenever they occur, as provided for under the Freedom of Information Act and the mandatory official contracts with the Publications Review Board. When Kermit Roosevelt made innocuous remarks about the role of the British in the SIS–CIA sponsored *coup d'état* against Mussadeq in *Countercoup*, the first edition was hastily withdrawn and censored before it had reached the bookstores. Comparison between the few first editions that slipped past the recall and the later edition reveals that the changes in text were limited to those passages that might have offended British sensibilities.[12]

When arriving at a conclusion about the integrity of the service, one is bound to note the absence of any Soviet Bloc defectors between 1948 and 1971, and the lack of success of operations such as the Berlin tunnel, despite heavy investment in Polish, Ukrainian and Czech émigré groups that turned out to be thoroughly penetrated. As has already been remarked, no less than three Soviet defectors who made approaches to the British during the critical period simply vanished. The Penkovsky operation, run jointly with the Americans, lasted a full eighteen months before it was wound up with embarrassing loss for SIS at least, and questions have even been raised about exactly when Penkovsky himself came under KGB control, as he certainly did towards the end.

The other counter-intelligence skills to be considered when examining SIS include the ability to spot false defectors, which has undoubtedly been an area of disagreement with the CIA. On several occasions the CIA has rejected defectors that have been accepted by SIS. The first was Boris Bakhlanov back in 1947, who was unable to establish his credentials with the Americans but was regarded as genuine by SIS.[13] More recently, a Canadian journalist, Peter Worthington, assisted in the defection of his translator, Olga Farmakovsky. She was married to a GRU officer and had been co-opted by the KGB to report on Worthington's contacts in Moscow. The CIA was unconvinced by her, but the British accepted her as an authentic. Although she is still banned by the American authorities, she lives in Toronto, partly due to the endorsement she received following her interrogation by SIS in Brussels.

When the US Congress heard evidence of defector handling in October 1987, some of the testimony was tacitly critical of the British treatment of Oleg Bitov, the foreign culture editor of a Soviet weekly who defected in Italy in September 1983 and was resettled in London. He later suffered severe depression, a common experience for many defectors, and in August 1984 he disappeared, having told friends he was about to enter hospital for cancer treatment. In reality, he had surrendered to the Soviet embassy and had been flown back to Moscow, where, uniquely, he was allowed to take up journalism again, a development that received wide publicity. SIS had minimal interest in Bitov's case, apart from a few interviews to establish whether he was willing to identify Soviet intelligence personnel operating in the West under journalistic cover. Once he had completed this chore, he was as free as anyone else to travel abroad, wherever he wished. Just as the CIA was powerless to forcibly prevent Yurchenko from redefecting, SIS had no legal standing to stop Bitov from visiting his embassy. Hardly a great success for either MI5 or SIS, but no catastrophe either, especially as Bitov had minimal intelligence value.

SIS's barren years produced few leads to spies operating in the UK, but since then its handling and safe receipt of Gordievsky, Rezun, Kuzichkin and Dzirkvelov demonstrates that times have changed, and no doubt enhances the status of SIS's CAZAB members. Although it must be admitted that there has only been one successful prosecution as a result of defector information in Britain since Lyalin betrayed three KGB illegals in 1971, which was Gordievsky's remarkable identification of MI5's renegade officer, Michael Bettaney, in the summer of 1983, it is also true to observe that the standards of legal proof required in British prosecutions is dauntingly high. However, the ease with which court proceedings can be transferred to private hearings, held in camera with only the lawyers and vetted juries present, must be a comfort for those eager to prevent the leakage of sensitive information. When the Bettaney trial took place, the only parts conducted openly were the introduction of the prosecution's case and the judge's sentence. The press and public were excluded from all the remainder, including Bettaney's final appeal, which was moved to a special room swept for listening devices.

In terms of operational ability, SIS generates considerable good-will around the world by opening its training facilities at Fort

Monkton, in Gosport, and in Lambeth, south London, to members of Commonwealth agencies. MI5 does the same and provides advisers to travel abroad and assist in the installation of telephone intercept stations and other technical undertakings. In this particular field SIS scores well, its well-guarded research centre inside the Hanslope Park complex having gained an international reputation for the development and manufacture of state-of-the-art gadgetry.

But whatever kudos SIS tries to attain by developing special kit in the hope of gaining favour with Allied services, it will always be reminded of its past sins and its unenviable record for treachery.

The British intelligence community has a reputation, apparently dating back to the early 1950s, of being unable to keep a secret. In the duplicity stakes, SIS scores high. This is ironical, given the very few penetrations experienced by MI5 and SIS. Insofar that prosecutions are any guide, only George Blake has been convicted of deliberately manoeuvring himself into a position where he could inflict serious damage. Since then, only Bettaney has attempted to do the same thing, and he was arrested in 1984 before he could even establish a dialogue with Arkadi V. Gouk, his chosen accomplice. By far the most serious case of Soviet espionage, perhaps during the entire post-war period, was that of Geoffrey Prime, the GCHQ analyst who, after he had been arrested in 1982 on an entirely separate, unrelated criminal offence, admitted having passed secrets to the KGB. He had resigned from GCHQ more than three years previously and had fallen out of touch with his Soviet controller.

The explanation for the unjustified reputation suffered by the British is in part the phenomenon of ideologically motivated moles, who were recruited before entering any sensitive post and then encouraged to burrow deep into what is known as 'the establishment'. No other intelligence structure has certain evidence of parallel cases, apart from the Canadian and American organizations which were also affected by what has been termed the 'Cambridge Comintern'. The concept of the mole, carefully hiding his true allegiance until he has climbed to a level where he can inflict exceptional damage, is a manifestation of sinister dedication. British preoccupation with class has heightened awareness of the paradoxical nature of the Communist-orientated member of the middle classes, enjoying all the privileges of rank, but secretly plotting the destruction of his society. Guy Burgess, Donald Maclean, Kim Philby and Anthony Blunt personify the contradictions. All came from relatively well-off backgrounds, attended expensive schools and moved among the elite of their generation at university. Yet there they embraced an alien culture and thereby tainted their contemporaries.

The drama of these renegades is emphasized by the knowledge that none was ever prosecuted. Burgess and Maclean defected in 1951, having been tipped off and assisted by Philby and Blunt. To add irony to an already piquant scenario, Philby was subsequently declared loyal in Parliament, and Blunt was to be decorated with a knighthood. Although Philby's eventual defection in January 1963 was impossible to conceal from the public, Blunt's involvement, to which he confessed in 1964 in return for an immunity from prosecution, was to be kept under wraps for a further fifteen years.

These events did nothing to inspire confidence in either SIS or the Security Service. When sanitized files were presented to the FBI in 1951 in order to explain away MI5's obvious ineptitude, William Sullivan spotted the documents as phonies straightaway. The CIA became increasingly frustrated with SIS's unwillingness to recognize Philby as a security risk and was appalled when he was brought back into the fold and allowed access to the SIS station in Beirut in 1956. In later years it seemed as though American suspicions about cover-ups were all too justified. Three other Communists who had gone underground at Cambridge were shown to have been in contact with Soviet intelligence officers and had escaped without penalty. John Cairncross, Leo Long and Alister Watson were all removed from access to secrets, but only after the damage had been sustained. No doubt there were others whose names were never disclosed. Was there a reluctance on the part of the authorities to prosecute because of the embarrassment factor, or was it really as was claimed that there was insufficient evidence to present to a jury, even behind closed doors?

The reality is that prosecutions are brought with vigour in England, some would say with rather too much enthusiasm. In March 1982, the Israelis informed MI5 that a junior British diplomat in Tel Aviv, Rhona Ritchie, had taken an Egyptian envoy as her lover. Ritchie admitted to having shown him just five classified telegrams and was sentenced to a suspended term of imprisonment. Was her offence wilful espionage or sheer infatuation and stupidity?

Each time a spy scandal emerges in London there is speculation about the impact felt on Anglo–American relations, but the fact is that the CIA and the FBI are very accustomed to working within a rigid legal framework and accept that there are perfectly respectable reasons for not pursuing a particular spy. After all, in the case of Harry Dexter White, whose identity as a valued Soviet source had been revealed in the VENONA signals intercept operation, the US authorities had used the expedient of recommending his promotion from the Treasury Department to the International Monetary Fund. White died of a heart attack three days after denying allegations of his covert membership of the Communist Party to a congressional committee in 1948.

The challenge facing the British security authorities in their attempts to deter espionage is the scale of the threat which is on a par with the situation in Washington. The difference is in the limited resources available to MI5 to maintain the blanket surveillance achieved by their American counterparts. The Soviets operate from a variety of different premises, including three different buildings in Kensington Palace Gardens: the embassy at number 13, which is also known as Harrington House: the service attaché's office at number 16: and the consular section on the Bayswater Road. There is also the trade delegation at 33 Highgate West Hill. In addition to the forty-two or so officially accredited diplomats, there are a further 200 Soviets in Britain. Some use the ambassador's country estate at Seacox Heath House in Flimwell, East Sussex; others are journalists working for *Soviet Weekly* and *Soviet News*, which share the Information Office in Rosary Gardens with Novosti, *Izvestia* TASS, *Socialist Industry*, *Pravda* and Radio Moscow.

There are also plenty of commercial covers in London, such as Aeroflot, and recent expulsions have shown that the KGB and the GRU are adept at inserting their personnel into them. Thus, Valeri A. Kotov, deputy managing director of the Razno metal merchandising company run from an anonymous block at 107 Curtain Road, Shoreditch, was PNG'd in September 1985, together with Valeri P. Ipatov of the Moscow Narodny Bank's branch in King William Street. An Aeroflot employee from the Piccadilly office had been sent home just five months earlier. Various agencies in London, such as the International Wheat Council, the International Cocoa Organization and the Maritime Commission, have also been used as vehicles for placing intelligence officers in England. Only a small proportion of the KGB and GRU personnel based in London are active case officers, but the remainder behave as though they are, acting as decoys to attract the attention of MI5's watcher teams away from their colleagues, who are engaged in surveying suitable dead-letter drops, rendezvous sites and all the rest of the routine tradecraft needed to communicate with agents. In order to confuse the watchers, they regularly engage complete strangers in conversation, switch taxis, and jump in and out of tube trains at the last moment. The one group that has yet to be detected in espionage in England is the sixty-five trade inspectors attached to companies throughout the country to exercise quality control over products destined for export to the Eastern Bloc. Unlike their compatriots in the capital, they are not subject to any travel restrictions and are, therefore, more difficult to keep under close supervision.

Deployed against this unknown figure of professionals are the field men and women of the Security Service who maintain permanent static observation posts overlooking all Soviet premises or, in the case of Kensington Palace Gardens, the 'choke points' at either end, and some selected residential accommodation. All the telephone lines are monitored, and until recently sensitive listening equipment was housed in one of the few palatial mansions in Kensington Palace Gardens in private ownership. Cyril Mills had retired from MI5 at the end of the war, but was very willing to have his living costs subsidized by his old employers. That particular operation was terminated when two inquisitive Soviet envoys were found clambering on his roof, in an apparent attempt to either steal or sabotage the apparatus. The battle is an unequal one because of the comparatively small number of British businessmen, diplomats and journalists in Moscow. This, of course, is one of the hazards of playing the game of intelligence on an uneven surface.

Yet in spite of Britain's in-built disadvantage, and in defiance of the obvious limitations that handicap other similar Western agencies, British perfomance in the intelligence field has undergone a striking improvement. Undoubtedly there was plenty of scope for progress, as can be seen from the remarkable absence of particular kinds of cases in the past. Take, for example, the issue of illegals. It has been the experience of most Western countries that the KGB will go to considerable lengths to develop the 'legend' of an individual and supply him with all the documentation needed for him to establish himself in his host community without arousing local suspicions. We have already examined the cases of Kaarlo Tuomi in America and Ludel Zemenek in Canada. Some have defected, others have been turned into double agents, but the background and training given to each has been roughly the same. If further proof was needed, Oleg Penkovsky supplied the complete text of a GRU training manual written by Lieutenant-Colonel I.E. Prikhodko in 1961, entitled *Characteristics of Agent Communicatioins and of Agent Handling in the United States of America*. This fascinating document, prepared on the basis of the author's experience as a GRU officer under UN cover in New York between 1952 and 1955, gives detailed guidance to prospective case officers on how they should conduct themselves while on hostile territory. In addition, Piotr S. Deriabin, the KGB officer who defected in Vienna in 1954, has confirmed that earlier that same year a directive had been issued from Moscow Centre demanding greater efforts to build illegal networks and reduce dependency on local Communist Party contacts, who were regarded as vulnerable. This instruction echoed a signal, sent two years earlier, which was supplied by Vladimir Petrov in Australia on the same subject:

> The aggravation of the international situation and the pressing necessity for the timely exposure and prevention of cunning designs of the enemy, call imperatively for a radical reorganization of all our intelligence work and the urgent operation of an illegal apparatus in Australia which could function uninterruptedly and effectively under any conditions.[14]

Having accepted that illegals are regarded by the KGB and the GRU as essential, and knowing that greater emphasis was placed on their development as early as 1952, it is odd that the British authorities failed to uncover a single case of an illegal until the Portland spy ring was wound up in January 1961, netting 'Gordon Lonsdale' and the two 'Krogers'. Between the arrest of Lonsdale and Reinhard and Sonja Schulze in 1985, no illegals were caught in England. To a counter-intelligence officer making extrapolations from espionage statistics, such an omission is damning. Accordingly the Schulze case, that of a husband-and-wife team of 'sleepers' waiting to be called into play, is something of a coup (see page 197).

More evidence to support the view that the position has improved significantly in recent times is to be found in the perceptible increase in PNGs, most of which must be attributable to Gordievsky's arrival in Britain in June 1982. In the eleven-year period between the mass expulsions of September 1971, based on Lyalin's testimony, and Gordievsky's appointment, there had only been two PNGs, that of

Viktor N. Lazin, a second secretary who was ordered to leave in August 1981, and Vadim F. Zadneprovsky, a GRU officer under trade cover, who went in February 1982. Thereafter, once the new counsellor had settled in, the situation changed quite radically. Captain Anatoli P. Zotov of the GRU was expelled in December 1982, followed closely by Vladimir A. Chernov, a translator at the International Wheat Council in January. At the time Moscow Centre may have blamed the recent defection to the British in October of Vladimir A. Kuzichkin for the sudden change in the KGB's fortunes. It knew that he had been responsible for blowing the cover of his old colleague Oleg S. Zuyenko, who had been thrown out of Tehran in January 1983. But it was not until April 1983, and the announcement that three Soviets were to be expelled, that matters really came to a head. Just before Easter the Foreign Office named three Soviets whose continued presence in London was unacceptable: the assistant air attaché, Colonel Gennady Primakov; a second secretary, Sergei Ivanov; and Igor Titov, the London correspondent of the *New Times* who also happened to be the KGB's deputy *Rezident*. However, there was an unexpected postscript to the episode.

On Easter Sunday itself Michael Bettaney made an approach to the beleaguered KGB *Rezident*, Arkadi Gouk. Although listed as a first secretary, and theoretically subordinate to Gordievsky, their official ranks were reversed in the KGB. Because Bettaney was then employed in MI5's K Branch, the counter-espionage division of the Security Service, and had been working on a reconstruction of the KGB's order-of-battle, he had been able to calculate when to make his pitch without fear of discovery by the surveillance unit. He also knew exactly whom to make his pitch to, because K Branch had already identified Gouk as the KGB *Rezident* in London, thanks to SIS's link with Gordievsky. On the initial occasion Bettaney slipped an envelope through the door of Gouk's apartment in Holland Park, taking advantage of the absence of MI5's watcher team from their static observation post located opposite the building. As for establishing his credentials, Bettaney volunteered information concerning the three Soviets whose expulsion had only just been announced.

Gouk's reaction to this windfall was odd. Instead of following the complex instruction contained in Bettaney's letter explaining how contact should be made, he sought advice from his deputy, who presumably denounced the offer as an obvious provocation. The rest, as they say, is history. SIS conducted a molehunt to track down the would-be traitor, and by September the Security Service had been tipped off to his identity. Gouk was PNG'd in May 1984, following Bettaney's conviction, and Gordievsky was assured that he would succeed Leonid Y. Nikitenko, the new temporary *Rezident*.

By the time Gordievsky was recalled to Moscow in May the following year, four diplomats, a trade official and an Aeroflot employee had been expelled from London. Given the escalation in expulsions in recent years the KGB might well have had good reason to suspect Gordievsky. After his exfiltration, another thirty-seven Soviets were PNG'd. But Gordievsky's value ley not so much in the apalling damage he had inflicted upon the GRU and KGB in London, but the cumulative effect he and Vladimir Kuzichkin had had on Soviet operations throughout the world. The trail of damage in the Department Three area, which included the UK, Scandinavia, Australia and New Zealand, was clear for all to see. During his second tour of duty in Copenhagen, when it is known that he had begun passing information to SIS, four KGB and three GRU officers were expelled and six Soviets were PNG'd in Norway. Further afield there was also the unmistakable signs of well-informed CAZAB counter-intelligence operations. Using the codename REDWOOD, Kuzichkin had been flown to Canberra early in March 1983 to identify the Soviet embassy's first secretary, Valeri Ivanov, as a KGB case officer. Ivanov, who had previously served in the trade delegation to London, had then been watched while he made an attempt to suborn a senior member of the ruling Labour Party. By the middle of the following month he was on a flight back to Moscow, having been caught red-handed.

The worldwide fallout caused by the data supplied by Gordievsky, Kuzichkin and FAREWELL proved catastrophic for the KGB's First Chief Directorate; simultaneously it had the effect of rehabilitating both the French and British services in the eyes of the other Western agencies. As well as the current cases that the three had been able to neutralize, they were able to expose the order-of-battle of practically every *Rezidentura* in the world, making it impossible for the officers concerned to conduct clandestine operations. Within a short time virtually every Soviet controller in the West rated to have any talent had been placed under surveillance by the appropriate security organ, thus rendering the KGB impotent. Truly an extraordinary achievement for the British service which, after all, had endured an unenviable reputation for too long .

British Espionage Cases

Name		Date of Arrest	Date of Conviction	Sentence	Conclusion
WILLSHER	Kathleen	Feb. 1946	4 May 1946	3 yrs	
MAY	Dr Allan Nunn	4 March 1946	1 May 1946	10 yrs	
SQUIRES	Maj. Richard				Defected East Berlin 1947
FUCHS	Dr E. J. Klaus	27 Jan. 1950	10 Feb. 1950	14 yrs	
NAPIER	Neville M.	Oct. 1960	20 Feb. 1951	4 yrs	
MACLEAN	Donald D.				Defected May 1951
BURGESS	Guy F.				Defected May 1951
CAIRNCROSS	John		Not prosecuted		
MARSHALL	William Martin	12 June 1952	June 1952	5 yrs	
CLARENCE	John	Oct. 1954	17 Dec. 1954	5 yrs	
PATCHETT	Cpl. Brian				Defected 2 July 1956
LINNEY	Brian F.	27 May 1958	18 July 1958	14 yrs	
WRAIGHT	Ft Lt Anthony	18 Feb. 1960	1 April 1960	3 yrs	
HOUGHTON	Harry F.	7 Jan. 1961	March 1961	15 yrs	
GEE	Ethel	7 Jan. 1961	March 1961	15 yrs	
KROGER	Peter	7 Jan. 1961	March 1961	20 yrs	Swapped
KROGER	Helen	7 Jan. 1961	March 1961	20 yrs	Swapped
LONSDALE	Gordon	7 Jan. 1961	March 1961	25 yrs	Swapped
BLAKE	George	3 April 1961	3 May 1961	42 yrs	Escaped 23 Oct. 1966
VASSALL	William John	12 Sept. 1962		18 yrs	
FELL	Barbara	30 Sept. 1962	7 Dec. 1962	2 yrs	
PHILBY	H. A. R. (Kim)				Defected Jan. 1963
MARTELLI	Dr Giuseppe	22 April 1963	Acquitted		
BLUNT	Prof. Anthony F.		Not prosecuted		Granted immunity April 1964
LONG	Leo		Not prosecuted		
WATSON	Dr Alister		Not prosecuted		
ROBERTS	Alfred	29 Nov. 1964	Acquitted		
CONWAY	Godfrey	29 Nov. 1964	Acquitted		

Name		Date of Arrest	Date of Conviction	Sentence	Conclusion
BOSSARD	Frank C.	15 March 1965	10 May 1965	21 yrs	
ALLEN	Sgt Percy S.	16 March 1965	10 May 1965	10 yrs	
DORSCHEL	Peter	18 June 1967	19 June 1967	7 yrs	
KEENAN	Helen	25 May 1967	25 July 1967	6 months	
BLACKBURN	Norman	25 May 1967	25 July 1967	5 yrs	
BRITTEN	Douglas	Feb. 1968	4 Nov. 1968	21 yrs	
BLAND	Clive		Feb. 1968	£50 fine	
OWEN	Will	14 Jan. 1970	Acquitted		
STROSS	Sir Barnett				Dead
PRAGER	Nicholas	31 Jan. 1971	14 June 1971	12 yrs	
MARTIANON	Constantinos	9 Sept. 1971	7 Dec. 1971	4 yrs	
COSTI	Kyriacos	9 Sept. 1971	7 Dec. 1971	6 yrs	
ABDOOLCADER	Sirioj H.	17 Sept. 1971	8 Feb. 1972	3 yrs	
HINCHCLIFFE	Leonard M.	11 Oct. 1971	17 April 1972	10 yrs	
BINGHAM	Lt David J.	5 Sept. 1971	13 March 1972	21 yrs	
RITCHIE	Rhona	19 March 1982	29 Nov. 1982	3 months	
PRIME	Geoffrey A.	28 April 1982	10 Nov. 1982	35 yrs	
ALDRIDGE	Cpl Philip L.	27 Nov. 1982	18 Jan. 1983	4 yrs	
HAMBLETON	Prof. Hugh G.	28 June 1982	7 Dec. 1982	10 yrs	
DAVIES	Paul J.	10 Dec. 1983	Acquitted		
BETTANEY	Michael	16 Sept. 1983	16 April 1984	23 yrs	
SCHULZE	Reinhard	27 Aug. 1985	7 July 1986	10 yrs	
SCHULZE	Sonja	27 Aug. 1985	7 July 1986	10 yrs	
BOTHWELL	Cmmdr John	16 Feb. 1986	Acquitted		
VAN HAARLEM	Erwin	2 April 1988	3 March 1989	10 yrs	

Soviet Officials Expelled from Britain

1952	KUZNETSOV, Pavel S.[1]	Second Secretary
1954	GUDKOV, Andrei F.	Air Attaché
	PUPYSHEV, Ivan V.	Air Attaché
1955	BARABANOV, Ivan I.	
1960	TOKAREV, Viktor N.	
1964	SOLOMARTIN, Vladimir I.	Trade Delegation
	SUVOROV, Georgi B.	
	TKACHENKO, Vadim A.	
1965	BOYAROV, Vitali K.	Second Secretary
1968	DUSHKIN, Yuri A.	Trade Delegation
	KUZNETSOV, Anatoli V.	
	LOGINOV, Vladimir A.	Trade Delegation
1970	STANLNOV, Boris C.	Third Secretary
	TYUKHIN, Leonid Y.	
1971	AKIMOV, Anatoli I.[2]	Counsellor
	AKSENOV, Aleksandr P.	
	ALEKSANDROV, Nikolai F.	
	ARTISHEVSKY, Evgenny I.	
	AYKAZYAN, Eduard	
	AZAROV, Ivan P.[3]	
	BARYNIN, Vasili F.	
	BIRYUKOV, Igor D.	Counsellor
	BOBARYKIN, Nikolai B.	Third Secretary
	BREYTIGAM, Mikhail F.	
	BUDANOV, Viktor G.	
	BUNIN, Vladislav	
	CHEREMUKHIN, Yuri S.	Third Secretary
	CHERNETSOV, Yuri Y.	First Secretary
	CHERTVERTUKHIN, Aleksandr N.	
	CHUSOVITIN, Valeri S.	Third Secretary
	DENISKIN, Aleksei N.	
	DYUDIN, Vladimir N.	Attaché
	FILATOV, Vladimir G.[4]	Counsellor
	FILONENKO, Viktor	
	GAMOV, Prokopi I.	First Secretary
	GENERALOV, Vsevelod N.[5]	
	GOLUBOV, Sergei M.[6]	
	GOLYAKOV, Anatoli S.	Attaché

GORLENKO, Evgenny Y.	
GRESKO, Aleksandr A.	Third Secretary
IVANOV, Anatoli N.	
KABATOV, Yuri B.	
KARELIN, Vladislav B.	Third Secretary
KARYAGIN, Viktor V.	Counsellor
KASHLEV, Yuri B.	Counsellor
KHMYZ, Vasili P.	Attaché
KLIMOV, Igor K.	Second Secretary
KOLODYAZHNY, Boris G.[7]	Counsellor
KOLYCHEV, Yuri K.	
KOMAROVSKY, Fedor P.	
KONDRATENKO, Yuri A.	First Secretary
KONSTANTINOV, Igor K.	
KOPEYKIN, Gennadi N.	
KORNYENKO, Yuri F.	
KOROBOV, Yuri I.	
KOTUSOV, Aleksandr I.	Attaché
KRYKUNOV, Nikolai K.	Second Secretary
KULIKOV, Ivan A.	Second Secretary
KUTUZOV, Evgenni I.	Second Secretary
KUZIN, Evgenni F.	Third Secretary
KUZMIN, Lori T.	Ass. Naval Attaché
KUZNETSOV, Georgi A.	Counsellor
KUZNETSOV, Yuri A.	
KVARDAKOV, A.P.	
LAPTEV, Igor K.	First Secretary
LAVKOVSKY, Yuri I.	
LAVROV, Valeri A.	
LAZAREV, Oleg B.	
LEONOV, Vladimir A.	
LEONTIEV, Leonid A.	Attaché
MAKARENKO, Boris V.	Second Secretary
MELNIK, Vladimir I.	Attaché
MESHKOV, Boris P.	Third Secretary
MOROZOV, Yuri V.	Third Secretary
OROBINSKY, Anatoli P.	Third Secretary
PANIN, Yuri I.	
PANKOVSKY, Viktor M.	Third Secretary
PAVLOV, Lev A.	

PEREBILLO, Boris D.
PETROVICHEV, Leonid Y.   Attaché
PETROVICHEVA, Emilya A.
POSINIKOVA, Lyudmila A.   Attaché
PRONIN, Vasili I.   Second Secretary
PROSHIN, Dmitri
PUSHKIN, Vladimir A.
RAGOZKHIN, Ivan P.
ROGOV, Leonid A.   First Secretary
RUNKOV, Aleksandr
SAKOV, Vladimir Y.
SAYENKO, Sergei   Journalist, Radio
                           Moscow
SEMENENKO, Stanislav N.   First Secretary
SEPELEV, Yuri F.   Counsellor
SERGEYEV, Yuri P.
SHERSTNEV, Lev N.
SIMBURTSEVA, Ludmila S.
SLEPOV, Aleksandr V.
SOIDRA, Ivo-Aat A.   Second Secretary
SOKOLOV, Sergei N.
SOROKIN, Dmitri I.   Second Secretary
TER-SARKISOV, Yuri M.
TROITSKY, Anatoli P.
TSUTSKOV, Nikolai
USTENKO, Eduard V.   Second Secretary
VASICHEV, Gennadi N.
VAYGAUSKAS, Richardas K.[8]   Vice-Consul
VEKLENKO, Viktor T.   Third Secretary
VISKOV, Y.N.
VORONIN, Yuri N.   Counsellor
YASAKOV, Viacheslav A.[9]   Third Secretary
YASHCHENKO, Anatoli A.   Third Secretary
YURASOV, Viktor V.
ZAVORIN, Ivan P.
ZELENEV, Vladimir A.
ZHERNOV, Leonid A.
ZHURAVLEV, Gennadi A.   Second Secretary
ZOLOTAREV, Artur
ZOTOV, Konstantin L.   Second Secretary

	ZOTOV, Viktor N.	
1972	SOKOLOV, Vladimir M.	
1981	LAZIN, Viktor N.	Second Secretary
1982	ZADNEPROVSKY, Vadim F.	Trade Delegation
	ZOTOV, Captain Anatoli P.	Naval Attaché
1983	CHERNOV, Vladimir A.	International Wheat Council
	IVANOV, Sergei	Second Secretary
	PROMAKOV, Colonel Gennadi	Air Attaché
	TITOV, Igor	Journalist, *New Times*
1984	GOUK, Arkadi V.	First Secretary
1985	BELAVENTSEV, Oleg Y.	Third Secretary
	BOGHDANOV, Mikhail Y.	Journalist, *Socialist Industry*
	CHERKASOV, Lt-Col Vadim	Military Attaché
	DARANOV, Viktor V.	Clerk
	GORELOV, Aleksandr T.	Embassy driver
	GRIGOROV, Vyacheslav	Aeroflot
	IPATOV, Valeri V.	Moscow Narodny Bank
	KALITIN, Vyecheslav I.	First Secretary
	KHOMUTOV, Igor F.	Technical
	KODINTSEV, Aleksandr A.	Novosti
	KOMOV, Yuri P.	Trade Delegation
	KORCHAGIN, Boris A.	First Secretary
	KOTOV, Valeri A.	Razno
	KRASAKOV, Oleg P.	Trade Delegation
	KUDIMOV, Yuri A.	Journalist, *Komsomolskaya Pravda*
	LOGUSH, Viktor O.	Trade Delegation
	LOS, Captain Oleg A.	Naval Attaché
	LYUBENKO, Vladimir I.	Trade Delegation
	MERELIKOV, Anatoli N.	Third Secretary
	MISHIN, Colonel Viktor A.	Air Attaché
	MISHUSTIN, Vyacheslav D.	Embassy guard
	MUZALEV, Viktor I.	TASS
	PEREPELKIN, Eduard V.	Trade Delegation
	PROKOPCHIK, Valeri V.	Trade Delegation
	ROZHKOV, Yuri P.	International Cocoa Organization
	SAFRONOV, Evgenny I.	First Secretary

	SAVENKO, Sergei I.	Journalist, Radio Moscow
	SAVVALEYEV, Mikhail D.	International Wheat Council
	TIMOFAYEV, Viktor V.	Trade Delegation
	TOKAR, Valeriy G.	Second Secretary
	VASILEYV, Dmitri M.	Attaché
	VIKULOV, Ivan I.	Anglo-Soviet Shipping
	VOLOVETS, Sergei A.	Journalist, Novosti
	YEZHOV, Yuri	First Secretary
	YEROKHIN, Aleksandr I.	Clerk
	ZAIKIN, Captain Viktor	Naval Attaché
1989	BAGIN, A. A.	Driver
	KOLODIN, Col Nikolai L.	Assistant Air Attaché
	KUDASHKIN, I. A.	Trade Delegation
	KUZNETSOV, Sergei V.	Third Secretary
	MAKARUKOV, Aleksandr V.	Attaché
	SMIRNOV, Lt-Col Evgenny A.	Assistant Air Attaché
	TUEV, Nikolai G.	Third Secretary
	ZHILTSOV, Mikhail G.	Assistant Naval Attaché
	KUZMIN, Igor M.	First Secretary
	PESKOV, Igor N.	TASS
	SAGAYDAK, Yuri P.	*Komsomolskaya Pravda*
	KOZLOV, Col Viktor I.	Military Attaché
	MARSHANKIN, Major A. G.	Assistant Military Attaché
	NOVOZHILOV, Sergei I.	Trade Delegation

7

La Piscine

> 'In secret services there needs to be an impec-
> cable code of conduct and extremely strict
> discipline.'
>
> Comte de Marenches, Director of SDECE
> 1970–81

Since April 1981, the French secret intelligence service has been known as the *Direction Générale de Sécurité Extérieur* (DGSE), but to insiders the organization has always been referred to as 'La Piscine' because of the proximity of its bleak, ten-storey headquarters, behind a walled compound at 128 Boulevard Mortier, to the local municipal swimming-pool in the rue de Tourelle, in north-east Paris.

The DGSE's change in name from SDECE was one of a series of reforms introduced by the then Director-General, Pierre Marion, an Air France executive who replaced the long-serving Alexandre de Marenches when the Socialists won the French general election in 1981. The SDECE's first Director-General had been André Dewavrin, de Gaulle's legendary intelligence chief, who masterminded resistance operations in France from London throughout the war. Like many of his contemporaries who had left families behind in enemy-occupied territory, Dewavrin adopted the *nom de guerre* of a Paris subway station, PASSY. In January 1942, de Gaulle placed him in overall charge of the *Bureau Central de Renseignements et d'Action* (BCRA), which combined the responsibilities of the two

154

Chiefs of the French Intelligence Service

SDECE

Henri Ribière	1946–51
Pierre Boursicot	1951–7
General Paul Grossin	1957–62
General Eugene Guibaud	1966–70
General Paul Jacquier	1962–6
Alexandre de Marenches	1970–81

DGSE (from 4 April 1982)

Pierre Marion	1981–2
Admiral Pierre Lacoste	1982–5
General René Imbot	1985–7
General François Mermet	1987–9
Claude Silberzahn	1989–

---

old French agencies, the *Deuxième Bureau* and the *Service de Renseignements*.

Soon after the end of hostilities Dewavrin, who had previously taught at the military academy at St Cyr, returned to the regular army, and a leading Socialist politician, Henri Ribière, took over the headquarters of the BCRA (which had become the SDECE in 1946), then located in the Avenue Henri Martin. One of Ribière's first acts was to have Dewavrin arrested for embezzlement of the BCRA's funds, which where discovered in a series of bank accounts in England. The SDECE Chief of Station in London, Captain Lahana, who was implicated in the misappropriation, attempted suicide. Dewavrin spent four months in military detention while the financial scandal simmered, and was then released . The investigation established that Dewavrin had not used the secret funds for his own use, but had arranged a huge loan to *France Soir* in return for the newspaper's support of de Gaulle. Dewavrin later demanded a judicial review of his imprisonment, which was ruled illegal, and he was reinstated with the rank of colonel, only to resign from the army early in 1948. In clearing him the Justice Minister announced that 'counter-intelligence is not conducted by altar boys...and Colonel Dewavrin must not be judged by the same standards as other civil servants'.[1]

SDECE Organization

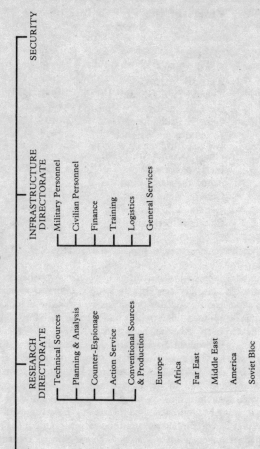

To make the affair all the more unpalatable, Ribière was badly injured when the brakes failed on his car, which was being driven at high speed. Sabotage was suspected, but never proved, and one of those thought responsible was Ribière's own ambitious deputy, Colonel Pierre Fourcaud. Although Ribière was not expected to emerge from a coma, he did so and continued to head the SDECE until the appointment of Pierre Boursicot, Director of the *Sûreté*, in 1951.

While all secret intelligence services occasionally have to endure an uncomfortable public exposure which brings them into disrepute whenever there is an embarrassing incident, SDECE appears to have experienced rather more unfortunate incidents than most parallel organizations. It acquired a particularly unsavoury reputation while fighting colonial wars, especially in Algeria, throughout the post-war period, and there have been examples of SDECE interference in domestic politics.

Twelve years after the PASSY business, events were to repeat themselves when the SDECE officer responsible for interrogating Dewavrin, Louis Favert, was himself embroiled in a scandal, which involved unvouchered funds being transferred to Swiss accounts and then being used for political purposes.

Even before *l'affaire PASSY*, French intelligence had a long history marked by controversy. In January 1941, two intelligence officers planted forged documents on de Gaulle's deputy, Admiral Emile Muselier, which suggested that he was collaborating with the Vichy regime and preparing to hand over a Free French submarine to them. He was promptly arrested by the British, but released from prison eight days later when the two plotters, named Collin and Howard, both Dewavrin's subordinates, were identified.

Another awkward incident occurred in December 1942, when a BCRA agent named Dufour escaped from custody at a Free French camp at Camberley and instituted legal proceedings against de Gaulle and Dewavrin alleging false imprisonment and torture. The case was settled out of court, but may have contributed to the lurid stories that circulated about the bodies of suspected collaborators buried in the basement of Dewavrin's headquarters at 10 Duke Street.

In subsequent years these embarrassments seemed mild indiscretions in comparison to the scale of SDECE fiascos that dogged successive French administrations. The scandals ranged from systemized assassination, kidnapping, penetration by Soviet agents and Corsican gangsters to international drug dealing. The catalogue of well-publicized débâcles is impressive, yet no French government ever fell because of SDECE's nefarious activities. Among the more notorious operations undertaken by SDECE were the ruthless *Barbouze* campaign conducted against the OAS, the 'Red Hand' assassination of German arms dealers during the Algerian war, the hijacking of Ahmed Ben Bella in 1955 and the kidnapping of Mehdi Ben Barka a decade later. Also worthy of mention is the indictment of Colonel Paul Fournier and Roger Delouette in April 1971 for importing ninety-six pounds of heroin into Port Elizabeth, New Jersey, and the arrest of André Lebay in France in similar circumstances. All three were SDECE officers of long standing. There was also SDECE involvement in the Marković affair, prompted by the unsolved murder of Alain Delon's Yugoslav bodyguard, who was himself widely thought to have been blackmailing Madame Pompidou, wife of the future president.

No French political scandal is considered complete unless there is an intelligence connection, and SDECE has rarely disappointed the conspiracy theorists. Yet the paradox of only a handful of ministerial resignations over the years is evidence that the French public are quite prepared to countenance even the most dubious enterprises, especially those like the sabotage of the *Rainbow Warrior* that are perceived to have furthered French national interests abroad. Even the Red Hand episode, a counter-terror campaign waged under SDECE's sponsorship, which is estimated to have caused the death of fourteen people and sunk five ships, did not stimulate much public debate.

French casualties from SDECE 'blowbacks' have been minimal. There were some resignations from Guy Mollet's government when Ben Bella was abducted en route between Morocco and Tunisia, and General Paul Jacquier took early retirement when a SDECE officer was implicated in Mehdi Ben Barka's disappearance in 1965. President de Gaulle also transferred responsibility for SDECE from the Prime Minister's Office to the Ministry of Defence. Similarly, Admiral Pierre Lacoste was forced to go for conspiring against Greenpeace in 1985.

In all of these incidents there was a complete absence of public outrage – in France at least. The Ben Bella affair was a skilful operation in which the King of Morocco's personal Super Constellation was diverted to Algiers while taking the Algerian resistance leader to an Arab League Summit in Tunis. When the plane landed it was stormed by French troops, who took the future president of an independent Algeria into custody. He was eventually released from Fresnes and flown to Geneva, but only after elaborate measures had been taken to protect him from assassination. At one stage Ben Bella was disguised as a gendarme, with one of de Gaulle's own bodyguards playing out his role.

SDECE's part in the Ben Barka imbroglio was at the request of General Mohammed Oufkir, the Moroccan Director of Security. Ben Barka, an exiled trade union leader and opponent of King Hassan's regime, was snatched off the streets of Paris by two SDECE agents in October 1965 and taken to Oufkir's villa in the suburbs, where, allegedly, he was tortured and then murdered. His body was never recovered, but as a result of the investigation that followed, Oufkir was permanently banned from returning to France. This, of course, was mere window-dressing, for SDECE's relationship with Hassan (and Mossad, which also had a hand in the operation) was actually enhanced.

Twenty years later SDECE's successor, the DGSE, was indulging in not dissimilar antics in New Zealand, when three teams of agents were dispatched to the Pacific with instructions to disrupt Greenpeace's anti-nuclear demonstrations. The operation culminated in the successful sinking of the *Rainbow Warrior* and the accidental death of a photographer, who had returned to the crippled ship to rescue his equipment. This tragic and unforeseen development prompted a major police enquiry in New Zealand and led to the arrest of two DGSE officers, Alain Mafart and Dominique Prieur. Despite the fact that both incriminated themselves in a very amateur fashion, the French government negotiated their releases from long terms of imprisonment.

But it is not the DGSE's proclivity for covert action, or its unsavoury past, that causes it to be treated as an outsider, if not a leper, by other Western intelligence agencies. It cannot be obvious indiscretion either, although Alexandre de Marenches, the SDECE chief until 1981, and Jean Rochet, Director of the domestic security apparatus, *Direction de la Surveillance du Territoire* (DST), until November 1972, have both written their memoirs.[2] Neither book is particularly illuminating and they certainly avoid breaching security.

The key to understanding the West's troubled relationship with the DGSE lies in the French political climate and the case of Jacques Paques, deputy head of NATO's press department, who was arrested in August 1963 in the act of supplying Vasili Vlassov with copious quantities of secret material.[3] France subsequently left NATO, much to the relief of the West's counterintelligence authorities, who had learned from Golitsyn that the country's administration was riddled with Soviet sources. Golitsyn's allegations were taken very seriously, and not just by the CIA's Counterintelligence Staff. One of those shaken by Golitsyn's charges of high-level penetration was SDECE's representative in Washington, Philippe Thyraud de Vosjoli. He was appalled by the evidence, as was General Temple de Rougemont, who was flown out with a team of five hand-picked experts especially to debrief the defector. Drawn from SDECE and the DST, they represented the most trusted men from inside the French intelligency community: the current DST Director, Daniel Doustin; Marcel Chalet, who would head the DST from 1975–1982; Louis Niquet; and Colonel René Delseny, then director of SDECE's counter-espionage section. Together they were introduced to Golitsyn by Jim Angleton. To their undisguised horror, the Soviet defector described a network, codenamed COLUMBINE, boasting a dozen SDECE officers which even reached into the Elysée Palace, and identified Jacques Foccart, de Gaulle's principal intelligence adviser, as a Soviet mole. Foccart was able to refute the claim, but there were other suspects too.[4]

Although the Paques case was something of a watershed for Allied–French relations, it would be incorrect to imply that all of NATO's woes were entirely centred on Paris. The organization has always been leaky, and it has experienced a series of spy scandals. Francis Roussilhe, who headed the International Secretariat's registry, was later exposed as a source for the Romanians, and Nahat Imre of NATO's financial section, a Turk arrested in 1968, had been working for the KGB for nearly twenty years. Ursel Lorenzen, who defected to East Germany in March 1979, had been betraying NATO secrets from its headquarters, where she had been employed as a secretary since 1966.

Golitsyn's observations about NATO were recognized as 'true bills' by the CIA, but the French seemed unenergetic, to say the least, in pursuing his leads. For example, Colonel René Bertrand, then head of SDECE's Research Directorate, was one of those suspected of being in the pay of the KGB, but no evidence was found against him and he continued in this post until removed in a purge organized by Marenches in 1970. Another possible mole, Colonel Charles d'Anfreville, threw himself out of a window in August 1969, when the DST arrived to interrogate him.

Golitsyn was able to demonstrate the depth of his knowledge of SDECE by telling de Rougement and de Vosjoli of changes that had been made in the organization since it had been restructured in 1958. He recalled having attended a lecture given by General Aleksandr Sakharovsky of the First Chief Directorate in July the following year in which the recent modifications had been outlined. He had also been able to establish his credentials by pointing out the fakes when presented with a mixture of forged and authentic NATO documents. As a consequence of Golitsyn's information, and SDECE's evident reluctance to take swift action, de Vosjoli took up temporary residence in Mexico after his tour of duty had ended and is now regarded in Paris as a defector to the US. One of the matters that prompted his desertion in November 1963 was the fulfilment of a prediction made by Golitsyn. During his debriefing he had mentioned a new super-secret unit within SDECE to gather military and scientific intelligence in the US, targeting specific areas of research that would assist France's independent nuclear deterrent. This tale was dismissed at the time, but when de Vosjoli returned to Paris in December 1962 for consultations with Colonel Marcel Mareuil, who was then in charge of liaison with foreign agencies, he discovered the defector had been right all along. To de Vosjoli's horror, Mareuil had proceeded to indoctrinate him into SDECE's new plan to build up networks within US military installations, in much the same way that Golitsyn had described. Needless to say de Vosjoli, who had enjoyed American hospitality in Washington since his arrival in April 1951, was appalled by the proposal. He guessed correctly that if the CIA ever supposed Golitsyn had been telling the truth, Franco–American relations, which he had worked so assiduously to develop, particularly during the Cuban crisis, would be gravely damaged, probably irreversibly. He was right. Even after Georges Paques had confessed to having worked for the Russians since 1944, none of Golitsyn's other claims had been investigated by SDECE. As de Vosjoli remarked, 'not a question was asked; no one wanted to know about other Soviet agents'.[5]

Nor was that the only reason for de Vosjoli to be anxious about

SDECE. He had played a crucial role in the build-up to the Cuban missile crisis by channelling information from his most reliable source in Cuba to the CIA. Somewhat against his will, de Vosjoli had been told to disclose his agent's identity to headquarters. A short time later, the Cuban was arrested and put on trial,[6] where his relationship with de Vosjoli had been accurately described by the prosecutor. There was also the cirumstantial implications of sensitive codeword intelligence that had been circulated in Washington under the cryptonym ARNIKA. De Vosjoli had passed some ARNIKA to Paris, only to learn that its source, Colonel Oleg Penkovsky, had come under Soviet control a short time later.

De Vosjoli's doubts about SDECE's integrity were compounded by some of the appointments made by General Paul Jacquier after he assumed command in 1962. He placed Colonel Leonard Hounou in overall charge of intelligence operations, apparently unaware that Hounou was widely thought to have been compromised by an attractive woman in a classic KGB honeytrap when he had been military attaché in Prague during the 1950s. One of Hounou's adversaries in SDECE was Georges de Lannurien, who had also served in the French embassy in Prague soon after the war and had lost most of an important network of agents. The exact circumstances of the disaster were unclear, but de Lannurien had been retained by Henri Ribière against the advice of his director of counter-espionage, Colonel Roger Lafont. There was no love lost between the two men, and eventually both were fired. None of Golitsyn's twelve spies was ever found, although Jacques Blaret, who worked on the staff of the SDECE representative in Prague, was arrested in 1967 and charged with passing secrets to the Czech STB.

De Vosjoli spent a year in Mexico dodging SDECE hit-teams before he returned to the CIA's protection and was resettled at Kendall, just outside Miami, in classic defector style, complete with a new identity. None of this inspired much confidence in SDECE, and it was gradually eased out of the informal Allied counter-intelligence exchanges that had been a characteristic of Western liaisons before the inception of CAZAB, from which the French have always been excluded. Mutual transatlantic mistrust was heightened after these events when the Canadians found evidence of covert SDECE activities on their territory. Worse still, they had good reason to believe that a couple of SDECE's illicit operations in Canada had been undertaken at Soviet behest. Was this RCMP paranoia or a manifestation of KGB penetration of SDECE? The CIA decided not to take any risks.

In recent years the French have taken steps to ingratiate themselves with their old allies. The purge mounted by Alexandre de Marenches when he took office in 1970 got rid of many officers associated with SDECE's embarrassments. Bertrand was one of the first to go, along with Colonel Jacques Hervé, the new head of counter-espionage who had only just returned to Paris from SDECE's liaison post in New York. Other victims included Colonel Paul Durand; Benoit Jeantet, the head of Special Operations; Colonel Bauchet; the technical services director, Major Callot; and his deputy, Captain Le Roy. Their departure was to have far-reaching consequences, but it would not be for some years that necessity forced improved liaison, at least between the DGSE, SDECE's new Socialist name, and the CIA.

What made the French suddenly more attractive were two separate events: certain breakthroughs achieved by the DGSE's cryptographic arm, the *Groupement de Contrôles Radio-électrique* (GCR), and a KGB walk-in at the DST's headquarters at 11 rue des Saussaies. The GCR is the equivalent of the NSA or GCHQ and is based at Domme in the Dordogne. Whether the GCR agreed to pool resources at one of its overseas intercept stations, or offered to share a certain product, cannot be ascertained, but more is known about the spy codenamed FAREWELL, mainly due to Yurchenko's helpful testimony.

The French had certainly not achieved much success with running Eastern Bloc sources. The one that lasted longest, a Czech named Pavel Sirodine, was executed by firing squad at Kharkov in 1968. But FAREWELL was really quite remarkable and undoubtedly authentic, because he was able to reveal the KGB's latest strategy: the illicit purchase, or theft, of Western technology. FAREWELL provided more than 4,000 documents from Directorate T, the scientific and technical branch of the elite First Chief Directorate, which showed how the KGB had collaborated with other components of Moscow's bureaucracy to target specific items in the electronics field. A secret acquisition section of the *Voenno Promyshlennaya Kossissiya*, the Soviet Military–Industrial Commission (the VPK), had been set up and agents dispatched abroad to buy or steal embargoed scientific *matériel*. It was industrial espionage on a grand scale, according to FAREWELL, who had a French middleman or 'cut-out' act as a courier and hand-deliver his first communication to the DST sometime in the spring of 1981. This initial letter was quite exceptional because FAREWELL identified himself as a senior Line X officer who had previously served in Paris in the 1960s. He gave some biographical details that matched data stored by the DST and pledged to supply further information in due course. No price was asked for, and the DST concluded that the source was probably the nostalgic Francophile he claimed to be, who was preparing his meal-ticket before defecting and retiring in the sun. During the following eighteen months FAREWELL kept his promise, and the DST was inundated with Soviet secrets on a scale that had not been seen in the West since Penkovsky. Then, in November 1982, as suddenly as the case had begun, FAREWELL went silent. A rumour circulated in Moscow that a senior KGB officer had been involved in a scandal. Apparently, he had rowed with his mistress, got drunk and then in a panic shot dead a member of the Moscow militia who had approached his car. The full details did not emerge for another three years, when Yurchenko told the CIA how FAREWELL had been sentenced to a long term of imprisonment for the policeman's murder.[7] Filled with remorse, FAREWELL had hinted at an even greater crime in a letter from his cell that was routinely intercepted and read. Yurchenko had been one of the KGB interrogators who had extracted a confession from FAREWELL, a statement that was to land him in front of a firing squad.

The DST responded to the loss of FAREWELL by compiling a massive dossier, which was circulated throughout the West, exposing the Line X operations in France. It led to the expulsion, on 3 April 1983, of forty-seven Soviet diplomats and the arrests of several unscrupulous East–West traders, who had been identified by FARE-WELL as having been active in illicit technology transfers.

Pierre Bourdiol, a sixty-six-year-old engineer with the huge Thomson conglomerate, who had been working on sensitive projects such as the Ariane European rocket, admitted to having supplied industrial secrets to the KGB for ideological reasons since 1970. FAREWELL also suggested that there was a senior KGB source inside Messerschmitt, but it took the BfV eighteen months to identify Manfred Rotsch, a chief engineer, as the spy. Rotsch confessed that he had worked for the KGB for the past seventeen years, and had used a miniature camera to photograph details of the Tornado fighter and an anti-tank missile he had helped design. His arrest by the BfV was regarded as a major coup, probably the most important spy identified in the Federal Republic since Gunter Guillaume back in April 1974.

Nor were all FAREWELL's tips restricted to Europe. Two important leads were taken up by the FBI and resulted in arrests. They both centred on sources run for the KGB by the Polish SB. FAREWELL described how Directorate T case officers would travel to Warsaw to collect huge quantities of classified documents, and he recalled that on one occasion, in June 1980, it had taken a team of five UB technicians all night to sort and copy the papers they had been sold. Much of the information concerned intercontinental ballistic missile defences and, in particular, the Minuteman project. There were enough clues in FAREWELL's reports to point to James D. Harper, a retired electrical engineer living in California. Harper's wife Louise had worked at a defence contractor, Systems Control, until her death early in 1983, and this company was the only common denominator in the material acquired by the UB. After his arrest, Harper admitted being paid $250,000 for classified data by Zdzislaw Przychodzien, a UB officer working under Polish Ministry of Machine Industry cover. Apparently, Louise Harper had allowed her husband access to secret material at weekends, and he had made the most of his opportunities.

The FBI also ran a separate investigation, in tandem with the Control Systems leak, into advanced radar research then being undertaken by the Hughes Aircraft Company on a US government contract. FAREWELL had learned of a technique known as 'silent radar', which was then in the experimental stage and allowed radar signals to be transmitted in an undetectable form. Hughes hoped to develop a system that would transform the electronic countermeasures market, but, according to the French, the KGB was monitoring every advance made. A molehunt ensued, and a Hughes engineer named William H. Bell, who had filed for bankruptcy in July 1976, was discovered to have found a new source of wealth, enough to finance regular visits to Europe. On 23 June 1983, Bell was confronted at work by the FBI and told that he had been betrayed by a Polish defector, an intelligence officer who had been operating under UN cover. Bell accepted this tale and promptly admitted his guilt. He then implicated his illegal controller, Marian Zacharski, and agreed to wear a microphone at their next rendezvous so that he could be caught too. Five days later Zacharski, who was supposedly the West Coast manager of Poland's state trading agency, engaged in an incriminating conversation with Bell and was arrested. Bell was sentenced to eight years' imprisonment and Zacharski received life. After FAREWELL's execution, Zacharski was exchanged in a spy swap and returned to Poland.

The dossier accumulated by FAREWELL's handlers had extraordinary implications. The return to 'leapfrog development' had enabled the Soviets to copy the infra-red guidance system of the Redeye and Stinger missiles, without doing the initial research. The BL-B bomber had been duplicated in the Soviet *Blackjack*, and the Antonov 72 transport bore a strong resemblance to the Boeing YC-14. There was also reason to believe that the US Navy's Mark 48 torpedo had been reproduced and that the USAF Awacs airborne radar technology had been borrowed for the Soviet equivalent. But not all the information bought by Directorate T had a military application. FAREWELL named Aleksandr Zaitsev as a Line X specialist attached to the Paris *Rezidentura*. Surveillance by the DST showed him to be in touch with a petro-chemicals analyst named Patrick Guerrier, who was then based at the state research centre in Paris studying the latest methods of exploiting underground gas deposits, a subject of considerable interest to the Kremlin. Guerrier was arrested on 30 March 1983 and was later sentenced to five years' imprisonment for his indiscretion; Zaitsev was one of the forty-seven Soviets expelled a few days later.

The FAREWELL episode had the effect of rehabilitating the French intelligence community in the eyes of other Western agencies, because it showed that the DST could run a Soviet agent successfully, a skill that had not been exercised much in the past. It also showed that the French could keep a secret, which was also something of a departure, and the expulsion of so many Soviet diplomats demonstrated a political resolve that had been entirely absent previously. In the West's perception, the DGSE's interests lay not in the East but in Africa, where puppet regimes had been supported and coups mounted occasionally to topple leaders who had fallen from favour in Paris. The sabotage of a Corsican separatist radio transmitter in Elba in 1980 illustrated that SDECE was still prepared to go to considerable lengths to achieve the Elysée Palace's dubious objectives, and the failures of its determined attempts to overthrow Ahmet Sékou-Touré in Guinea in April 1960, November 1965 and April 1974 were surely proof that SDECE did not enjoy a monopoly on wisdom or resources in the region, as many believed. Neverthless, both the CIA and SIS would admit that such a small organization, employing less than 2,000 civilian and military personnel, with an estimated budget of $50 million, can get results. SDECE is credited with having correctly forecast the date of the Yom Kippur War in 1973 and accurately predicted the Soviet invasion of Afghanistan in 1979. In addition, it greatly enhanced its influence by assisting the Saudis to resist an attack on the Grand Mosque in Mecca in November 1979. SDECE's willingness instantly to airlift highly sophisticated logistical support to the trouble, backed by a team of specialist advisers to supervise the equipment's deployment, won the organization many friends. The price paid, in the West, was the accusation that SDECE's Director, Alexandre de Marenches, had developed too close a relationship with the Arabs, and in particular Sadoun Chaker, then Chief of the Iraqi Secret Intelligence Service.

SDECE's separation from too close involvement with purely partisan undertakings was supposed to be one of the gains flowing from the 1965 decision to place SDECE under the Ministry of Defence; yet, as events twenty years later were to prove, the move simply switched responsibility for SDECE from one politician to another. The *Rainbow Warrior* saga was to raise numerous points of principle, both operational and political, that have not received wide consideration outside the DGSE, even though the background to the episode itself is quite well known.

In brief, a long-term clandestine surveillance operation had been underway for some years to protect French nuclear testing in the Pacific from interference by protesters. Alexandre de Marenches, who retired in June 1981, states that 'in my time we organized a number of operations in which the people seeking to monitor our experiments encountered mechanical problems ... a few backhanders made sure that a large number of boats suffered breakdowns and damage, but there were never any deaths. Never! That is counter-productive – the work of amateurs.'[8] This disposes of the suggestions mooted from time to time that the Greenpeace incident was a one-off accident. It was part of a larger, longer strategy, and 'if these exercises were not talked about, it was because they were successful'.[9] It is also clear that even though the DGSE had got rid of the so-called 'Action Services' that had given it such a notorious reputation, it had not dispensed with the concept of plausible deniability. In the event, several senior officials, including the Director, Admiral Pierre Lacoste, and even a politician, Defence Minister Charles Hernu, paid the price for failure, but not for lack of attempted cover-ups.

The operation itself had been prepared with considerable skill. An experienced agent, Christine Cabon, had been infiltrated into Greenpeace to conduct a reconnaissance and had left the scene in May 1985, well before the sabotage teams arrived the following month. Altogether eight DGSE saboteurs were involved, including Louis-Pierre Dillais, commandant of the underwater combat school at Aspretto in Corsica, and Colonel Jean-Claude Lesquier, head of the Action Division since November 1984. All had good cover and took textbook precautions to avoid gathering together or establishing a link between themselves. The main team of three petty officers sailed to New Zealand on a chartered yacht with a contract agent, Dr Xavier Maniguet, who convincingly played the role of a wealthy playboy on vacation. Their support group, consisting of Commander Alain Mafart and Captain Dominique Prieur, masqueraded as a pair of Swiss honeymooners, while the overall mission co-ordinator, Lieutenant-Colonel Dillais, moved about independently from his base, a room on the seventh floor of the Hyatt Kingsgate Hotel in Auckland, which conveniently overlooked the harbour.

The *Rainbow Warrior* docked in Auckland on 7 July, and within forty-eight hours two limpet mines with delayed action fuses had been placed in position. The sabotage team were on board the *Ouvea*, well out of territorial waters and en route to Norfolk Island when the explosive charges went off on the evening of 10 July, accidentally killing a member of the ship's crew, Fernando Pereira. Those remaining in New Zealand, Dillais, Mafart and Prieur, were supposed to continue their leisurely holidays and then fly home some ten days later after the initial fuss had died down. Such clues that had been left behind, notably an abandoned Zodiac dinghy used to carry the frogmen and their mines close to the target, could not be traced to anywhere incriminating. Although the inflatable was French-made, it had been bought for cash in London by one of the team who had used a false name when checking into his hotel for a single night. They had covered their tracks with commendable professionalism and probably would have gone undetected, but for a vigilant local resident who had spotted the wet-suited saboteurs loading equipment aboard Mafart's rented Toyota van. Suspecting he was watching thieves who had been looting yachts moored in the harbour, the witness made a note of the van's registration number and reported the incident to the local police.

But for the complete absence of clues and suspects, this lead might have been overlooked: the police were grasping at straws when they traced the rented van to the two Swiss honeymooners. There was still no evidence of their involvement in the sabotage, but at a critical point Mafart's tradecraft failed. His and Prieur's cover story held up well, but he was in difficulties when he was asked why, if he was on vacation, he had kept a detailed record of his expenditure. Mafart replied glibly that it was simply force of habit. But if he was not on business, challenged his interrogator, why had he deliberately falsified some of his hotel receipts? There would be no purpose in exaggerating his expenses unless he was going to reclaim them. Mafart lapsed into silence and later made a telephone call to an unlisted number, at La Piscine. When the Auckland police asked their French counterparts to trace the number in Paris, they were told that it did not exist. Thus, one quite avoidable lapse identified Mafart as at least a conspirator, and another then betrayed an official French involvement.

The DGSE has repeatedly tried to divert attention away from these awkward blunders by implying that other forces were at work to ensure the operation failed. De Marenches, for example, suggested that the Zodiac was bought in London from 'a salesman who was either a *bona-fide* opposite number in the British services, or a reserve officer in the same Service...that was not a mistake – it was a provocation!'[10] In fact, the proprietor of the shop had no intelligence connections, and the British played no part in undermining the operation because they were never in a position to do so. De Marenches has also hinted darkly that 'somebody has made use of the Greenpeace Affair. I would not go so far as to maintain it was the Russians',[11] which is his way of suggesting exactly that, adding that 'certain appointments and sackings in 1981 destabilized the organization to a dangerous degree'. In reality, the operation's failure was caused by nothing more complex than sheer ineptitude on Mafart's part.

Up until the *Rainbow Warrior* fiasco, the DGSE was kept on a very loose rein by its ministerial masters and funds had been administered by the Service itself, having been cleared on a quarterly basis by the Director-General with the Prime Minister. Extra expenditure had been available with the authority of the President, a procedure that in practice had been handled at private secretary level. The Greenpeace scandal raised serious questions about the way the DGSE spent its budget and doubts about political account-ability, after the official Tricot enquiry had virtually exonerated everyone from involvement. As one might expect, de Marenches has strong views on the issue, asserting loftily that

> matters relating to the Special Services are, by definition, apolitical: they pertain neither to the left nor to the right, but to a much higher plane, that of the French nation. ... The question of whether those in power in France should be able to act with total impunity in such matters, without scrutiny by Parliament or any sort of monitoring, is very hard to answer. The Americans, more particularly the Carter administration, were responsible for the break-up of the CIA. They succeeded in doing, in a few short years, what the KGB could never have achieved even in its wildest dreams. They presided over the self-destruction of the American Services, including the FBI.[12]

This interpretation of the metamorphosis experienced by the CIA is hardly borne out by the facts, but it does reveal an attitude that is uniquely French and explains why the French public was largely unmoved by the affair, and no government fell because of the furore. In the US, Watergate was enough to destroy a president, even though the central issue concerned a burglary, not a murder; and in London, a mere call-girl scandal, involving a politician who was not even of Cabinet seniority, proved sufficient to topple an admin-istration that had been in power for thirteen years. De Marenches remained convinced that the Greenpeace scandal only 'gave politics a bad name', but it was rather more than that. Domestically, the repercussions were still detectable four years later, when the DGSE underwent its third change in management since Lacoste's depar-ture, and Claude Silberzahn, one of the trusted Elysée Palace officials who had investigated the affair for President Mitterrand, replaced General Mermet. Clearly the insertion of a civilian at the top of the DGSE is a significant development, and it remains to be seen what impact the appointment has. Certainly, if FAREWELL had not restored the French intelligence community's image, La Piscine would have found itself without a role, and perhaps without any friends.

8

The Institute

One of the myths widely current in the United
States is that of the efficacy of Israeli intelligence; it is simply not very reliable in its
coverage of its primary target, the Arab world
surrounding Israel's narrow boundaries. The
Jewish communities that used to inhabit the
Arab countries today are gathered in Israel,
viewed by most Arabs with abhorrence. Thus
Israeli intelligence can rarely count on ideological volunteers inside the Arab target. Furthermore, except for their now-established
embassy in Egypt, they havé no embassies in
the Arab countries from which to conduct
operations. So they must try to find recruits
without a local base, from afar, a very difficult
task.[1]

Archie Roosevelt

Most conventional histories of the Israeli Secret Intelligence Service
lay emphasis on how Mossad developed out of the Haganah, the
Jewish underground resistance force, and was firmly established as
the branch responsible for political intelligence-gathering after the
British mandate ended in 1948. This is a somewhat romantic
interpretation of events, and the truth is rather different.

When the State of Israel emerged in 1948, its intelligence community remained in chaos. The information and security service,

Directors of Mossad	
Isser Harel	1951–63
Meir Amit	1963–8
Zvi Zamir	1968–74
Yitzhak Hofi	1974–81
Nahum Adoni	1982–

known as *Sherut Yedioth* but always referred to as *Shai*, actually consisted of five separate components, all competing with each other and answering to different ministries. They were the political intelligence section *(Machlakit Medinit)*; counter-espionage and internal security *(Sherut Bitachon Klali)*; military intelligence (*Sherut Modiin*); police branch of military intelligence (*Sherut Modiin Shel Mate Artzi*); and naval intelligence and security (*Sherut Modiin ve Betachon Kohot Ha Yam*). These diverse agencies had no centralized organization or co-ordinated command system, and it was not unusual to find all of them represented in Israeli diplomatic missions abroad, sometimes running the same agents. Conflicts inevitably arose and inter-department fights were frequent, in spite of the common cause they all shared. But it was not until April 1951 that Prime Minister David Ben-Gurion and his Cabinet became increasingly alarmed at the jealousy that threatened to jeopardize Israel's preparedness and authorized Reuven Shiloah to take whatever measures he deemed necessary to restructure Israel's security and intelligence apparatus. The result was the creation of Mossad or, to give 'the Institute' its full Hebrew title, *Mossad Letafkidim Meyouchadim*, a special political intelligence service independent of the Ministry of Foreign Affairs, which was allowed to retain a research division (*Machleket Hackeker*).

Shiloah, who died after a car accident in 1959, is arguably Mossad's true father, for he was the chairman of a secret body, the Committee of Heads of Services, or *Va'adat Rashei Hasherutim*. Nevertheless, he hardly earns a mention in most popular writing about Israeli intelligence. Born in Jerusalem, the son of a rabbi, he was originally a teacher, and he spent some years in Iraq as a journalist on the *Palestine Bulletin* before working as a liaison officer with the British authorities for the Jewish Agency. He later

Mossad Organization

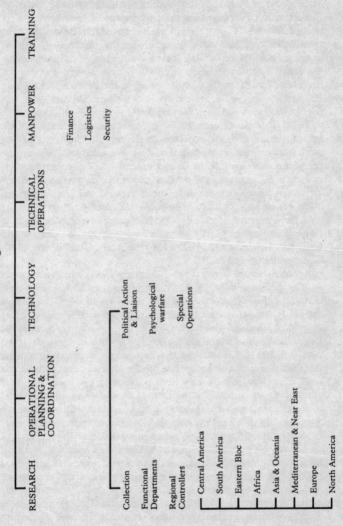

RESEARCH

OPERATIONAL PLANNING & CO-ORDINATION

TECHNOLOGY

TECHNICAL OPERATIONS

MANPOWER

TRAINING

Collection

Functional Departments

Regional Controllers

Political Action & Liaison

Psychological warfare

Special Operations

Finance

Logistics

Security

Central America

South America

Eastern Bloc

Africa

Asia & Oceania

Mediterranean & Near East

Europe

North America

developed a close relationship with the British SOE and, based in Cairo and Bari, arranged for the recruitment of Jewish volunteers to operate behind enemy lines in the Balkans. After the war, he went to America to gather financial support for the purchase of weapons and was later posted to Washington, ostensibly as a diplomat with the rank of minister, but really to negotiate a special status for successive Israeli intelligence personnel inside the fledgling CIA.

It certainly served American interests to assist Shiloah. Although the Soviet Union had been the first power to give formal recognition to Israel, its attitude changed when Stalin realized the scale of his miscalculation and had to come to terms with the fact that the new, post-colonial independent state was unlikely to become the compliant client or satellite he had anticipated. The Americans had had their own reasons for backing the emerging Jewish state and welcomed Shiloah's overtures. One of the first and most influential members of Israel's lobby within the US intelligence community was Jim Angleton, formerly OSS's counter-intelligence chief in Italy, later head of the CIA's embryonic Clandestine Service and finally, in December 1954 until his retirement, Chief of the CIA's Counterintelligence Staff.

Angleton was to have a profound influence over Mossad's unique relationship with the CIA, but many of the friendships he enjoyed with individual Israelis predated even the CIA and went back to his days in Rome, when he was in regular contact with Jewish refugees from the Holocaust who were using all their ingenuity to evade the British controls on illegal emigration to Palestine and planning for a post-mandate homeland. Angleton remained in Rome, manoeuvring though the arcane world of Italian politics to ensure the Communists were excluded from power, until November 1947 when he was appointed assistant to Colonel Donald H. Galloway, the new head of the Clandestine Service, and played a crucial role in setting up a Soviet Division within the new CIA. Angleton's remarkable career is shortly to be documented, when more of his achievements will come into the public domain, but suffice to say here that, with his loyal subordinate, Ray Rocca, he effectively dominated three aspects of CIA operations: agent-running in Italy, liaison with Tel Aviv and anti-Soviet CI operations. Rocca, who stayed on in Rome until 1953 before returning to Washington to head the Counterintelligence Staff's research and analysis unit, eventually became Angleton's deputy and retired from the Agency with him in 1974.

With such weighty supporters it was inevitable that Mossad would be granted an unofficial favoured-nation status with the CIA. Nor was this a one-sided relationship. With Jewish emigration from the Soviet Union gradually increasing there was a wealth of intelligence to be obtained from émigré screening programmes.

The modern Mossad has undergone a few changes from the original organization, some prompted by its perceived failure to give any warning to the Cabinet of the 1973 Yom Kippur War, which found Israel quite unprepared for the concerted Arab attack. A special commission of enquiry was set up to investigate the débâcle and recommended various improvements, including the creation of a research and evaluation unit in Mossad.

For many years Mossad's headquarters were located inside the main army compound in the heart of Tel Aviv, which also housed echelons of the military intelligence service, but it is now accommodated in a large office block directly across the road. Altogether about 500 officers work for Mossad, with about 1,500 support personnel. Shin Beth, the security service which moved from Jaffa in June 1970 to specially constructed premises just north of Tel Aviv, employs around 1,000, of whom 550 hold officer rank. In much the same way that its Western counterparts operate from embassies around the world, Mossad runs outstations under diplomatic cover, but it does so handicapped by a single marked disadvantage. Whereas the British and Americans enjoy protected facilities in Moscow, at the heart of their main target, and *vice versa*, the Israelis possess almost no diplomatic representation in Arab countries, and Mossad's principal objective is to assess Arab capabilities and intentions. Accordingly, Mossad is unusually reliant on liaison with allied services and is forced by circumstances to invest heavily in 'illegal' networks.

Mossad takes its own internal security extremely seriously and, as a secret report by the CIA makes clear, its senior staff 'conform to the highest professional standards of integrity and honesty and impose these standards on the lower echelons'.[2] That, however, is not to say that the Israeli intelligence community is immune from hostile penetration. There have been at least three bad examples of security lapses. The first, Professor Kurt Sitte, was a Gentile of Sudeten Czech origin, who had studied nuclear physics at Edinburgh, Manchester and Syracuse before taking up a teaching post at Haifa's Institute of Technology. He is believed to have been recruited into a Communist resistance cell at Buchenwald concentration, camp and was sentenced to five years' imprisonment for passing secrets to the Czechs in February 1961. In September the following year, Aharon Cohen, the leftist MAPAM Party's expert on the Middle East, was convicted of spying over a period of fourteen months for the Soviets; he received five years, which was later halved on appeal. Dr Israel Beer, on the other hand, was a long-term KGB agent, who had been put in touch with Moscow in Austria several years before he emigrated to Palestine in 1938. There he had been active in the Haganah and had been promoted to the rank of lieutenant-colonel during the War of Independence, ending his overt military career as an aide to army Chief of Staff, General Yigael Yadin. Thereafter, he had turned to academic pursuits, writing an acclaimed history of the 1948 war and heading the military history faculty of Tel Aviv University, and had been appointed deputy chief of the military intelligence service with responsibility for liaising with the Defence Minister on intelligence matters. However, after a tip from the CIA, probably as a result of information from either Michal Goleniewski or Anatoli Golitsyn, Beer was arrested in April 1962 and sentenced to ten years at a trial which was conducted in camera. He died in prison four years later.[3] Nor was this an isolated incident of Soviet activity in Israel.[4] As early as 1950 no less than three NCOs, Uri Winter, Gustave Gulovner and Sergeant-Major Reicher, had been convicted of spying for the Soviets, and since then there is ample evidence to suggest that Israel is considered an important target for KGB and GRU illegals. No doubt a number have slipped into the country along with authentic Soviet emigrants.[5]

These examples of Eastern Bloc espionage caused Mossad and Shin Beth to review their policy of employing former members of European Communist Parties who had renounced Marxism. Mossad regarded such individuals as well qualified to undertake clandestine missions, but its confidence was not shared by other components of the Israeli intelligence structure. In any event, all employees undergo an intensive screening procedure, accompanied by checks with a foreign Jewish community if appropriate. This provides a measure of protection for the government from hostile penetration by impostors, but is not foolproof.

Mossad enjoys an unrivalled reputation, only part of which is truly justified, although the CIA rates it as 'among the best in the world'[6] using 'expert personnel' and 'sophisticated techniques', of the kind that enabled it to eavesdrop on a scrambled telephone conversation between President Nasser and King Hussein, right at the height of the Six Day War in 1967. Certainly, the agency enjoys tremendous support from the public, an appreciation prompted by 'the historical development of Israel and the long continuing struggle against the Arabs',[7] according to the CIA. It is also unscrupulous in a good cause, and 'if the government requested the execution of a certain task, legal or illegal, it would be accomplished'.[8] In fact, Israeli law allows Mossad to do almost whatever it wants. Article 29 of the Basic Law states, in a sentence reminiscent of Catch-22, that 'The Government is authorized to carry out on behalf of the State, in accordance with any law, any act whose implementation is not lawfully entrusted to any other authority.' Thus, because there is no other Israeli law governing intelligence and security functions, the government is entrusted with them. Backed by such imprecise and ambiguous legislation, Mossad has a free hand to mount risky, high-profile operations of the sort witnessed at Entebbe in July 1976 and Tunis in October 1985, which enhanced its reputation for mounting imaginative schemes with a good success rate.

Before examining Mossad's operational prowess in some detail, we should turn to the international conditions that the agency has to survive in. Many observers believe that the lack of diplomatic representation in target countries is compensated by the existence of indigenous Jewish communities in virtually every country of the world. Whilst Mossad would like to believe that this is the equivalent of an untapped pool of local talent willing to co-operate with it, experience shows that worries about divided loyalty work both ways, and Mossad prefers not to take unnecessary risks. Nor can it automatically rely on American support in every eventuality. Indeed, Mossad's second principal target is the United States, particularly its secret policy decisions affecting Israel and scientific intelligence. There is plenty of evidence of Israeli espionage against the US.[9] The CIA report on Mossad recovered from the US embassy in Tehran in 1979 cites numerous examples of hostile behaviour, recalling an attempt to blackmail a clerk at the consulate-general in Jerusalem, the discovery of numerous listening devices planted by Shin Beth, including some found in the ambassador's office and the military attaché's residence, and 'two or three crude attempts to recruit marine guards for monetary reward'.[10] Nor is such activity confined to inside Israel's borders, a recent example in the US being that of

Jonathan J. Pollard, a Jew employed by the Naval Investigative Service, Pollard was a specialist researcher at the Intelligence Support Centre at Suitland, Maryland, just outside Washington, and in June 1984, after five years' service, he was transferred to the Anti-Terrorism Alert Centre in the NISC's Threat Analysis Division. Here he had access to large quantities of classified material, which was considered by some to be ill-advised as Pollard had already been warned about leaking information to the South African military attaché. Despite this initial brush, and the temporary suspension of his security clearance, Pollard made contact with an Israeli intelligence unit in New York.

The question of whether this particular operation was formally authorized, or whether it was run, albeit with plausible deniability by Mossad, is still a matter for debate, so the personalities involved should be examined. Pollard's first controller was Colonel Aviem Sella, the air-force officer who commanded the famous airstrike against the Iraqi atomic reactor in 1981, and was then living with his wife in Manhattan and taking a graduate course at New York University. In November 1984, Sella introduced Pollard to Yossi Yagur, a staff member of the Israeli consulate in New York, and Rafael Eitan, a veteran intelligence officer and Mossad's former Chief of Operations. In that role he had taken part in the abduction of Adolf Eichmann from Buenos Aires in 1960, and directed the hit team dispatched to track down and eliminate the Black September terrorists who had attacked the September 1972 Olympic Games at Munich. He was later appointed an adviser on terrorist matters to Prime Ministers Menachem Begin and Yitzhak Shamir. In 1965, he had been implicated in the disappearance of nearly a hundred kilos of enriched uranium, enough to build ten nuclear bombs, that was widely believed to have ended up at the Dimona research centre, Israel's secret atomic plant in the Negev Desert. A routine inventory check of a nuclear factory in Apollo, Pennsylvania, by Atomic Energy Commission inspectors revealed an extraordinary discrepancy in the fuel stocks, and the CIA was alerted when the installation's lack of records was blamed on a mysterious fire the previous year. The Agency noted that the company's president, Zalman Shapiro, was a regular visitor to Israel, where he had close links with the Minister of Defence, and concluded that Mossad had engineered the transfer of uranium. It cited traces of enriched uranium detached at Dimona, and the Israeli air-force's development of a training programme to teach pilots the techniques of delivering nuclear weapons, as indications that the Apollo plant had been the source of Israel's raw material. However, the AEC commented that the CIA's final report contained 'circumstantial evidence and much color', but was insufficient for the purposes of a presecution.

Officially, Eitan ran the Defence Ministry's Scientific Affairs Liaison Bureau, known by its Hebrew acronym LEKEM, and early in 1985 he arranged for Pollard to receive training in espionage techniques in Israel. Thereafter, Pollard routinely delivered secret documents to the home of Irit Erb, purportedly a secretary at the Israeli embassy in Washington.

Pollard and his wife were eventually placed under surveillance in November 1985, when it became clear that he had been taking documents home without authority. They unsuccessfully tried to gain asylum at the Israeli embassy and were arrested as they left the premises. By this time Sella and Miss Erb were already on their way back to Tel Aviv. Although Sella was to be indicted on espionage charges in the US, he was promoted to the rank of brigadier-general upon his return home and was given the command of the important Tel Nof airbase. Neither could be interpreted as punishments for a rogue officer mounting his own renegade operation. For his part, Eitan was appointed chairman of Israeli Chemicals, a huge state-owned corporation.

Mossad is clearly not handicapped by the political considerations that shackle other Western agencies. Indeed, a large proportion of Israel's modern politicians have served in either Mossad itself or one of the other intelligence components. The current Prime Minister, Yitzhak Shamir, for example, spent ten years in Mossad. This is now something akin to a tradition founded on the backgrounds of many of the country's first leaders, who took an active part in the Second World War and thereafter in the underground resistance to the British mandate. Many proved themselves to be adept at organizing illegal immigration and smuggling arms, all useful preliminaries to developing the political will to support hazardous enterprises from positions of authority. Thus, government and intelligence have become integrated to an extraordinary degree, allowing Mossad considerable freedom of action, even when operations go badly wrong, as happened in July 1973 when an assassination squad sent to kill Ali Hassan Salameh in Norway shot the wrong man and six of the group were apprehended. Such an incident would have grave political repercussions in any capital except Jerusalem. Another unique advantage enjoyed by Mossad is its close relationship with the regular diplomatic corps, the leading members of which have also invariably had some involvement with intelligence matters.[11] Unlike Britain and the United States, and even the Soviet Union, where the respective ministries of foreign affairs tolerate an uneasy relationship with the intelligence establishment, ever mindful of the diplomatic consequences of a bungled operation, Israeli officials 'serve as valuable auxiliaries to their covert colleagues, whose diplomatic cover is diligently maintained'.

Is is not unusual for an Israeli embassy in any particular country to be staffed with former citizens of that country, thus giving the mission a highly specialized view of the local situation. Mossad draws upon this experience and benefits from another singular blessing: the dedication with which Israeli diplomats cultivate friendships in the host community. This is not accidental, and obviously makes their full-time intelligence personnel more difficult to identify. Another element that tends to confuse those seeking to construct an accurate order-of-battle for Mossad, or for a single diplomatic mission for that matter, is the practice of frequently switching *noms de guerre*, and Hebraicizing European or Yiddish birth names.

Nor is this support limited to the civil service. Many leaders in the field of commerce and industry enjoy intelligence or security backgrounds, and it is not unusual for the divisions between government service and the private sector, sharply drawn elsewhere in the world, to be deliberately blurred in Israel. But in spite of these attributes, there are plenty of hurdles that Mossad is obliged to overcome before it can start to engage the Arabs on equal terms.

The major handicap, apart from the absence of immunity-protected bases from which to operate inside hostile territory, is the relative absence of Arab walk-ins, and the consequent need to undertake deep-cover operations. The feature shared by the major protagonists in the intelligence game played by the superpowers is the heavy reliance of each on walk-in volunteers. The KGB, as we have seen, compensates for the relatively insignificant grade of most of its sources by a dependence on illegals. Mossad does the same, and two cases stand out.

Eliahu Cohen was an Egyptian-born Jew, who was one of the few conspirators to avoid arrest following the military intelligence service's ill-fated terror campaign waged against British and American installations in Alexandria in 1952. After escaping to Israel, he was recruited by Mossad, adopted the identity of a dead Syrian émigré and went to live in Argentina. He was accepted by the local expatriate Arab community and used his credentials, established there in the guise of a wealthy textile merchant sympathetic to the new Ba'athist regime, to facilitate a move to Damascus, where he operated undetected for just over four years until January 1965. His capture was a consequence of poor tradecraft. When the police burst in on his apartment, he had been transmitting from his illicit radio for more than an hour. He was hanged publicly in May 1965.

While Cohen was cultivating senior military and political figures in the Syrian capital, Mossad ran a similar operation in Cairo, using Wolfgang Lotz. Half Gentile and German in origin, Lotz built up a legend as a former Afrika Korps officer and opened an equestrian centre in the Nile Delta, a short distance away from a secret military base where German rocket experts were helping to build two Egyptian missiles, the Al-Kahir and the Al-Zafir. Both were designed to have a long range to reach targets 'south of Beirut'. In reality, Lotz had spent the war in the British army and had subsequently fought with the Haganah. He even married a German woman, although he already had a wife in Israel, to improve his cover. He was eventually arrested in February 1965, after being implicated in a terror campaign to wreck the Egyptian plan to build a viable rocket.

Dr Heinz Krug was the first victim, and he was abducted in Munich in September 1962. Formerly the administrative head of the Stuttgart Jet Propulsion Laboratory, he had signed up, along with several colleagues, to assist in an Egyptian long-range rocket programme. He was never seen again. Two months later, on 27 November 1962, a series of letter bombs, posted from Germany and addressed personally to individual German technicians, were delivered to their offices in Cairo. One, labelled to Wolfgang Pilz, a veteran rocket engineer who had worked with von Braun at Peenemünde, exploded and badly injured his secretary. Another killed five local workers when it was opened. In February 1963, Dr Hans Kleinwachter, an electronics expert, was shot when he returned home to Lörrach. The police never found his assailant, but they did recover a significant clue from the abandoned getaway car: a forged passport in the name of Ali Samir. It was later realized that Ali Samir was actually a senior officer in the Egyptian intelligence service! That Mossad had thoroughly penetrated Egyptian security became obvious when one of its agents, using the name Yoseph Ben-Gal, was arrested in Switzerland on a charge of threatening the daughter of Professor Paul Goerke, one of the first Germans to go to Cairo to develop a navigation system for the Egyptian rockets. When Ben-Gal was caught, he was accompanied by Otto Joklik, who had himself been employed in Cairo to build an atomic warhead. Both men were tried in Basle in June 1963 and sentenced to two months' imprisonment for harassing Professor Goerke's family, but they were released immediately because of the time they had already spent in custody. More importantly, Mossad used the court as a stage to reveal the involvement of German scientists in helping President Nasser acquire an atomic bomb, a disclosure that was to have profound consequences. The Bonn government, of course, was hugely embarrassed by the German presence in Cairo and took steps to discourage others from engaging in military contracts abroad. However, the public airing of Mossad's blatant technique of intimidation was rather less welcome by Tel Aviv and resulted in a major row in the Cabinet, which ended with Isser Harel's resignation. The first Director of Mossad, or *Memuneh*, took the view that Israel's objective of deterring further German co-operation had been achieved. The Prime Minister disagreed, insisting that behind-the-scenes diplomatic pressure on the Adenauer administration would have been more appropriate.

When Lotz joined in the intimidation campaign in 1964, writing anonymous letters to named German expatriates assuring them that reprisals would be taken against them and their families unless they abandoned their work and returned home, it became clear to the Egyptian security authorities that there was still a Mossad asset at liberty. Whether he was identified by a tip from a foreign source, as Lotz later claimed, or betrayed by his own poor tradecraft, remains unknown, but he was sentenced to life imprisonment and flown home in an exchange of prisoners in February 1968.[12] In a curious and mischievous twist, Lotz confessed his espionage, but denounced the local representative of the West German BND, Gerhard Bauch, as his controller. Not surprisingly, this caused a major rumpus and Bauch only narrowly avoided being put on trial alongside Lotz.

The debate on the relative wisdom of Mossad's campaign itself was the first of its kind for the organization and, paradoxically, followed an operation that, in spite of Lotz's arrest, might reasonably be judged a success. Certainly, the Egyptian missile programme collapsed. The only previous dispute of this kind, from which Mossad had ended a beneficiary, was the Lavon affair in 1954, when its military intelligence networks in Egypt had been rounded up so comprehensively by the feared local security apparatus, the *Mukhabarat*. On that occasion the Minister of Defence, Pinhas Lavon, had overstepped his authority by sanctioning a wave of sabotage incidents centred on Alexandria. The political fallout was caused not so much by the subsequent trial of eleven participants, of whom two were executed and one committed suicide, but the admission that their targets, official premises owned by the British and American governments, had been selected so as to undermine Nasser's standing in London and Washington. This was truly a Machiavellian strategy, and one that Mossad had to distance itself from.

That Mossad played no part in the Lavon fiasco is generally accepted, but that is not to say that the agency is not prepared to undertake remarkably risky missions which do not always end as intended. The abduction of Adolf Eichmann from Argentina in May 1960 led Isser Harel to express concern about 'the need to carry out a clandestine action in the sovereign territory of a friendly country',[13] but evidently whatever misgivings he may have had were not shared by his successors. The murder of Ahmed Bouchiki, an Arab waiter, in Lillehammer on 21 July 1972 took place while General Zvi Zamir, the *Memuneh* since 1968, was actually in Norway, albeit in another town forty miles away, conferring with his chief of European operations, Georg Manner. In a case of mistaken indentity Bouchiki was ambushed and shot dead upon his return from work. The first two Mossad agents of the hit-team to be caught, Dan Aerbel and Marianne Gladnikoff, were taken into custody at Oslo's Fornebu airport, returning their rented Peugeot to the car-hire firm, in a scene reminiscent of the one to be repeated almost exactly thirteen years later on the other side of the world in a suburb of Auckland. Suspicious neighbours had noted the car's index number while it had been parked outside Bouchiki's apartment. When Aerbel was questioned by the police, he produced an emergency telephone number in Tel Aviv, which happened to be connected directly to Mossad's operations centre. When Marianne Gladnikoff was asked where she had stayed in Oslo, she volunteered the address of Mossad's safehouse where two other members of the team had taken refuge. They were promptly arrested too. The Norwegian Security Service, the *Overaaksningstjeneste*, then headed by Gunnar Haarstad, gradually pieced together the backgrounds of those arrested. One had been an Israeli diplomat in Paris until 1969, while another had worked at the same embassy as a chauffeur. Haarstad was later to realize that Mossad had fielded at least eleven agents in a complex operation that had many ramifications. The bullets that killed Bouchiki had been fired from weapons that ballistic tests proved had been used in the shootings of Wadal Zwaiter in Rome in October 1972 and Basil Al-Kubaissi in Paris in April 1973. Five of those arrested were convicted of second-degree murder, but none served more than twenty-two months in prison; the sixth, Yigal Eyal, turned out to have diplomatic immunity and was expelled. None was extradited to face charges elsewhere.

The Lillehammer débâcle had few long-term ill effects for Israel, but Mossad could hardly have anticipated that, even if it could lay some claim to the moral high ground after Black September's assault on the Olympic Games. The massacre of eleven of the nation's top athletes had prompted Prime Minister Golda Meir to promise retribution. By the time the Lillehammer operation was in the planning stage, twelve Palestinian members of Black September had already been tracked down and eliminated, three being shot dead in Beirut on 9 April 1973 in a joint operation executed by Mossad and a team of naval commandos.

Mossad's willingness to ignore international law and conventions was ably demonstrated, this time without loss of life, when the Dimona nuclear facility required a new source of uranium after the US Atomic Energy Commission had cut the illicit conduit from Apollo, Pennsylvania. The ingenious solution was a compliant German-registered company, Asmara Chemie, which supposedly traded in industrial solvents for the soap manufacturing industry. Asmara purchased, quite legitimately, a 200-ton consignment of uranium oxide, declaring the end-user to be a practically bankrupt Italian firm making textile dyes. In a separate move an elderly tramp freighter, the *Scheersberg A*, was purchased by a dormant shipping enterprise, Biscayne Traders, whose ownership had been concealed behind layers of inpenetrable corporate veils. On 15 November 1968, the *Scheersberg A* loaded its cargo of uranium, packed into 560 metal drums, at Antwerp. The original crew had been paid off and replaced with a smart team of fit young sailors. Once the formalities had been completed, the *Scheersberg A* sailed, bound for Genoa – but turned up empty in the middle of the following month in Palermo, where most of the original crew were rehired.

Where had the *Scheersberg A* been? What had happened to the cargo? The relevant pages of the ship's register were missing, and it was not until Dan Aerbel was arrested in Oslo nine years later that the truth was discovered. In his confession to the Norwegian *Overaaksningstjeneste*, Aerbel admitted that he had once hired a Swiss lawyer to register a Liberian company called Biscayne Traders. Evidently, Mossad had been behind the illegal acquisition of the *Scheersberg A*'s cargo of uranium. As had been the case with fuel that went missing from Apollo three years earlier, the disappearance had almost gone unnoticed. There had been no bodies to be found, no bills left unpaid, no complaints from irate officials. If Aerbel had remained silent, the operation would have been a complete success.

Aerbel also revealed that, unusually for Mossad, orthodox tradecraft, which dictates that separate clandestine operations should be compartmented and not run together, had been rejected with the *Scheersberg A*. A detailed analysis of the ship's movements while under Biscayne Traders' ownership showed that after the uranium success the freighter had been utilized again by Mossad at the end of December 1969. On this occasion the operation was run jointly with the Israeli navy in an effort to extract five embargoed gunboats from Cherbourg. Although the fast patrol craft had been built to Israeli specifications and had been paid for in full, President de Gaulle had banned their release after the Six Day War. Mossad's solution to the problem had been the creation of Starboat, a Panamanian registered corporation, which declared its intention to bid for North Sea oil-rig supply contracts. As a first step to trading in this specialist field, it opened negotiations with the French authorities to buy the embargoed Israeli gunboats. A deal was agreed, and on Christmas Day 1969 Starboat crews, looking remarkably like Israeli navy regulars, decided to test the engines of all five boats simultaneously. The only serious obstacle to racing them straight to Haifa was their limited range. At a cruising speed of 22 knots they would need to be refuelled at least once along the 3,000 mile journey, and after the loss of the *Eilat* in the war during the previous year the depleted Israeli navy possessed no long-range, ocean-going ships suitable for the task except, of course, Mossad's covert asset, the *Scheersberg A*. Although no proof exists, there is strong circumstantial evidence to suggest that, early on the morning of 26

December, the old steamer held a rendezvous with the five gunboats somewhere in the Bay of Biscay, while supposedly carrying a load of industrial sand from Almeria to Brake in West Germany. By New Year's Day, Biscayne Traders had made arrangements to sell the *Scheersberg A*, at a substantial loss, and soon afterwards the company wound itself up. The director who issued the instructions to dissolve it was Dan Aerbel, who had never even seen his ship.

As a rule it is only when an operation goes wrong that the details emerge into the public domain. Successes usually remain unsung unless there is some clear overriding objective, probably political in nature, that makes a disclosure attractive. The Lillehammer incident not only implicated Mossad in the two episodes in which the *Scheersberg A* had played a part, but unequivocally linked Mossad to institutionalized, state-sponsored murder. Nor was Lillehammer an isolated incident. The ballistic evidence demonstrated that two other unsolved shootings had been Mossad's work, but at least one of them had not left an innocent man dead. Although Wadal Adel Zwaiter was best known as a Palestinian poet, and the translator of *A Thousand and One Nights* from Arabic into Italian, and ostensibly employed part-time by the Libyan embassy as an interpreter, this long-time resident of Rome was actually the local representative of Black September. His brother had been expelled from West Germany after the Munich massacre and he had been implicated in the first El Al hijacking, that of a Boeing 707 to Algeria, and the bombing in August 1972 of another El Al flight bound for Tel Aviv, which fortuitously managed to return to Rome safely after the device had gone off in the plane's armour-lined baggage hold. Zwaiter had been killed on 16 October 1972 by twelve bullets as he approached his apartment, and the two gunmen had escaped in a getaway car containing two accomplices. None was ever caught.

The weapon used in Zwaiter's murder, a distinctive long-barrelled .22 Beretta, was identical to the one that fired some of the nine shots that killed Dr Basil Al-Kubaissi in Paris six months later. The Iraqi professor, who was intercepted by two assailants outside his smart hotel near the Place de la Madeleine on 6 April 1973, was believed to be Black September's quartermaster in Europe, responsible for storing and distributing explosives and weapons. Once again, the gunmen had disappeared, but the Lillehammer incident proved Mossad's complicity in well-planned and well-executed killings in three different European countries, all considered sympathetic to

Israel and all hosting Israeli diplomatic missions and liaising directly with Mossad.

The fear of upsetting local sensibilities seems low on Mossad's list of priorities, as other Mossad operations demonstrate. This is odd, considering its membership of the KILOWATT group, which is solely concerned in combating Arab terrorism. Its members are drawn from the counter-terrorist agencies of all the European Community countries, plus Switzerland, Norway, Sweden and Canada. KILOWATT meets regularly in secret session and provides a forum for the non-attributable exchange of data concerning Palestinian extremists. However, despite its privileged position as virtually the only non-European member (apart from Canada), Mossad routinely takes 'active measures' on friendly soil, even at the risk of jeopardizing relations. Of course, its ties to individual countries are often quite complex, as is well illustrated by France's somewhat ambiguous attitude to Israel. It has supplied large numbers of Mirage aircraft, and the Israeli Kfir fighter-bomber is really a Mirage copy, built under licence. However, when the DST arrested Abu Dauod in January 1977 on a West German extradition warrant charging that he he had planned the Black September attack in Munich, he was released within a few days. It was later disclosed that Dauod had entered France under SDECE's sponsorship. Certainly, the DGSE has continued to take a close interest in the PLO. Christine Cabon, part of the reconnaissance team on the *Rainbow Warrior* mission, is known to have penetrated the PLO in Beirut in 1984, in the guise of an interpreter, and at the time of the explosion in Auckland was traced to an archaeological dig outside Tel Aviv, where she was on a similar assignment under an academic cover that proved too thin. Yet despite a formal request to detain her from the New Zealand police, the authorities in Tel Aviv allowed her to slip quietly home in 1985.

Mossad has never been inhibited from mounting operations on French soil, as was shown again in April 1979 when the core of a nuclear reactor destined for Iraq was blown up while in a warehouse in Seine-sur-Mer awaiting shipment. In June the following year, the head of Iraq's atomic programme was shot in a Paris hotel. These events were the prelude to another daring mission, the destruction on 7 June 1981 of the Osiraq research reactor at Tuwaitha, just outside Baghdad, shortly before its construction had been completed. Even though fourteen Israeli fighters had been seen to execute the mission, there was much speculation at the time that precision bombing could not possibly account for the scale of the damage inflicted. The suspicion was that several Mossad saboteurs had been infiltrated into the French firm awarded the building contract, and radio-controlled charges had been placed skilfully around the core itself to ensure total devastation.

Mossad's sensitivity to the development of an Arab nuclear capability is matched by its determination to keep all aspects of the Dimona research centre secret. Located in the Negev, just forty miles north-east of Beersheba, work began on the installation sometime in 1957, and it was initially disguised as a textile factory. Later the official cover was changed to a 'pumping station' and it was not until December 1960, when the CIA obtained conclusive photographic evidence from a U-2 flight of the existence of a nuclear reactor at Dimona, that Ben-Gurion announced Israel's 'peaceful' atomic project.

Since then security at the site has remained rigid. Most of the plant is deep underground and the area is ringed with Hawk and Chaparelle surface-to-air missiles, which are known to have brought down at least one Israeli air-force plane that strayed into the restricted airspace by accident.

The only person to have given a first-hand account of Dimona's activities is Mordechai Vanunu, a Moroccan-born Jew who worked there from November 1976 to October 1985, before moving to Australia in 1986. As well as smuggling a camera into the establishment to take fifty-seven photographs, Vanunu revealed that the top-secret processing plant, located several levels below the surface, had stockpiled enough weapons-grade plutonium to arm 150 nuclear and thermonuclear devices. He also confirmed what the CIA had suspected since September 1979, when a VELA surveillance satellite had recorded an inexplicable double flash of extraordinary intensity high over the uninhabited Prince Edward and Marion Islands in the southern extreme of the Indian Ocean: that the Israelis had collaborated with South African scientists to build and test a small nuclear bomb. There has been a long history of military co-operation between Pretoria and Tel Aviv, dating back to 1955 when the Uzi submachine-gun was licensed for manufacture in South Africa. Since then there have been sales of Centurion tanks and *Reshef* fast patrol-boats. Furthermore, the CIA was already aware of the secret atomic research centre run by the South Africans at Valindaba, in the Kalahari. According to Vanunu, South African technicians were regular visitors to Dimona.

Vanunu's revelations eventually received worldwide publicity on 5 October 1986, but not before Mossad had been tipped off by ASIO about his allegations. Mossad acted swiftly, using an attractive agent to lure Vanunu from London, where the *Sunday Times* was preparing to publish his story, to Rome. The circumstances of Vanunu's abduction from there on 30 September are still shrouded in mystery because his subsequent trial in Jerusalem, at which he was sentenced to eighteen years' imprisonment for espionage, was held in camera. Nevertheless, it is believed that once on Italian territory Vanunu was drugged and then smuggled aboard an Israeli ship bound for Haifa. Once again Mossad had shown its readiness to engage in high-risk operations and get away with them. The CIA believes that the Vanunu affair was just one example of several cases where Jews who had been of service, particularly to the intelligence community, and typically involving some post-operational trading with the *Mukhabarat*, have been kidnapped and placed on trial in Israel. News of these events, which usually result in a ten-to fourteen-year sentence, is suppressed.

If the British authorities had taken any comfort from the apparent scrupulousness Mossad had exercised while in London, their complacency was to be dashed in June 1988 when a Palestinian terrorist, Ismail Sowan, was convicted of hoarding arms and sentenced to a lengthy term of imprisonment in spite of his plea that he had been supplying information to the Israelis. For good measure, London's Mossad representative was expelled as well.

Mossad has attained a unique reputation for ruthless efficiency and has exploited it to great advantage all over the world, with a special emphasis on Africa where 'the Institute' has cultivated the Kenyan and Liberian security services, helped establish the Ghanaian Military Intelligence Service and been 'active in Zaire',[14] according to the CIA. Through a secret agreement known as TRIDENT, Mossad has also trained the Turkish National Security Service and run joint operations with the pre-revolutionary Iranian SAVAK, the group's third member. By March 1979, Mossad had established formal liaison with numerous countries in the Western Hemisphere and opened two regional stations, in the Rio de Janeiro consulate, which had accommodated training staff to assist the Argentines, and in Caracas. Other countries willing to co-operate with Mossad include Mexico, Nicaragua, Costa Rica, Panama, the Dominican Republic, Colombia, Ecuador and Peru. The breadth of Mossad's official contacts are remarkable, given the diplomatic limbo which Israel is supposed to endure theoretically. Mossad has links via its regional centre in Singapore with Thai, Taiwanese and South Korean agencies, and has exchanged 'technical equipment and information'[15] with the Japanese. It has even got an accredited representative in Jakarta, the capital of Muslim Indonesia, even though he is obliged to operate discreetly under commercial cover.

Although many of these contacts may incidentally offer peripheral information relevant to Mossad's prime target, the Arab states, if seems unlikely that liaison achieves much hard data, especially as most European countries are unwilling to offend Arab feelings. As regards the United States, the traffic is not entirely one way. Mossad can trade three exceptional advantages. Firstly, it has immediate access to a highly cosmopolitan population, a high proportion of which consists of émigrés with first-hand knowledge of places and subjects that may be of vital importance to the CIA. In short, Mossad is sitting on a vast human resource, which is uniquely eager to co-operate and provide authentic information. Mossad's assistance in the CIA's Soviet emigrant screening programme is considered essential. Secondly, the Israelis possess a wealth of logistical intelligence obtained from captured Arab hardware, almost invariably of Soviet design or manufacture. For the items that have not been recovered on the field of battle, Mossad is willing to mount expeditions to steal them. In one such raid in December 1969, the Egyptian radar installation at Ras Ghaleb on the Red Sea was completely disassembled, loaded on to helicopters and flown across the frontier.

Thirdly, Mossad can also supply useful sites from which Middle East signals traffic can be intercepted, like the one atop Mount Hermon, just forty miles south of the Syrian capital. Although the NSA operates several covert facilities in Turkey and has access to the British 'take' in Cyprus, the revolutions in Iran and Ethiopia have forced the closure of some key listening-posts. Even the long-established antenna fields close to the Soviet frontier with Turkey had to suspend operations when Washington imposed an arms embargo in July 1975. Later, in May 1977, the base at Kagnew in Eritrea was abandoned, and two years later the huge NSA centres at Kabkan, Meshed and Behshahr had to be evacuated. No doubt the Israelis grasped the opportunities presented by these setbacks, but there is little to compare with managing one's own assets. Quite apart from other considerations, it allows better assessments to be made by the analysts, who can double-check against information from alternative sources.

For political reasons Mossad gets few chances to take on walk-ins, but in the face of adversity it does employ false-flag techniques to recruit agents and simultaneously conceal Israeli involvement. In some respects the Israelis do well at running agents, and Shin Beth has plenty of levers that can be used against Palestinians: offers to release blocked bank accounts or other assets frozen in 1948, the release of families from detention, business opportunities and even old-fashioned bribery. The CIA says that, 'Among the Arabs, money has been especially effective. Appeals have also been made successfully to other Arab vulnerabilities such as jealousy, rivalry, fear and political dissension.'[16] But from Mossad's viewpoint, such methods are regarded as potentially counter-productive, so it selects 'its agents almost exclusively from persons of Jewish origin....The recruitment of Gentiles is comparatively rare.' That, of course, is not to say that useful sources are discouraged. Alfred Frauenknecht, a Swiss engineer with access to the blueprints of the Mirage III's latest jet engine, sold Mossad thousands of original plans that he had been employed to destroy, until he was arrested in Winterthur in September 1969. In his case the motivation was money, combined by subtle but continuous reminders of the Holocaust. Frauenknecht had revealed in conversation to an Israeli diplomat that his conscience made him believe that Switzerland shared part of Germany's wartime guilt, and this was exploited to the full by his Mossad controller, who operated from the embassy in Rome so as not to compromise the declared Mossad liaison officer at Berne. As regards funds, Frauenknecht was estimated to have received around $85,000 to encourage his moral stand. Such generosity is not uncommon. A journalist in Paris, who passed on titbits of political gossip, was paid $1,000 a month; when he was 'gently but peremptorily' let go,[17] he was given a severance lump sum which amounted to $1,000 for every year he had helped Mossad.

Mossad will 'appeal to Jewish racial or religious proclivities, pro-Zionism, dislike of anti-Semitism, anti-Soviet feelings (if applicable) and humanitarian instincts'.[18] If all else fails, the recruiter will adopt the role of an intelligence officer from a completely different country. This system was used to snare Munir Redfa, a top Iraqi fighter pilot who was persuaded by his lover, whom he believed to be an American, to fly his MiG-21 to Israel. A member of the Maronite Christian minority, his loyalty to the Ba'athist regime had been undermined by his participation on missions into Kurdistan to bomb and strafe Iraqi Kurds. He finally defected, in August 1966, having been refuelled at an American airfield in Turkey and escorted by US Phantoms for the rest of the flight to Israel. When Redfa's story was eventually made public, it was stated firmly that he had overflown Jordan before landing in Negev, so as to avoid compromising the Turkish base.

Redfa was resettled in Israel and his experience was certainly better than that of Mahmoud Himli, the Egyptian pilot who, two years earlier, had flown his Yak trainer into Israel in protest against missions then being flown to support Royalists in the Yemen. Himli was given a new identity and moved to Argentina, but he was traced to Buenos Aires by the *Mukhabarat* and abducted. Brought back to Cairo by ship, he was convicted of treason and executed by firing squad.

Mossad's need to resort to false-flag operations is significant in that it shows how weak the organization is at acquiring highly placed assets inside the Arab establishment. Short-term sources willing to trade tactical, security intelligence for the release of a relative from a prison in Gaza is one matter, but it is no substitute for the top-level walk-in. Mossad's difficulty lies in the rarity of that particular commodity in the Middle East. Israel's total unpreparedness for the Yom Kippur War is eloquent testimony of how inadequate Mossad's agent-running operations were at that time. Since then steps have been taken to improve the situation, and a huge investment has been made in hardware for the interception of communications. The CIA believes that 'Israeli signals intelligence successes against the Arabs in the past were of such high order that the Israelis had less need than at present for good agent operations against the enemy. Part of this success was due to poor Arab communications security.'[19] In recent years, however, the Arabs have introduced sophisticated measures to protect their radio channels, thus presenting Israel with an even greater challenge.

Having one's intelligence-gathering apparatus put to the test periodically by the advent of a full-scale war, and more frequently by terrorist attacks, is a discipline that few other countries have to live with.

9

Endgame

'I don't like to use the word game, but they take defensive measures, denials and deceptions: and we do too. We want to deny them information that we don't want them to have. They want to deny information that they don't want us to have. And therein is the challenge of an effective intelligence collection agency.'[1]

For the optimists who believed *glasnost* and *perestroika* would herald a reduction in Soviet espionage, Mikhail Gorbachov must have been a disappointment. In fact, all the evidence suggests that, as far as the Kremlin is concerned, there are three vital imperatives that compel the KGB and the GRU to redouble their efforts. In the technology field the drive to modernize has created an infinite demand for automated equipment and computer hardware. The CPSU policy-makers are acutely aware of the domestic pressure to reduce military spending and make life more tolerable for ordinary people, who are enjoying increasing access to the Western media. Espionage is one way of squaring the circle. At a military level, force reduction agreements emphasize the necessity for effective verification procedures, and the Soviets are understandably keen to deter cheating. The arrangements for on-site inspections provide an unprecedented opportunity for what amounts to institutionalized, legitimate spying. Finally, as the treaties limit the nuclear arsenals of the superpowers, and the balance of ballistic missiles is more finely drawn, the need to monitor developments in the strategic defence arena becomes more vital. Even a relatively insignificant breakthrough in, say, laser weaponry can have quite a disproportionate impact on the 'Star Wars' equation. Accordingly, there is a determination in the KGB to keep right up to date with any research conducted in France or the NATO countries that might have defence applications. The current DCI, Judge William Webster, has observed that,

> despite all these detente-type initiatives of Gorbachov, the intelligence-collecting activities of the Soviets have, if anything, increased around the world. And that calls for an increased counter-intelligence capability on our part.... We continue to be in a kind of a race, to stay ahead in technology, a race to make sure that our military capabilities, our defensive capabilities, are equal and better than theirs. So they have an interest in stealing our secrets and knowing our intentions and capabilities, recruiting assets in order to provide them with that information.[2]

In the area of conventional intelligence-gathering, it is clear that the KGB has profited from concentrating its efforts on agents with access to signals data. According to Yurchenko's testimony, a special department was created within the First Chief Directorate to exploit sources such as the Walker family. Relatively low-level assets, with NCO rank, seem especially vulnerable and the potential harvest of secrets exceptionally useful. The KGB's ability to run the Walkers for so long demonstrates its operational prowess and must have enhanced the organization's standing with the Red Navy in particular. Some attention should be given to the way in which the spy ring was eventually rolled up. Although Harvey Barnett, Director-General of ASIO, has suggested in his memoirs, *Tale of the Scorpion*,[3] that the Walkers were betrayed by Yurchenko, the entire network had already been arrested when the KGB officer defected. Yurchenko is known to have arrived in Rome late in July 1985 and defected at the end of the month, but all the Walkers had been taken into custody in mid-May after a lengthy investigation. Accordingly, while Yurchenko may have had an impressive meal-ticket, the Walkers were not part of it. In fact, it was John Walker's wife who originally tipped off the FBI to the fact that her unfaithful husband was a traitor. There is, therefore, good reason to suppose that the KGB's tradecraft retained its integrity, and it was the FBI's dogged pursuit of Jerry Whitworth's anonymous attempts to do a deal with the authorities, combined with telephone calls from Barbara Walker, which started in November 1984, that led to the final identification of the spies. Thus, their case officer, Aleksei G. Tkachenko, should not have been blamed for the collapse. The KGB's methods played no part in assisting the investigation, and there is every chance that the haemorrhage of classified material would have continued undetected if Whitworth had not sought to negotiate immunity.

While the KGB must have regarded the Walkers as a veritable goldmine, their loss ought to have been considered a disaster. Similarly, although the pragmatists might have argued that neither Ronald Pelton nor Edward Howard was currently employed by US intelligence agencies, the sheer depth of knowledge they represented was unsurpassed. The elimination of so many sources during 1985, the so-called 'year of the spy', must have had more than a transitory effect on the First Chief Directorate. When combined with the known KGB and GRU defectors during this period, plus those whose details have yet to be disclosed, and the cumulative damage caused by at least three agents in place, Gordievsky, Kuzichkin and FAREWELL, the conclusions are inescapable: the First Chief Directorate has not just been rendered temporarily impotent, but actually eliminated from the game.

Human intelligence operations do not develop overnight. They require support through local facilities provided by legals. But legals can only hope to evade hostile surveillance by maintaining a plausible cover, using good tradecraft and avoiding attracting unwelcome attention. If a well-informed source has itemized a complete order-of-battle, drastic measures are called for to repair the damage. All the active case officers will have to be presumed compromised and reassigned; and security will not be restored until the remainder of the station or *Rezidentura* has been replaced with unknown faces. Given the limited resources of most agencies, such an exercise cannot be completed quickly and, in any event, will create considerable inconvenience. If the insight gained represents anything more than a brief glimpse, or a mere snapshot, of current activities, the disruption may prove irreversible. When the data supplied by FARE-WELL, Kuzichkin, Gordievsky, Yurchenko, Bokhan and the rest is added together, there can be few KGB personalities of any experience or talent left to operate without fear of continuous surveillance. The mere knowledge that one's cover is blown is sufficient in most cases to sap confidence and undermine morale. This, in turn, leads to excessive caution in handling assets and may even give borderline, uncommitted agents a severe dose of bad conscience. In any event, the adoption of excessive security routines, such as 'tail-shaking' or 'dry cleaning' as the counter-surveillance techniques are called, will itself alert the watchers to the initiation of non-diplomatic behaviour. None of these phenomena are particularly conducive to good agent-running.

In these circumstances failure will beget failure. Career intelligence officers who have been compromised may opt for accepting a gangplank pitch in preference to a deskbound future. Agents may turn themselves in rather than risk becoming a defector's meal-ticket. A senior *apparatchik* may switch sides instead of responding to a recall signal, which, in all probability, will herald disciplinary proceedings. Even those who have been accumulating information on a contingency basis, for possible use in the future, may be motivated to act swiftly while the data still has some currency.

This is the exact sequence of events that has handicapped the First Chief Directorate. Certainly, its Line K personnel in the Western Hemisphere has been utterly compromised. No case officer can be confident that he has not been identified by one of his contemporaries who has undergone a lengthy debriefing in a secluded farmhouse in Maryland or Virginia. Indeed, it is likely that he will have had to suspend operations until a (perhaps untried) replacement can be established and indoctrinated.

From the hierarchy's viewpoint, the solutions hardly commend themselves. Greater reliance on illegal networks brings its own special hazards, and they take time to build. Wholesale reorganization, unpalatable though it may be, is the only long-term remedy. But in a highly structured bureaucracy such as the KGB, where the staff enjoy a favoured place in the *nomenklatura*, the career implications are less than attractive.

On the assumption that large-scale purges, in the Yagoda style, may be judged to be counter-productive and lead to further intelligence losses, and in consideration of the certainty that there are too many vested interests to allow the First Chief Directorate to be wound up, there is a limited path for the Kremlin strategists to follow. The most logical route is to devote more energies to the training and infiltration of illegals, preferably using Eastern Bloc services to carry out the preliminaries and use untainted legals to provide the necessary support. There is already evidence that exactly this remarkable change in trends has already started. In mid-December 1988, Vlastimil Lubvik, the first secretary at the Czech embassy in New Delhi, disappeared and sought asylum in England, bringing to an end a series of misfortunes that had hampered the STB's operations in England since his transfer from London to India. Earlier in April an illegal, Erwin van Haarlem, had been arrested at his flat in Hertfordshire, caught in the act of transmitting a signal to Prague. Five months later the assistant air attaché, Major Bedrich Kramar, the military attaché, Major Vlastimil Netolicky, and Pavel Moudry from the commercial section had all been PNG'd. These events had the familiar characteristics of a well-placed defector's meal-ticket, and no doubt Lubvik has earned his entitlement to resettlement and a pension. In a similar case in July 1986, an illegal East German HVA husband-and-wife team, Reinhard and Sonja Schulze, were found to be building themselves cover in a London suburb, conveniently close to Heathrow airport. More recently in California in January 1988, a US navy Master-at-Arms 1st Class, Wildredo Garcia, was sentenced to twelve years' imprisonment for selling classified documents concerning submarines based at the Mare Island Naval Shipyard to an unspecified Eastern Bloc middleman for $800,000. In Canada, an illegal of Hungarian origin, Stephen B. Tatkai, was arrested in June 1988 and convicted of spying on a US navy installation at Argentia, Newfoundland, on behalf of the Soviets. A couple of months later two more illegals, Sandor and Imre Kercsik, were charged in Sweden with having run a retired US army sergeant, Clyde L. Conrad, in West Germany. All these separate cases had significant common denominators: they had centred on illegals operating for Eastern Bloc services as surrogates for the Soviets. Care had been taken in all to maintain a distance between each operation and the local Soviet legals. Of Soviet involvement there was no doubt, for the tasks assigned to van Haarlem at least could be deduced from the lists of British defence companies with SDI contracts found in his apartment, together with the names and addresses of émigré organizations linked to Russian dissident groups. Since the discovery of illegals is an extraordinarily rare event in England, the manifestation of two significant cases in succession in the same country cannot be dismissed lightly. Nor can the curious emphasis placed on Soviet satellite services. In the past these agencies have been used by the KGB for a specific, relevant reason. Quite often it has been because of a family connection of the target individual with a particular country. Expatriates can be very susceptible to threats or blandishments made in regard to family left in the old country. The Czechs and Hungarians have proved themselves to be especially adept at this form of coercion, yet, in the examples cited here, this behaviour can be discounted.

There is also evidence that what might be termed conventional espionage, concentrated on Soviet legal *Rezidenturas*, is on the wane. When Lieutenant-Colonel Yuri Pakhtusov was PNG'd in Washington in March 1989, he was the first to have been expelled since the hasty departure in December 1988 of Mikhail Katkov, a member of the Soviet UN mission in New York. Remarkably, no Soviet officials were thrown out of the US in either 1985 or 1987 – the previous year that had the distinction of zero expulsions was 1971. Whatever might be said about silent PNGs, there is a clearly perceptible change taking place in the way that the KGB is going about its business, and the indications are that the role of the First Chief Directorate has been transformed.

Figures for expulsions are, as previously stated, generally inaccurate as guides to anything more than overt, declared PNGs, and espionage statistics should be interpreted with great caution, but the escalation in the number of espionage prosecutions in the West, and especially in the Soviet Unions's principal target, the United States, is undeniable.

Although the bar graph opposite shows the rise in espionage arrests in the US between 1970 and 1988, with a remarkable peak in 1984, it should be noted that these figures, based on Department of Justice statistics, include diplomats who were arrested but successfully claimed diplomatic immunity and thus won their release. Most, of course, were subsequently expelled. But the figures include cases of non-Soviet Bloc espionage, such as Hou Desheng, the People's Republic of China military attaché, and Zang Weichu, an official from the PRC consulate in Chicago, who were caught on 21 December 1987 receiving classified documents in a Chinese restaurant in Washington from an NSA employee. Although this was an FBI operation, it is typical of another recent phenomenon that has influenced the growth in espionage statistics. Although their existence is largely unknown to the public, there are several other

Espionage Arrests in the US

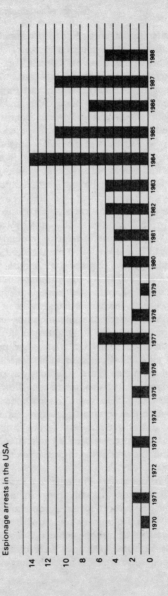

Espionage arrests in the USA

US counter-intelligence agencies in competition with the FBI, which all run their own provocation exercises. Indeed, the Naval Investigative Service and the Air Force Office of Special Investigations are especially active in mounting a particular kind of sting known as a 'controlled walk-in' against Soviet targets. Sometimes this will result in a Soviet contact being cultivated for a couple of years until there is an advantage to be gained from winding up the case. This happened with YOGI, an AFOSI volunteer, who supplied Colonel Vladimir M. Ismaylov of the GRU with especially prepared material until June 1986, when he was arrested in the act of servicing one of YOGI's dead-letter drops.[5] The reason for bringing the case to a conclusion was retaliation for the expulsion of Eric Sites from Moscow.

These kinds of provocations can occasionally lead to unexpected windfalls. In December 1981, an NIS agent, William H. Tanner, posed as a walk-in at the East German embassy in Washington, claiming to be a disgruntled naval officer stationed at the US Navy Electronic Systems Engineering Center at Charleston, and managed to obtain $21,000 for bogus information. But instead of being run by diplomats, Tanner was passed to an HVA illegal, Professor Alfred Zehe, a former exchange student based in Mexico. Zehe was eventually arrested while attending an academic conference in Boston on 4 November 1983, and later swapped (together with three other convicted spies) for twenty-five people imprisoned in the Eastern Bloc. Four months later Ernst Forbrich, another HVA illegal of seventeen years' standing, was caught in almost identical circumstances in Clearwater Beach, Florida. He was sentenced in June 1984 to fifteen years' imprisonment. As well as providing confirmation that certain diplomatic personnel suspected of espionage are, indeed, covert intelligence officers, and identifying the occasional illegal, the controlled walk-ins have the deterrent function of teaching the opposition to be wary of those that are not under any supervision.

Many of the service intelligence operations are those run against potential walk-ins. Usually they are initiated in response to an attempt by a suspect to make contact with a hostile intelligence agency. If the preliminary communication is by letter or telephone to premises which are the subject of regular interception, specially trained substitutes, posing as KGB officers, are dispatched to take matters a stage further and to receive any classified material on offer.

Since 1985, there have been five such incidents in the US, and in each a conviction has been obtained and the documents at risk recovered.

Although superficially an impressive response to the espionage threat, George Kalaris, who succeeded Jim Angleton as the CIA's Chief of Counterintelligence, is highly critical. He regards the US counter-intelligence effort to have

> failed miserably to have carried out its mission. ... The quality of performance by the components of the government agencies charged with CI responsibilities has improved susbstantially over the past decade. Yet that improvement has not prevented severe damage from being inflicted by hostile intelligence services. The CI system as a whole has proved to be inferior to the excellence of its component parts.[6]

Kalaris considers that 'the present counterintelligence response to the multi-faceted threat is fragmented',[7] and argues for central control of the CI function of all the various separate services, along the lines adopted in Britain, France and Israel. He also warns that traditional American liaison with external organizations may be abused, as happened with the Pollard case, and the CIA 'may find itself co-operating in intelligence and CI matters with countries simultaneously operating against the United States'.[8]

Whether the Kalaris analysis is correct or not, the damage sustained by the US in recent years has been described by the Select Committee on Intelligence as 'jeopardizing the backbone of this country's national defense' to a degree that may potentially be 'altering the course of history'.[9] This might be an exaggeration, but in reaching a conclusion on the CIA's relative performance, it is clear that not everyone is convinced that the Agency has met its responsibilities in full. Certainly, no final judgment can be based solely on counter-intelligence criteria, for although the episodes described above are the daily routine of the West's counter-espionage community and are bound to attract the attention of the media at the consequent trial, court-material or expulsion, they are proportionally only a small percentage of the US's intelligence activities. The overwhelming majority of intelligence-gathering is undertaken without attendant publicity. Determining exactly what the ratios are is fraught with difficulty; but, if expenditure is any guide, the CIA itself 'controls less than ten per cent of the combined national and tactical intelligence efforts', according to the Senate Intelligence Committee.[10] The CIA, DIA and all the other related agencies are dwarfed by the NSA, in much the same way that in Britain its counterpart, GCHQ, employs more than double the combined strengths of the Security and Intelligence Services and enjoys a vastly greater budget.

In spite of the post-war ascendancy of signals intelligence organizations as dependable sources of information, there have been enough failures to maintain the value of the clandestine services and the human factor. The NSA's predecessor, the Armed Forces Security Agency, gave no warning of the invasion of South Korea in 1950. Indeed, Dean Rusk, then an assistant Secretary of State, assured a congressional committee that there was no chance of an invasion of South Korea by the North just days before the war started. The GCR was of no help to the French in Vietnam; the Israeli Signal Corps was taken by surprise in the Yom Kippur offensive in 1973; and GCHQ gave positively misleading advice prior to the Argentine assault on the Falklands in 1982. But if 'the Company' itself can be judged to be subordinate to the NSA in some respects, the DCI is compensated by his retention of responsibility for co-ordinating the collection and distribution of all American intelligence, and thereby maintains a unique and commanding position. Certainly, the CIA has been transformed from the days when President Eisenhower complained that he had to learn of the 1956 Suez invasion from the newspapers, or when Allen Dulles told the Senate Foreign Relations Committee on 16 January 1959 that Castro had 'no Communist leanings', two weeks after he had seized Havana. That, of course, is not to say that the CIA has recently acquired a monopoly on wisdom. Its stated opinion, in August 1978, that Iran was not in a pre-revolutionary stage proved somewhat flawed and demonstrated that the Agency still had shortcomings when it came to political analysis in the Middle East.

Relations between intelligence agencies in the West depends upon a hard currency of worthwhile information. Whatever the events of the past, and the defection of the SDECE representative in Washington must have been a bitter pill for de Vosjoli's superiors to swallow, the as yet undisclosed Soviet data obtained by the GCR, combined with the gems supplied by FAREWELL, ensure that liaison with Paris was transformed from an unimportant sinecure into a conduit of strategic significance. US links with Israel have also experienced bad patches. Although there may have been an element of plausible deniability in Mossad's involvement with Jonathan Pollard, there was no chance of concealing the death of thirty-four members of the NSA's ship *Liberty* off the Sinai Peninsula in June 1967. The floating intercept station had been put out of action after a prolonged attack by Israeli fighter-bombers and torpedo-boats soon after the outbreak of the Six Day War, and at the time few Americans who had been indoctrinated into the *Liberty*'s SIGINT mission had accepted Tel Aviv's official explanation of an unfortunate 'miscalculation'.[11]

Mossad regards itself as being in a high-risk business and has demonstrated its willingness, time and again, to mount clandestine operations against friendly governments. Some of these operations, like the series conducted to keep the Dimona research centre supplied with uranium, have been executed with great finesse, but others, like the fiasco at Lillehammer, have been too terribly flawed. The Israelis have also experienced Soviet penetration, even though many of the cases have been unpublicized.

Oddly enough, the strength of personal relationships between British and American intelligence personnel has ensured that, regardless of the efforts of Philby and Blake, there has not been a necessity for SIS to buy its way back into acceptance in the French fashion. Had there been such a need, the shared debriefings of Lyalin, Kuzichkin, Rezun and Gordievsky would have been more than sufficient, but CAZAB, the real key to the West's counter-intelligence successes, has proved the bedrock upon which Anglo–American co-operation is based. The CIA's establishment in London is its largest overseas station, and all the US service intelligence agencies work much more closely with their counterparts, including the police Special Branch, than is generally supposed.

There is a special equation to be made that balances the relative assets and liabilities of the six agencies examined here, which participate in the game of intelligence, and it is possible to discern a profit-and-loss account for each. There are three fundamental categories referred to in the introduction: integrity, operational capability and product exploitation. In the first group we have taken the opinion of insiders into account and the views of other professionals, and then examined individual performance in terms of counter-intelligence skills. This latter field has been hard to define and extrapolated from such statistics as can be gathered. Thus, by any standards the First Chief Directorate of the KGB has been crippled by defectors, the GRU less so. The CIA has been the principal beneficiary, receiving such a volume of East–West traffic that the Frankfurt base, where most of the initial debriefing is conducted, has acquired the title 'Westport Station'. According to the CIA's own classified assessments, it has dealt with around 800 defectors 'of intelligence interest', although the number of real insiders from the KGB or the GRU who have opted for a new life is considerably less than this inflated aggregate implies (see pages 122–3). Within that group are the thirty self-confessed dispatched disinformation agents that surfaced between 1951 and 1967. A second survey, conducted by the Counterintelligence Staff six years later, could only identify a single confirmed disinformation defector in the period up to January 1973, perhaps indicating that the CIA had refined its skills and deterred the Soviets from resorting to that particular method of peddling bogus data. SIS has also demonstrated a marked improvement in its ability to attract and hold defectors in recent years, and even the DGSE has had sufficient success to enhance its standing.

The ability to deter treachery is virtually impossible to quantify, but the remarkable number of American NCOs succumbing to espionage for economic reasons contrasts sharply with the very limited group of Western spies known to have eluded detection in the Soviet Union. According to the Russian intelligence historian Nikolai Yakovlev, there have only been 'a few isolated instances'[12] of Soviets being recruited by the West, and there is good reason to believe him. By their nature the successes are unlikely to be trumpeted from the rooftops, but the general view is that the examples of Popov, Penkovsky, Tolkachev, FAREWELL and Gordievsky are extraordinarily rare exceptions. In more than four decades it is impossible to recall realistic Soviet equivalents to the Walker family, Geoffrey Prime or Gunter Guillaume. Neither Kalinin nor Nilov acquired the same notoriety as Blake or Philby. The other side of the same coin is a capability to run successful penetrations and spot false defectors. While the Soviets have had very limited experience of luring intelligence professionals to Moscow, they have shown a patient willingness to invest long-term and wait many years to get an illegal of the the the calibre of Robert Thompson or Karl Koecher into a position of worthwhile access.

The historical evidence of the Rote Kapelle and Gouzenko's revelations suggest that the past masters of developing large-scale espionage networks are the GRU. Even in the Soviet Union the organization is cloaked in secrecy and, from what little the West knows, it is in quite a different league to the KGB. Witness the case of Rudolf Abel, the so-called KGB masterspy who was arrested without a shred of evidence that he had ever seen a classified document. The only person implicated in the same episode was a lowly sergeant, who had once been employed as a mechanic in the US embassy's motor pool in Moscow. When Gouzenko defected in 1945, there were worldwide implications, and a dozen agents were arrested and convicted. Ten years later Vladimir Petrov made a similar move in Australia, but was unable to supply enough evidence to imprison a single spy. This was not a matter of limited knowledge on Petrov's part. As *Rezident* he knew the full story, but there had been precious little in the way of illicit activity to disclose. Whereas the KGB has been dogged persistently by poor security, with even its strongest cases being compromised by defectors, the GRU has suffered few comparable setbacks. While neither the DGSE nor Mossad operate on the same scale, it is fair to note that they have both suffered hostile penetration, with Mossad probably enjoying the highest degree of internal security, thanks largely to its unique ethnic and historical background.

Thus, when arriving at a conclusion concerning relative integrity, one is bound to award high marks to the GRU, with Mossad a close second, leaving the other services as also-rans.

The position in regard to operational capability is rather different. Included in the criteria for assessing this group is the political environment in which the agencies exist, which, in turn, takes into account the sanctioning of assassination (expressly prohibited by the US); the readiness to indulge in covert action (as exercised by the DGSE); and the willingness of the relevant authorities to consent to black propaganda. Certainly, the KGB is the leader in the field when it comes to freedom of discretion, with even the Israeli and French governments having to pay a price, albeit of small value, for failures such as Lillehammer and *Rainbow Warrior*. However it could be argued that the limitations endured by the modern British and Americans in particular give their services a moral superiority over their rivals and opponents, and thereby a concealed advantage.

Operational prowess takes in the practicalities of handling walk-ins (demonstrably excellent by the British, even with their limited experience); the treatment of defectors (with insufficient long-term provision by the CIA); the establishment of moles (once clearly a monopoly enjoyed by the Soviets); the management of double agents (a craft being perfected by the Cubans as Soviet surrogates); resourceful exfiltrations (undertaken with ruthless determination by Mossad); and the provision of adequate resources. In this latter class the CIA excels, boasting impressive training facilities and state-of-the-art communications technology. Only the KGB's facilities at Bykovo and Kuchino, and the GRU's headquarters at Khodinka, compare with 'the farm', Camp Peary in Virginia. Neither the British equivalent, at Fort Monckton in Gosport, nor the DGSE's centres at Beuil in the Alpes Maritimes, and Noisy-le-Sec on the outskirts of Paris, are anything like as elaborate. Whilst Mossad's headquarters in Tel Aviv have a high reputation, there can be little doubt that only the CIA, KGB and GRU compete on an equal footing.

When it comes to technology, the CIA probably has the edge, but Soviet ingenuity should not be underestimated. On several occasions, particularly in the highly specialized area of clandestine listening devices, the Soviets have surprised Western experts with their mastery of remote-powered bugs and electronic counter-measures. They have also been the first to develop reliable burst transmitters and other sophisticated paraphernalia, such as miniaturized document copiers and concealed cameras. None the less, the Agency devotes large sums of money to the development of new methods of intelligence-collection and, accordingly, must be regarded as the heavyweight. Certainly it routinely relies on satellites for communicating with its assets, thereby reducing the chances of interception, while the KGB has misled some of its illegals in North America into believing that their signals were being relayed via satellite, when, in fact, they were receiving conventional broadcasts from Cuba.

In addition to communications technology and training facilities, there are two other items that ought to be taken into consideration: the deployment of agents and the co-operation of 'honourable correspondents'. As we have already seen, Israel is at a tremendous disadvantage because of its lack of diplomatic premises in its target countries. As a result, Mossad is obliged to lean heavily on liaison and illegals. The British have a diminishing number of overseas stations to which SIS can post its staff, and those that survive cutbacks offer fairly transparent cover. The Americans and Russians, on the other hand, use a wealth of business and other fronts to act as vehicles for their personnel. With the expansion of tourism in the Eastern Bloc, it may well be that the previous advantage of maintaining 'denied areas' enjoyed by the Soviets will be negated. However, they are undoubtedly compensated by the power exercised by both the GRU and KGB when it comes to co-opting extra helpers. A *Rezident* can demand immediate support from the local Soviet colony, and no TASS or *Izvestia* journalist could risk refusing a request for assistance. The same level of help would not be expected by a CIA station chief from the American media. But when it comes to voluntary aid from the private sector, it is the French who have the upper hand. A surprising proportion of businessmen working away from Paris consider it their patriotic duty to forward reports to the nearest DGSE representative, in contrast to the British approach which involves the discreet protocol of seeking consent from a company's chairman before an approach can be made to a particular employee. Following the well-publicized experiences of Greville Wynne and James Swinburn, two British businessmen who underwent imprisonment having been caught spying by the KGB and Egyptian *Mukhabarat* respectively, SIS does not get many amateur volunteers. Against that handicap should be weighed SIS's unique asset, the British honours system. Several senior members of the American intelligence hierarchy have been honoured, such as Louis W. Tordella, Deputy Director of the NSA for sixteen years, who was awarded an honorary knighthood upon his retirement in 1974. Similarly, Anatoli Golitsyn was thrilled with his reward of an honorary CBE in 1963 for having collaborated with MI5. These decorations cost the taxpayer nothing, but they are of inestimable value to the recipients. The nearest the CIA can come to competing with such an inducement is its privilege, enshrined in the 1947 National Security Act, to grant a limited number of US citizenships annually, bypassing the usual formalities.[13] The corresponding Soviet prerogative, to offer residency permits to defectors allowing them to settle in Kuibyshev (a drab industrial city more than 500 miles from Moscow), as accepted by Guy Burgess in 1951, seems captivating but hardly appealing.

In conclusion, when it comes to operational prowess, it must be acknowledged that, despite some shortcomings in the thorny area of counter-intelligence, the CIA seems to benefit the most from its huge financial investment in a bewildering array of collection systems, ranging from atomic-powered sensors to submarine cable-tapping.

The GRU comes a close second, with SIS attaining a new ascendancy, achieved through bitter experience, in the counter-intelligence field. This leaves the KGB, Mossad and the DGSE to reflect upon former glories. At least all three can be consoled with the thought that, prior to 1909, the British Secret Service was widely believed to dominate the intelligence sphere, although it had yet to be created![14]

The question of product exploitation is the third and last factor to be looked at. Which agency has a reputation for reliability and timely dissemination? What is its relationship with the providers of SIGINT? Does it have an overall role in the development of national intelligence assessments and the formulation of policy? Following the Cuban missile crisis, the CIA consistently has been the dominant department of government in playing these roles and, over the years, its status has been enhanced, reaching a pre-Irangate peak when DCI Bill Casey achieved Cabinet rank, a position that was not given to his successor. Almost in parallel, Viktor Chebrikov, the then KGB Chairman, lost his membership of the Politburo.

Despite the CIA's miscalculation over the Shah of Iran's prospects in 1978, the Agency has recovered much of the lost ground, especially in its analysis of political developments in the Middle East. Its paramount function of supplying intelligence to the White House, combined with the DCI's duty as a co-ordinator of the product from all the other US intelligence disciplines, puts the Agency into a class of its own in comparison with the five other services examined here. The DGSE Director, by comparison, is a lowly bureaucrat; likewise the British SIS Chief has only a deputy secretary's grade in the civil service and is answerable to the Chairman of the Joint Intelligence Committee and the Cabinet Intelligence Co-ordinator. In February 1971, the head of the GRU, Colonel-General Pyotr I. Ivashutin, was promoted to army general and, although senior to his KGB counterpart, Yuri Andropov, was still subordinate to the Chief of the General Staff and his deputy.

Selecting the pre-eminent service of the six studied here is no easy task, but, having laid down the ground rules, the decision almost made itself. Once the popular prejudices concerning Mossad's ruthless efficiency, or SIS bungling treachery, have been discarded, it can be seen that there are particular standards that can be applied to each, whatever their size, budget, image or history. Instead of taking an intelligence supremo's word for it, for example, that his organization has recently acquired a Soviet Bloc defector, a politician will seek to know such critical details as what service he belonged to? How impressive was his meal-ticket? How long was he active in place before he finally defected? Have his credentials been authenticated? Is he ideologically motivated? What can his information be traded for to Allies? Is he likely to redefect? Similarly, the taxpayer may like to be reassured on the training facilities offered to other agencies; the current status of liaison with particular countries; the relative integrity of a service; the level of co-operation it receives from amateurs; and the proportion of staff deployed overseas. In short, is the outfit supplying value for money?

Of course, there may be good reasons for sidestepping some of these topics, but it may bring to an end those unsatisfactory encounters between bemused politicians and supercilious intelligence bureaucrats, where the latter would nod knowingly and give vague assurances that 'things are going well, but take time to develop', or other unconvincing platitudes.

That espionage has a future cannot be doubted, whatever the protestations made in Moscow by Viktor Chebrikov, the former Chairman of the KGB, who gave an unprecendented interview in September 1988,[15] shortly before his replacement, which heralded a series of extraordinary public relations exercises. Suddenly Western defectors became available for interview; spies such as Karl Koecher and Edward Howard[16] were produced for selected journalists; George Blake appeared on television and was the subject of a long article in *International Pravda*;[17] even the disgraced Vitaly Yurchenko was allowed to talk to an American writer for six days. However, all this *glasnost* is unlikely to change the games of intelligence played by East and West alike. Indeed, the indications are that world leaders are likely to turn to intelligence more often. After all, two of the world's leaders, President Bush and Yitzhak Shamir, boast solid intelligence backgrounds, and Mikhail Gorbachov demonstrated his confidence in his new KGB Chairman, Vladimir Kryuchkov,[18] by including him in his entourage to the Washington Summit in December 1987. According to Yurchenko, Kryuchkov has attempted to redeem the First Chief Directorate's lost reputation by developing an entirely new branch, known as Directorate 'R', for research, whose personnel operates abroad under academic as well as diplomatic cover, outside the local *Rezidenturas*. This has enabled its members to avoid the attention of local security services.[19]

There are other indications that the games will continue to escalate: Richard F. Stolz Jr, the CIA's new Serbo-Croat-speaking chief of the Clandestine Service, is not known as a detente-style appeaser. He is an old hand, who had operated in Frankfurt and Sofia before his expulsion from Moscow in 1965 'for subversive activities'.[20] He later headed the CIA stations in Belgrade and Rome. The signs are that in an era of arms control agreements and the new increased emphasis on verification, there will be even more pressure from the policy-makers for accurate data. This, the collection of strategic intelligence, is just one of the games of intelligence played by the six members of the major league. Some have deserved reputations for political analysis, while others have to endure crippling handicaps. All will continue to embarrass their countries, but, so long as politicians fear surprise attack, their intelligence agencies will be required to participate in Kipling's 'great game'.

APPENDIX I

Books Written by CIA Insiders

After his retirement, Allen Dulles began a tradition with *The Craft of Intelligence* in 1965 that he followed up the next year with *The Secret Surrender* and *Great True Spy Stories*. Long before Dulles had joined the CIA he had written an account, *The German Underground*, of the resistance to Hitler in Germany and his role in it. Following his example, three further DCIs were to write their momoirs. William Colby's *Honorable Men: My Life in the CIA*; Stansfield Turner's *Secrecy and Democracy: The CIA in Transition* and Bill Casey's *The Secret War Against Hitler* were all released after they had left the Agency; Turner experienced great difficulty in obtaining clearance and Colby was fined for not bothering. Ironically, Turner had been responsible for prosecuting Frank Snepp for breaking his contractual obligations by surreptitiously releasing *Decent Interval*. For Casey, publication of his wartime memoirs took place shortly after his death.

Many of their subordinates followed the example set by their DCIs and recalled their experiences, generally in uncritical terms. Into this second category fall E.C. Mike Ackerman's *Streetman*; William J. Barnds's *The Right To Know, Withold and To Lie*; Melvin Beck's *The Secret Contenders: The Myth of Cold War Counter-Intelligence*; Scott Breckenridge's *The CIA and the US Intelligence System*; Michael Burke's *Outrageous Fortune*; William Coffin's *Once To Every Man: A Memoir*; Chester L. Cooper's *The Lion's Last Roar: Suez 1956*; Miles Copeland's *The Game of Nations* and *The Real Spy World*; Peter de Silva's *Sub Rosa: The CIA and the Uses of Intelligence*; Wilbur Crane Eveland's *Ropes of Sand: America's*

Failure in the Middle East: William Hood's case history of Major Piotr Popov of the GRU, entitled *Mole*; Howard Hunt's *Undercover: Memoirs of an American Secret Agent* and *Give Us This Day*, his version of the Bay of Pigs affair, in which he participated; Edward Hunter's *Attack by Mail*, *The Black Book on China* and *Brainwashing in Red China*; William R. Johnson's *Thwarting Enemies at Home and Abroad*; Edward Geary Lansdale's *In The Midst of War: An American's Mission to South-East Asia*; Gordon G. Liddy's *Will*; and James McCargar's *A Short Course in the Secret War*, under the pseudonym Christopher Felix. Lyman B. Kirkpatrick, who headed the Operations Division before being put into a wheelchair by polio in 1952, has written *The Real CIA*, his study of Second World War intelligence failures, *Captains without Eyes*, *The US Intelligence Community: Foreign Policy and Domestic Activities* and *Espionage and Propaganda in the 1970s*. There have also been Cord Meyer's *Facing Reality*, a memoir from the Station Chief in London who also masterminded the CIA's covert action programme against the Soviet Union; Sig Mickelson's *America's Other Voice: The Story of Radio Free Europe and Radio Liberty*; George O'Toole's *Encyclopaedia of American Intelligence and Espionage*; David Atlee Phillips's *The Nightwatch: 25 Years of Peculiar Service*, *Secret Wars Diary* and *Careers in Secret Operations*: the ill-fated U-2 pilot Francis Gary Powers's *Operation Overflight*; Archie Roosevelt's *For Lust of Knowing: Memoirs of an Intelligence Officer*; his cousin Kermit's account of the Mussadeq coup in Iran, *Countercoup*, which had to be withdrawn almost before it reached the bookstores and reprinted after protests from the British intelligence authorities; Harry Rositzke's *The CIA's Secret Operations*; Thomas Bell Smith's privately printed *The Essential CIA*; Vernon Walters's *Silent Missions*; and Donald Wilber's *Adventures in the Middle East*, from which several passages were deleted by the Agency's Publications Review Board.

Philip Agee's original exposé, written largely in Cuba and first published in London, *Inside the Company: A CIA Diary*, was the first of the genre; subsequently he contributed to *Dirty Work: The CIA in Western Europe* and *Dirty Work 2: The CIA in Africa*. His latest is an autobiographical account of his struggle to publish, entitled *On the Run*. Victor Marchetti's *The CIA and the Cult of Intelligence*, written with a State Department official, John Marks, was the subject of prolonged litigation, which resulted in the book being published with portions of the text deleted. Sylvia Press's *The*

Care of Devils recalls her bitterness at being dismissed from the CIA. Other books include Patrick McGarvey's *CIA: The Myth and the Madness*; Ralph McGehee's *Deadly Deceits: My 25 years in the CIA* (spent mainly in South-East Asia); Joseph B. Smith's *Portrait of a Cold Warrior: Second Thoughts of a Top CIA Agent*; Frank Snepp's controversial memoir of Saigon, *Decent Interval*; and, finally, John Stockwell's account of the guerrilla conflict in Angola, *In Search of Enemies*.

There is a long-standing convention of CIA officers, particularly analysts, preparing erudite papers on their chosen fields of study. Among those who have reached a wider audience than the classified community is Dr Ray Cline, once Station Chief in Taiwan and the CIA's Deputy Director. He has written the very readable *Secrets, Spies and Scholars*, among many other titles. Most of the books in this group are specialist treatments by experts on narrow subjects. They include the very comprehensive *Intelligence and Espionage: An Analytical Bibliography* written by a former Athens Station Chief, George Constantinides; Drexel Godfrey's *Basic Elements of Intelligence*; Richard J. Heuer's *Quantitive Approaches to Political Intelligence*; Roger Hilsman's *Strategic Intelligence and National Decisions*; Dr Sherman Kent's *Strategic Intelligence for American World Policy*; Klaus Knorr's *Foreign Intelligence and Social Sciences*; William L. Langer's *In and Out of the Ivory Tower*; Herbert E. Meyer's *Real World Intelligence*; the respected Walter Pforzheimer's *Bibliography of Intelligence Literature*; Fletcher L. Prouty's *The Secret Team: The CIA and its Allies in Control of the United States and the World*; Raymond Rocca's impressive *Bibliography on Soviet Intelligence and Security Services*; Theodore Shackley's *The Third Option: An American View of Counter-insurgency Operations*, from the former Station Chief in Saigon; R. Harris Smith's *OSS: The Secret History of America's First Central Intelligence Agency*; Thomas F. Troy's *Donovan and the CIA: A History of the Establishment of the Central Intelligence Agency*; and Jack Zlotnick's *National Intelligence*.

Of the outsiders who choose not to mention their CIA connections, the following are prominent: James Burnham's *The Web of Subversion: Underground Networks in the US Government*; Robert W. Komer's *Bureaucracy at War: US Performance in the Vietnam Conflict*; and, dealing with a related subject, Paul D. Henze's *The Plot to Kill the Pope*.

This is all a rich vein from which to divine a composite view of the Agency, but, alas, its fecundity prevents this kind of approach. While in the case of other organizations it is possible to determine some universally accepted opinions, virtually every possible prejudice can be justified by selected quotations from insiders.

APPENDIX 2

Books Written by KGB and GRU Insiders*

Ismail Akhmedov	*In and Out of Stalin's GRU*
Piotr Deriabin	*The Secret World*
Ilya Dzirkvelov	*Secret Servant*
Anatoli Golitsyn	*New Lies for Old*
Igor Gouzenko	*The Iron Curtain*
Svetlana Gouzenko	*This Was My Choice*
Anatoli Granovski	*I Was an NKVD Agent*
Aleksandr Kaznacheev	*Inside a Soviet Embassy*
Nikolai Khokhlov	*In the Name of Conscience*
Yuri Krotkov	*I Am From Moscow*
Gordon Lonsdale	*Spy*
Aleksei Myagkov	*Inside the KGB*
Vladimir Petrov	*Empire of Fear*
Elizabeth Poretsky	*Our Own People*
Vladimir Rezun	*The Aquarium*
Vladimir Sakharov	*High Treason*
Rupert Sigl	*In the Claws of the KGB*
Maurice Shainberg	*Breaking from the KGB*
Grigori Tokaev	*Comrade X*
	Betrayal of an Ideal
Ruth Werner	*Sonia's Rapport*

*This list is limited to intelligence officers who have written books, and deliberately omits those released by Soviet agents, such as John Vassall (*The Autobiography of a Spy*, Sidgwick & Jackson, London, 1975) and Michael Straight (*After Long Silence*, W. W.

Norton, New York, 1983), who have published accounts of their espionage activities.

APPENDIX 3

Criteria by which To Judge a Nation's Intelligence Service

1. *Integrity of Service:*
   - A) Opinion of insiders
   - B) Views of other professionals
   - C) Receipt of defectors
   - D) Ability to run successful cases
   - E) Counter-intelligence skills
     *Ability to spot false defectors
     *Ability to catch spies
     *Success in deterring treachery
     *Status of liaison with Allied CI

2. *Operational Prowess:*
   - A) Political environment
     *Sanction of assassination
     *Consent to covert action
     *Permission for black propaganda
   - B) Handling of walk-ins
   - C) Treatment of defectors
   - D) Planting moles
   - E) Management of double agents
   - F) Resourceful exfiltrations
   - G) Tactical capability

                              *Training facilities
                              *Communications
technology
                              *Deployment of tactical
agents
                              *Co-operation of
honourable correspondents

3. *Product Exploitation*:

    A) Timely dissemination
    B) Reputation as a reliable
        source
    C) Relationship with SIGINT
        agencies
    D) Overall role in development
        of intelligence assessments

Notes

Introduction

1 The Swedish Intelligence Service, the *Försvarsftaben Operativ Enhęt*, was replaced on 1 July 1989 by the *Underrattelse och Säkerhetsenhet* (Intelligence and Security Unit), headed by Colonel Lennart Frick.

1: The Company

1 Thomas Powers, *The Man Who Kept the Secrets* (Weidenfeld, London, 1979), p. 53.

2 The CIA's official handbook includes the organizational chart, but omits any details regarding the Operations Directorate, which is the largest component of the clandestine service. Formerly known as the Plans Directorate, its structure was first disclosed by Philip Agee in his *Inside the Company: CIA Diary* (Stoenhill, New York, 1975).

3 Dale Peterson, assistant to Herbert E. Hetu of the CIA's Office of Public Affairs, was a naval officer who had been brought into the Agency by Stansfield Turner. He had previously been widely quoted, in September 1978, following the mysterious death of John Paisley. See William Corson, Susan Trento and Joseph Trento, *Widows* (Crown, New York, 1989).

4 The figure of forty OSS traitors is based upon testimony from Elizabeth Bentley. Among the best-known Soviet sources were: George Zlatovsky and his wife Jane Foster, who were indicted on espionage charges but not extradited from Paris; Duncan Lee; and Helen Tenney. For further details, see William Corson and Robert Crowley, *The New KGB* (Morrow, New York, 1985) and Hayden B. Peake's Afterword to Elizabeth Bentley's *Out of Bondage* (Ivy Books, New York, 1988).

5 More recently, Yurchenko was given permission to be interviewed by

the American author and journalist Ronald Kessler, who intends to write his biography.

6 Carver's opinion quoted in 'Hearings before the Permanent Sub-committee on Investigations (Federal Government's Handling of Soviet and Communist Bloc Defectors)' (Washington, 1988), p. 248.

7 Richard Helms in *ibid.*, p. 261.

8 Tom Polgar in *ibid.*, p. 711.

9 Mark Wyatt in *ibid.*, p. 925.

10 In addition, a KGB major-general, as yet unannounced, defected to the US in April 1985 from East Germany (*US News & World Report*, 3 February 1986).

11 Ogorodnik was given the cryptonym TRIGON by the CIA and, at one time, was believed to have been compromised unintentionally by an indiscreet member of the National Security Council. It would now seem that Karl Koecher is a better candidate for having alerted the KGB to TRIGON's existence.

12 Furnival Jones, quoted in David Leigh, *The Wilson Plot* (Heinemann, London, 1989), p. 31.

13 The debate concerning Yurchenko's *bona fides* still continues. Several counter-intelligence experts have cast doubt on the validity of his evidence and his apparent failure to clear up certain suspected penetrations, like that of SASHA.

2: Company Business

1 Dr Ray Cline, *The CIA under Reagan, Bush and Casey* (Acropolis, Washington, 1981), p. 171.

2 William Weisband was an ASFA clerk who betrayed the existence of the VENONA Soviet decryption project to the KGB in 1948, an act invariably attributed to Kim Philby, who was not indoctrinated into the programme until the following year. The only reference to Weisband's case in the public domain is in Corson and Crowley, *op. cit.*, p. 216.

3 In addition to forty-seven trade missions in the West, the Soviets operate some 300 separate import–export organizations.

4 'KR' is a Russian abbreviation of *Kontra Razvyedka*, or counter-intelligence. See page 81 for a more detailed account of the KGB's internal structure.

5 According to the State Department, when Mikhail Katkov was declared persona non grata on 18 December 1987, he became the forty-second Soviet official assigned to either the Soviet UN mission or to the UN Secretariat to be expelled for espionage since 1950.

6 See William C. Sullivan's *The Bureau: My Thirty Years in Hoover's FBI* (W. W. Norton, New York, 1979), p. 184.

7 For a detailed account of Vaygauskas's activities in London see Leigh, *op. cit.*

8 For a detailed account of Dubberstein's involvement with Wilson, Terpil and the Libyans, see Peter Maas, *Manhunt* (Random House, New York, 1986).

9 For the best account of Karl Koecher's espionage, see Ronald Kessler, *Spy Vs Spy* (Scribner's, New York, 1988).

10 William Webster, quoted in Thomas B. Allen and Norman Polmar, *Merchants of Treason* (Delacorte, New York, 1988), p. 206.

11 In the *Church Committee Report* Devlin was given the pseudonym 'Victor Hedgman'.

12 *Church Committee Report*, p. 41.

13 *Ibid.*, p. 51.

14 *Ibid.*

15 *Ibid.*, p. 86.

16 CIA cable, 30 May 1961, quoted in *ibid.*, p. 214.

17 DCI McCone to Richardson, drafted by William Colby (then Chief, Far East Division), *ibid.*, p. 221.

18 See, for example, Powers, *op. cit.*, p. 163.

19 Colby in the *Church Committee Report*, p. XV.

20 Bob Woodward, *Veil* (Simon & Schuster, New York, 1987), p. 388.

21 Theodore Shackley, *The Third Option* (McGraw-Hill, New York, 1981), p. x.

22 *Senate Investigations Committee Report*, p. 425.

23 *Ibid.*

24 *Ibid.*, p. 131.

25 *Ibid.*, p. 132.

26 *Ibid.*, p. 285.

27 *Ibid.*, p. 27.

28 See also David C. Martin, *Wilderness of Mirrors* (Harper & Row, New York, 1980), and Henry Hurt, *Shadrin* (McGraw-Hill, New York, 1981).

29 The discovery of an atomic-powered remote sensor, placed on a mountain close to the Indian frontier to monitor Soviet nuclear tests, was exploited in hostile propaganda alleging that the device's atomic fuel had contaminated the source of the Ganges.

30 There is a curious contradiction between the French language edition of DCI William Colby's memoirs *Honorable Men* (Presse de la Renaissance, Paris, 1978) and the Agency-cleared version published in the US (Simon & Schuster, New York, 1978) regarding AZORIAN's success.

3: A Cuban Game of Bluff

1 Dr Ray Cline, *Secrets, Spies and Scholars* (Acropolis, Washington, 1976), p. 195.

2 For Thyraud de Vosjoli's own account, see *Lamia* (Little, Brown, Boston, 1970), pp. 295–7.

3 For further details of Sergei M. Kudriavtsev's colourful career, see page 108.

4 The individual US units manning these stations are listed in Jeffrey T. Richelson and Desmond Ball, *The Ties That Bind* (Allen & Unwin Australia, 1985), p. 329.

5 The US intercept bases in Iran were closed following the 1979 revolution.

6 Soviet telemetry was also intercepted from a USAF base at Bada Bier, near Peshawar, northern Pakistan, which was closed in 1967.

7 Powers was convicted of espionage and subsequently swapped for 'Colonel Rudolf Abel' on 10 February 1962. His treatment contrasts with that received by a Bulgarian, Lieutenant Milusc Sokolov, who crash-landed his MiG-17 on 20 January 1962 on a Jupiter base at Acquaviva in Italy. Sokolov had flown so low to photograph the site that he accidentally clipped a treetop. He was initially charged with spying and then released.

8 Colonel V. V. Meshcheryakov was later promoted to colonel-general, deputy chief of the GRU and head of the Military Diplomatic Academy, based on Narodnogo Opolchenia Street, Moscow.

9 Both the CIA and the NSA were particularly interested in the development of a huge antenna field, covering some twenty-eight square miles near Lourdes. The Soviet SIGINT station became operational in 1960 and currently employs an estimated 2,000 Soviet technicians.

10 The NSA's role in the missile crisis was first revealed by James Bamford in *The Puzzle Palace* (Houghton Mifflin, New York, 1982), p. 215. Walter Laqueur speculates about the SIGINT contribution in *World of Secrets* (Weidenfeld, London, 1985), p. 163.

11 SAM missiles were regarded as entirely defensive in nature because their maximum slant range was about twenty-five miles, whereas the coast of Florida was ninety miles away.

12 See Roosevelt's account in *For Lust of Knowing* (Weidenfeld, London, 1987), p. 468; Chester L. Cooper headed the briefing team and also described these events in *The Lion's Last Roar: Suez 1956* (Harper & Row, New York, 1978), p. 260.

13 Cline, *The CIA under Reagan, Bush and Casey*, p. 221.

14 Soviet secrecy was so intense that troops bound for Cuba were not told of their destination, so they packed arctic clothing and skis.

15 SNIE 85–3–62, p. 8.

16 The exact number of Soviet personnel stationed in Cuba during this period is unknown, but the CIA's figure was certainly an underestimate. It is now believed that about 42,000 Soviet troops went to Cuba, although the American reports ranged from 4,500 in October to a peak of 10,000–12,000 in November, when the presence of four mechanized infantry regiments was noticed.

17 Castro later complained that if Cubans had been involved in the deployment, all the military hardware would have been disguised as agricultural machinery. There is some evidence to show that Khrushchev believed the sites had been camouflaged, but a breakdown in communications had prevented the relevant order from reaching its destination.

18 Anderson's U-2 was reportedly destroyed in error, without the Kremlin's authority by the senior Soviet officer at the Los Angeles SAM battery, General Igor D. Statsenko. See James G. Blight and David A. Welch, *On the Brink* (Hill & Wang, New York, 1989) p. 369.

19 Cline, *op. cit.*, p. 222.

20 Secret intelligence indicates that all the warheads were aboard the *Poltava*, which sailed from Odessa in mid-October with a false cargo manifest declaring her destination as Algiers. In fact, the vessel held a rendezvous with three Soviet Northern Fleet submarines in the Atlantic, but on 24 October, the day the blockade was announced, the *Poltava* turned around and returned to Russia. NRO analysts also reported that none of the Cuban bunkers was manned by well-armed KGB troops, as was the case in the USSR.

21 Oleg Penkovsky, *The Penkovsky Papers* (Wheatsheaf Books, Brighton, 1988), p. 223.

22 The day after Anderson's death, another U-2 pilot accidentally veered deep into Soviet territory over the Chukot Peninsula without incident, en route to a suspected nuclear test site in the Soviet Arctic.

4: The Neighbours

1 Thomas Polgar, *The KGB: An Instrument of Soviet Power* (The Intelligence Profession Series no. 3, AFIO), p. 15.

2 *Ibid*.

3 Abel died on 16 November 1971. His grave in Moscow is inscribed with the birth date '11 July 1903' and his true name 'William Genrykovich Fisher'. Neither detail conforms with British birth records.

4 The Krogers' passports were granted by a Cambridge-educated consular official, Paddy Costello, who was then based in Paris. In 1955, he

was appointed Professor of Russian at Manchester University and was later investigated as a suspected Soviet agent.

5 Molody's aunt, Tatiana Piankova, was the art director of a French ballet company. Her sister, Evdokia Konstantinova Naumova, had been Molody's mother. See the *People*, 21 March 1965.

6 The scale of Golitsyn's meal-ticket is a matter of dispute. His critics insist that Georges Paques was the only important Soviet agent he unmasked. The British Security Service held him in high regard because he alerted them to John Vassall, although it was Nosenko who provided the clues that eventually identified the Admiralty clerk as a Soviet agent, and Barbara Fell. Both were arrested in 1962 following tip offs from the CIA. Golitsyn's detractors point out that apart from Paques none of his leads concerning the French resulted in arrests, and his information concerning a Norwegian spy, Indgeborg Lygren, turned out to be embarrassingly incorrect.

7 Krotkov ended up writing novels in Spain, where he died.

8 William Hood, *Mole* (W. W. Norton, New York, 1982), p. 14.

9 Polgar, *op. cit.*

10 'Soviet Intelligence Operations Against Americans and US Installations Abroad: An Analysis of Soviet Doctrine and Practice', a CIA document recovered from the US embassy in Tehran and published in *Documents from the US Espionage Den*, vol. 51.

11 The UN Secretariat employs approximately 450 Soviet officials. Until March 1986 the permanent Soviet UN Mission comprised of 250 accredited diplomats. This figure was reduced by agreement to 170 in April 1988, and compares to the French delegation of just fifteen diplomats and fifty support staff.

12 Cord Meyer, *Facing Reality* (Harper & Row, New York, 1980), p. 314.

13 David Dallin's wife, Lilia Estrine, had first-hand experience of Soviet espionage. She had been editor of *The Bulletin of Opposition* with Trotsky's son, Leon Sedov, before his murder in Paris in 1938.

14 Ray Rocca, *Bibliography on Soviet Intelligence and Security Services* (Westview Press, Boulder, Colorado, 1985), p. 108.

15 George C. Constantinides, *Intelligence and Espionage: An Analytical Bibliography* (Westview Press, Boulder, Colorado, 1983), p. 74.

16 Levchenko quoted on dustjacket of *Chekisty* (Lexington Books, Lexington, Mass., 1988).

17 Rezun's literary output has attracted some criticism, particularly from Dmitri K. Simes, an associate of the Carnegie Endowment for International Peace who described 'Suvorov's' fourth book as 'the functional equivalent of a consumer fraud'.

5: Navigators from the Aquarium

1 Vladimir Rezun, *Soviet Military Intelligence* (Hamish Hamilton, London, 1984), p. 40.

2 Weiss was identified by the decryption of his telephone number, PAD 7501, in GRU wireless traffic. The only declassified reference to Weiss is in the CIA's study entitled *The Rote Kapelle* (University Publications of America, 1979), p. 100.

3 MI5 reported that 'the Robinson Papers, apart from Weiss, did not give any positive lead to spies in situ in the UK', *ibid.*, p. 96.

4 *Ibid.*, p. 342.

5 *Ibid.*, p. 100.

6 Vladimir Kostov defected in Paris on 27 June 1977. He subsequently wrote *The Bulgarian Umbrella* (Harvester Wheatsheaf, Brighton, 1988).

7 Although not an SB officer, Wladyslaw Tykocinski proved an invaluable source when he defected to the USA from his post as head of the Polish Military Mission in Berlin on 16 May 1965.

8 Ladislav Bittman (now Dr Lawrence Martin) in testimony to Senate Sub-committee on Investigations, p. 57.

9 Laszlo Szabó, quoted in 'Soviet Intelligence Operations Against Americans and US Installations Abroad', p. 11.

10 Viktor Kravchenko wrote two books about his experiences, *I Chose Freedom* (Robert Hale, London, 1947) and *I Chose Justice* (Scribner's, New York, 1950), and was sued for defamation by the Soviet government in Paris in 1949. The Soviets lost the case and never tried to take legal action against a defector again.

11 Kim Philby, in Phillip Knightley, *Kim Philby: KGB Masterspy* (Deutsch, London, 1988), p. 435.

12 Major Richard Squires vanished in Germany in 1947 and was reported to have written *On the Path to War*, published in East Berlin. His name was eventually removed from the Army List in June 1967 and posted formally as a defector.

13 John Disco Smith is referred to by Harry Rositzke, *The KGB: The Eyes of Russia* (Doubleday, New York, 1981), p. 164, and by Pauly V. Parakal, *Secret Wars of the CIA* (Sterling Publishers, New Delhi, 1984), p. 94.

14 Aleksandr Shelepin, quoted in 'Soviet Intelligence Operations Against Americans and US Installations Abroad', p. 13.

15 *Ibid.*, p. 51.

16 Office of the Assistant Chief of Staff for Intelligence, Department of the Army, *Ibid.*, p. 18.

Games of Intelligence

Notes to Tables on Pages 122–3.

There are only two books devoted exclusively to post-war Soviet defectors: Gordon Brook-Shepherd's excellent *The Storm Birds* (Weidenfeld, London, 1988) gives detailed accounts of the cases of Rastvorov, Khokhlov, Deriabin, Vladimir and Evdokia Petrov, Golitsyn, Nosenko, Lyalin, Cheboratev, Nikolai Petrov, Hovanesian, Sorokin, Rezun, Levchenko and Gordievsky. Vladislav Krasnov's *Soviet Defectors* (Hoover Institution, Stanford, California, 1985) reproduces an authentic KGB wanted list covering the period May 1945–April 1969, together with a detailed analysis of the 470 *perebezhchiki* (defectors) mentioned therein.

The KGB list, obtained from *Possev*, the official publication of the NTS émigré organization, contains the names of just fifteen intelligence defectors from either the KGB or the GRU. Curiously, although it includes Vladimir M. Proletarsky, better known by his cover name, Vladimir Petrov, there is no entry for his wife Evdokia, who was also an intelligence officer. Krasnov lists the two Petrovs in a category of known defectors omitted from the Possev list (p. 180) without realizing that 'Petrov' was a *nom de guerre*. Also omitted are such well-known intelligence defectors as Anatoli Granovsky, Rupert Sigl, Bogdan Stashinsky, Kaarlo 'Tuomi' and Reino Hayhanen, all of whom would appear to qualify for an entry by their NKVD/KGB status.

In addition to the above, Professor Krasnov lists a further eleven defectors who switched sides between May 1969 and his publication date. Of that group Aleksandr Sakharov is described in error as having been a KGB officer (p. 206), whereas he was simply an academic and denies any KGB connections. This leaves a grand total of thirty confirmed intelligence defectors between 1945 and 1985.

A few on the *Possev* list are not described in full, and so there may be one or two who were not obviously KGB or GRU. It may also be that some defectors, such as Hayhanen and Sigl, conceivably may have been known to the KGB by another name which is listed.

The chart on pages 122–3 is strictly limited to intelligence personnel, either directly employed or, like Kiselnikova and Gezha, merely co-opted recruits. Some, like Hayhanen, Runge and Zemenek, are not of Soviet origin. It is as comprehensive as possible, having been drawn from largely open sources. A point to note is that although the CIA often talks of 'unlisted' intelligence defectors, thereby implying that a substantial number have slipped across without attendant publicity, these claims cannot be substantiated by reference to the Possev list. One common characteristic of the intelligence defectors on the wanted list is the endorsement of a trial in absentia by the Military Collegium of the Supreme Court of the USSR. This is a sure indication of a KGB or GRU background, because 'only the most grave cases involving high treason' (Krasnov, p. 94), amounting to twenty individuals, merit such a distinction. Accordingly, there is good reason to suppose that the true number of Soviet intelligence defectors is closer to the author's calculation than the vague CIA claim.

Nevertheless, some doubt still surrounds some of those listed here. 'Anton', 'Boris' and the 1983 redefector have never been officially identified beyond the details disclosed here. Similarly, Vladimir A. Ignaste is acknowledged as a KGB defector by John Barron in *KGB* (Hodder & Stoughton, London, 1974, p. 436), and by Krasnov (p. 173), who also lists Lyudmila Petrovna Ignaste. No additional data is known.

1 Ronald Hingley, *The Russian Secret Police* (Hutchinson, London, 1972). Burlutsky is also mentioned in Robert Conquest, *The Soviet Deportation of Nationalities* (1960), p. 51.

2 Hayhanen's story is told in Louise Bernikow, *Abel* (Trident, New York, 1970).

3 'Tuomi' is the name given to this illegal by Barron, *op. cit.*, p. 258. His true name is unknown.

4 Goleniewski is included here because he was a KGB agent as well as a Polish UB officer. He subsequently acquired some notoriety because of his claim to be the Czar's son Alexei and was the subject of a biography by Guy Richards (Devin-Adair, New York, 1966), based on numerous interviews.

5 Hendrik van Bergh used the pseydonym 'Karl Anders' to write Stashinsky's version in *Murder to Order* (Devin-Adair, New York, 1967).

6 Nosenko's controversial case is best documented by Edward J. Epstein, a confidant of Jim Angleton. See *Legend* (Arrow, London, 1978).

7 Olga Farmakovskaya's defection is recounted by Peter Worthington, *Looking for Trouble* (Key Porter, Toronto, 1984).

8 Rositzke, *op. cit.*, p. 241.

9 Kiselnikova is listed on the basis that she was a co-opted worker for the KGB, see Barron, *op. cit.*, p. 245.

10 The circumstances of Lyalin's defection received widespread publicity at the time, in September 1971, but it was not until Peter Wright told Chapman Pincher about his role for six months as an MI5 agent that his true significance became known. See *Their Trade is Treachery* (Heinemann Australia, Victoria, 1987), p. 103. When Wright collaborated with Paul Greengrass for *Spycatcher* (Sidgwick & Jackson, London, 1981), they mistakenly made the date February 1970, eighteen months too early (p. 343). This, combined with their inability to spell the name of the MI5 case officer who handled Lyalin (A. M. 'Tony' Brooks, DSO, MC), undermined his credibility, or so claimed Brooks in letter to the Special Forces Club newsletter (Autumn 1988, p. 9).

11 Few details are known about the circumstances of Konstantin Nadi-

rashvili's defection. See Krasnov, *op. cit.*, p. 195.

12 Barron, *op. cit.*, p. 356. Zemenek is better known as 'Major Rudolf Hermann'.

13 Christopher Dobson and Ronald Payne, *The Dictionary of Espionage* (Harrap, London, 1984), p. 99.

14 'Boris' is sourced in Dobson and Payne, *ibid.*, p. 19, to an April 1983 article in the *Daily Telegraph* written by them. They also attribute the recent expulsions 'within a short period' of five Soviets from London, forty-seven from Paris and Yevgenni Barmyantsev from Washington to information from 'Boris'. This explanation seems improbable, bearing in mind what is now known about FAREWELL, who supplied the DST with sufficient data to compromise the forty-seven Soviets in France, and the fact that Colonel Barmyantsev was the victim of an FBI controlled walk-in, John Stine, who had been targeted originally against another GRU officer, Vyacheslav Pavlov (see page 48). Dobson and Payne were also wrong to say that 'two other Russians were expelled with Barmyantsev'. His was an isolated case, and a brief study of the other four Soviet expulsions in that year show that they had no connection with him. The only other GRU officer removed from Washington in 1983 was Yuri Leonov, who was not expelled until 20 August, as a consequence of another quite separate FBI-controlled walk-in operation. While the circumstances of Skripko's departure from New York are unknown, Mikheyev and Konstantinov, both based at the UN, were PNG'd after they each made an unsuccessful recruitment pitch. As regards the five 'ordered to leave Britain', these would appear to be Zotov and Chernov, PNG'd in December 1982; and Primakov, Ivanov and Titov, who followed in April. Since all these cases are linked to Vladimir Kuzichkin, it would seem that 'Boris' probably does not exist, or, if he does, that he was not responsible for the coups credited to him.

15 Gezha is believed to have been a journalist co-opted to do occasional work for the KGB, see Nigel West, *The Friends* (Weidenfeld, London, 1988), p. 165.

16 *Ibid.*

17 *Ibid.*, p. 161.

18 Father Vladimir Ignaste is acknowledged by Barron, *op. cit.*, p. 436, as a 'former officer or agent of the KGB'.

19 This unnamed defector is cited by Donald Jameson in David Wise, *The Spy Who Got Away* (Random House, New York, 1989), p. 237, as an example of a 'plant' who subsequently redefected.

6: The Friends

1 Reinhard Gehlen, *The Service* (World Publishing, New York, 1972), p. 211.

2 *Time*, 6 February 1978, p. 26.

3 Chester L. Cooper, *The Lion's Last Roar: Suez 1956* (Harper & Row, New York, 1978), p. 70.

4 Joseph B. Smith, *Portrait of a Cold Warrior* (Ballantine, New York, 1976), p. 139.

5 Following Kuzichkin's defection SIS supplied a copy of his initial debriefing to the CIA, which leaked it to Tehran. In consequence some 200 members of the Tudeh (Communist) Party were executed and the remaining functionaries imprisoned. In addition, eighteen Soviet diplomats with clandestine Tudeh links were expelled.

6 See Jon and David Kimche, *The Secret Roads* (Secker & Warburg, London, 1954), p. 195, for a detailed account of the sabotage.

7 See David Leigh, *High Time* (Heinemann, London, 1984), for Howard Marks's biography.

8 Owen's painful interview with the Security Service was witnessed by Leo Abse, then Labour Member of Parliament for Pontypool.

9 Wright, *op. cit.*, p. 342.

10 Leonid A. Makarov was expelled on 2 February 1984, together with Stanislav Tsyibotok, Yuri A. Anisimov, Mikhail Outkin and Anatoli A. Artamonov.

11 Weibel's GRU contact, Viktor Kedrov, left the Soviet Trade Mission in Copenhagen to be Vice-President of Etorg, the State Electronorg-Technika Company in Moscow. More recently he turned up in Geneva attached to the Soviet negotiating team at the Vienna disarmament talks.

12 See the *Wall Street Journal*, 6 November 1979: 'The Coup against Countercoup: How a Book Disappeared'. McGraw-Hill pulped 7,500 copies of the first edition and only an estimated 400 books escaped the ban. The original version contains several references to the Anglo–Iranian Oil Company, which have been replaced by 'British Intelligence'.

13 Bakhlanov's memoirs, written under the pseudonym 'A. L. Romanov', and entitled *The Nights Are Longest There*, were translated by Gerald Brooke, a university lecturer who had been swapped for the Krogers in July 1969.

14 Directive quoted by Vladimir and Evdokia Petrov, *Empire of Fear* (Deutsch, London, 1956), p. 265.

Notes to Tables on Pages 149–53.

1 Kuznetsov subsequently was based in Belgrade and was appointed Soviet ambassador to Indonesia in 1972.
2 Akimov had been an Amtorg official in New York, 1962–6.
3 Azarov had served in Washington, 1951–4 and 1961–2.
4 Filatov had previously been at the UN in New York, 1966–7. He was appointed Soviet ambassador to Gabon.
5 Generalov, a GRU officer, was expelled from the US in 1962.
6 Golubev had been a member of the Soviet delegation to the UN in New York, 1961 and 1963–4.
7 Kolodyazhny had previously served in the GRU *Rezidentura* in Washington as first secretary, 1958–63.
8 Vaygauskas had been at the UN in New York, 1960–3, and at Montreal for Expo '67 in 1967.
9 Yasakov had attended Cornell University, 1965–6.

7: La Piscine

1 Quoted by Philippe Thyraud de Vosjoli, *Lamia* (Little, Brown, Boston, 1970), p. 150.
2 See Alexandre de Marenches, *The Evil Empire* (Sidgwick & Jackson, London, 1988), and Jean Rochet, *Cinq ans à la tête de la DST* (Plon, Paris, 1985).
3 According to Golitsyn, Paques's principal Soviet case officer was General Ivan Agayants, who had been attached to the Paris *Rezidentura* with the identity of 'Ivan I. Avalov'.
4 According to declassified CIA papers contained in *The Rote Kapelle* a large number of the cryptonyms found in wartime Soviet intelligence wireless traffic were found to refer to influential agents close to de Gaulle. One, for example, was discovered to be Jacques Soustelle, whom de Gaulle appointed head of his intelligence staff in 1943, and Minister of Information in 1945.
5 de Vosjoli, *op. cit.*, p. 316.
6 Although the name of this agent has not been disclosed, it may have been Pierre Owen de Ure, a Frenchman then resident in Cuba who was arrested in September 1963 and described in the local press as a CIA spy.
7 FAREWELL's true name has not been released by the DST. See Thierry Wolton, *Le KGB en France* (Grasset, Paris, 1986), p. 246.
8 de Marenches, *op. cit.*, p. 160.
9 *Ibid.*
10 *Ibid.*, p. 163. In spite of these remarks, de Marenches remains a great Anglophile, having married a Scot, Lady Lilian Witchell, in 1954.

11 *Ibid.*, p. 159.
12 *Ibid.*, p. 165.

8: The Institute

1 Roosevelt, *For Lust of Knowing*, p. 447.
2 'Israel: Foreign Intelligence and Security Services' survey published for internal use only by the CIA's Directorate of Operations Counter-Intelligence Staff, p. 12, in *Documents from the US Espionage Den*, no. 11.
3 There remains some doubt about Beer's real identity. Inconsistencies in his Austrian background suggest he may have been a Soviet illegal who simply adopted the real Beer's identity.
4 A thirteen-strong Syrian network rounded up by Shin Beth in 1958 is believed to have been Soviet-organized. It included three Arab members of the Israeli Communist Party, one of whom was a Party branch secretary.
5 Two Soviet moles, Shabtai Kalmanovich and Marcus Klingberg, are currently serving prison terms for espionage.
6 CIA Survey, p. 15.
7 *Ibid.*, p. 12.
8 *Ibid.*
9 A recent example is the acquisition of cluster-bomb technology from a US defence contractor following a ban on its export in 1982. In 1985 Israeli agents tried to buy electro-plating equipment for use on tank barrels, also the subject of an embargo. In 1986 the Israelis were caught attempting to steal a classified aerial reconnaissance photographic unit from its manufacturer in Illinois.
10 *Ibid.*, p. 30.
11 David Kimche, until recently the Director-General of the Israeli Foreign Ministry, had previously been Mossad's Head of Station in Tehran.
12 Lotz's father-in-law was General Hans-Heinrich Worgitzsky, formerly the BND's chief in Bremen, and appointed Gehlen's deputy in 1957.
13 Isser Harel, *The House on Garibaldi Street* (Deutsch, London, 1975).
14 CIA Survey, p. 24.
15 *Ibid.*, p. 23.
16 *Ibid.*, p. 22.
17 *Ibid.*, p. 23.
18 *Ibid.*, p. 22.
19 *Ibid.*, p. 13.

9: Endgame

1 DCI William Webster interviewed by Jim Lehrer, PSB TV, 1 February 1989.

2 *Ibid.*

3 A nineteen-year veteran of ASIS, Harvey Barnett, was appointed ASIO'S Director-General in 1976. He retired in September 1981 and was succeeded by Mr Justice A. E. Woodward. The title of Barnett's memoirs, *Tale of the Scorpion* (Allen & Unwin, London, 1988), reflects ASIO's registered cable address: Scorpion.

4 They were followed on 25 May 1989 by four other expulsions: Jan Pavlicek, the press attaché; Dr Helena Krepelkova, second secretary; Jan Sarkocy, third secretary; and Rudolf Kasparovsky, a technical adviser.

5 For a comprehensive study of AFOSI's counter-intelligence operations, see Special Agent David J. Crawford, *Volunteers* (US Government Printing Office, 1988).

6 George T. Kalaris, 'Counter-intelligence in the 1990s', *International Journal of Intelligence & Counter-intelligence*, vol. 2, no. 2, p. 181. Prior to his counter-intelligence appointment, Kalaris had served at Jakarta and Vientiane and headed the CIA stations in Manila and Brasilia.

7 *Ibid.*, p. 183.

8 *Ibid.*, p. 182.

9 'Meeting the Espionage Challenge: A Review of United States Counter-intelligence and Security Programs', Report of the Senate Select Committee on Intelligence, 3 October 1986.

10 Quoted by James Bamford, *Puzzle Palace* (Sidgwick & Jackson, London, 1982), p. 3.

11 The most detailed examination of this incident can be found in *Attack on the USS Liberty* by William D. Gerhard of the National Security Agency Central Security Service, declassified on 11 July 1983.

12 Nikolai Yakovlev, *CIA Target: The USSR* (Progress Publishers, Moscow, 1982), p. 93.

13 The 1947 National Security Act entitles the DCI to sponsor up to 250 aliens for US citizenship a year. Sections 313 (a) and 313 (c) of the Immigration and Nationality Act also allow the CIA to use its discretion in awarding US citizenship, although the present authority stands for 125 only.

14 Those convinced that the British Secret Intelligence Service has a continuous history dating back to Queen Elizabeth I are referred to Professor Sir Harry Hinsley's *British Intelligence in the Second World War* (HMSO, London, 1979), p. 16n, which insists that SIS 'only came into separate existence in 1909'.

15 Viktor Chebrikov's translated interview, see *Foreign Broadcasts Infor-*

mation Service, Soviet Union, 88–171, 2 September 1988, pp. 28–34.

16 Karl Koecher was the subject of Ronald Kessler's *Spy vs Spy* (Scribner's, New York, 1988), and Edward Howard was interviewed by David Wise for *The Spy Who Got Away* (Random House, New York, 1988). In January 1988 Phillip Knightley was given access to Kim Philby in Moscow, which resulted in *Philby: KGB Masterspy* (Deutsch, London, 1988).

17 Viktor Adriyanov, 'The Spy Who Came in from the Cold', *International Pravda*, vol. 11, 12 November 1988, pp. 9–11.

18 The newly installed Vladimir Kryuchkov was sufficiently confident in January 1989 to welcome the US ambassador, John Matlock, to a ninety-minute meeting at his Dzerzhinsky Square headquarters.

19 Andrei S. Parastayev, first secretary in Washington, has been named as a Directorate R member by John Barron ('The KGB's Deepest Secret', *Reader's Digest*, November 1988, pp. 94–6); and Valeri Zemskov's appointment as minister counsellor at Canberra was opposed in 1986 by ASIO Director Alan K. Wrigley on the same grounds. Both were identified by Yurchenko in August 1985.

20 Richard Stolz's biographical details are mentioned in Julius Mader's *Who's Who in the CIA* (Mader, Berlin, 1968), p. 500, and updated by Philip Agee in *Dirty Work* (Lyle Stewart, Secaucus, NJ, 1979), pp. 669–70.

Index

234

Index

237

Index

Index

Index